WAVERS & BEGGARS

DR. WARREN BRUHL,
TODD LOVE BALL, JR.

WAVERS
&
BEGGARS

New Insight and Hope to End Poverty and Global Challenges

Dr. Warren Bruhl,
Todd Love Ball, Jr.

WESTBOW
PRESS®
A DIVISION OF THOMAS NELSON
& ZONDERVAN

WestBow Press books may be ordered through booksellers or by contacting:

WestBow Press
A Division of Thomas Nelson & Zondervan
1663 Liberty Drive
Bloomington, IN 47403
www.westbowpress.com
1 (866) 928-1240

Because of the dynamic nature of the Internet, any web addresses or links contained in this book may have changed since publication and may no longer be valid. The views expressed in this work are solely those of the author and do not necessarily reflect the views of the publisher, and the publisher hereby disclaims any responsibility for them.

Any people depicted in stock imagery provided by Thinkstock are models, and such images are being used for illustrative purposes only.
Certain stock imagery © Thinkstock.

ISBN: 978-1-5127-4021-9 (sc)
ISBN: 978-1-5127-4022-6 (hc)
ISBN: 978-1-5127-4020-2 (e)

Library of Congress Control Number: 2016906852

Print information available on the last page.

WestBow Press rev. date: 06/27/2016

"There is only one God and He is God to all; therefore it is important that everyone is seen as equal before God. I've always said we should help a Hindu become a better Hindu, a Muslim become a better Muslim, a Catholic become a better Catholic. We believe our work should be our example to people. We have among us 475 souls—30 families are Catholics and the rest are all Hindus, Muslims, Sikhs—all different religions. But they all come to our prayers."

Mother Teresa

"A way has to be found to enable everyone to benefit from the fruits of the earth, and not simply to close the gap between the affluent and those who must be satisfied with the crumbs falling from the table, but above all to satisfy the demands of justice, fairness and respect for every human being."

Pope Francis
Address to the Food and Agricultural Organization, 6/20/13

To my family,

There are not enough words to express the appreciation I possess for God providing the family I was born to and the family He provided to me as a husband and father. My wife, Marka, has been an inspiration and teacher to me, showing me the way to love unconditionally, giving to others generously, and weathering life's challenges by my side with an enduring and loving spirit. Each of my children has singularly shown me how to love beyond ways I thought I was capable. It was a moment I will never forget when I realized I loved my children and wife so much that *I would take a bullet for them.* This is the ultimate sacrifice and it is this awareness of how profound love can implant in our heart, giving me faith to love God and know He loves every one of us.

God has always been by my side through every trial, victory, and moment of doubt. Though I have doubted, he has never doubted me. I thank God for my wife Marka and my three children, Austin, Montana, and Sage. I am also more thankful than ever for my mother, Sandy Taylor and Kenny, my stepfather. They demonstrated through their actions and not their words how to love our brothers and sisters who have the greatest need but are often most forgotten. At the end of this book, I have provided a tribute to my mother, Sandra Taylor, which speaks to her selfless love. This book is a tribute to the family I know and the family I do not yet know but will one day meet here or in heaven.

Dr. Warren Bruhl

Thank You

This book is made possible by the heroic, deeply moving *everyday life* billions of people live around the world. Their stories have been our motivation to create a movement that will bring understanding and compassion for the challenges they face every day. We've learned from spending time with people living on the edge of survival in poverty that there isn't much difference between their lives and the lives we have living in privilege in America. Often, the only difference we have noticed is that we were born in America where more opportunities exist, while they were born into poverty in a chaotic troubled part of the world. Nonetheless, the families we've gotten to know have inspired us to move forward, to learn more and write with a desire to help change the circumstances that still cripple millions of people from ever getting ahead. It is our vision that *Wavers & Beggars* will become a social movement and a platform to educate young children who have the resources and ability to do something amazing to help under-resourced people. We want to discover a world where our young leaders take a stand and say, "No More! I will not sit back and let people suffer this way any longer without doing something!"

As we have detailed in **Wavers & Beggars***, the first step toward change is the willingness to act.*

We thank our families for supporting our vision and desire to travel often and use resources—every trip and project we undertake takes time and resources that could be used elsewhere. We'd also like to thank our editor, Mrs. Becky Hodgin, who was extremely kind and dedicated in reading our initial manuscript, giving needed feedback, and then rereading it over again to make sure our message was clear. As well, we thank Dr. Angela Zolper for the final edits she provided and feedback from Dr. David Neubauer, Ms. Carrie Barnett, Dr. Jeff Kahrs, and Ms. Jean Bons. Providing illustrations and our logo design for Wavers & Beggars, Mr. Wayne Potrue generously gave his creativity and time to our project. Moreover, we appreciate the wonderful work of Chiromission and Drs. Todd Herold, Jean-Claude Doornick, Aura Tovar, Jason Gerard, Tiffany Thornton, Deb Morrone, and Mr. Jeff Cobelli. Chiromission leaders have provided the support for much of our sports charity work in the Dominican Republic and have been amazing leaders to emulate and work alongside in our international efforts. Always demonstrating selfless love, Dr. Scott Smith, our Dreamweaver director, and his wife Heidi, has been inspirational. They've dedicated themselves to serving the poor and shown through actions and not words, the love of Christ. Their children, Beret, Cari, and Scotty have all been servants of the poor and led by example. We are also grateful for our relationships with Willow Creek Church's Gift in Kind Ministry and the selfless dedication of Mr. Frank Davis leading this project. We thank Mr. Ken Taylor and Mrs. Sandy Taylor for their kind and warm hospitality in opening up their home in Kenya and teaching us from their twenty-five years of experience working with the poor. Though Sandra has now passed, their thoughts and experience were invaluable in our learning curve and determining where we needed to seek guidance to write this book. Warm thanks to Mr. Joseph Nkaapa for his dedication to local leadership and demonstrating God's love in a new and fresh way. His work with Dreamweaver International has been a blessing. Final thanks are given to Mr. Owino Chapman, who heads our Gear for Goals project in Kenya, for his selfless dedication to changing the lives of youths in East Africa. Each time we speak with Joseph and Owino, they share their time and knowledge generously to help us shape and grow as stewards of God's blessings. Often 'the seen' is not what it appears, and certainly we have discovered this while writing this book, getting to know different cultures. Perspectives change when there are local people who live in the issues and share their insight.

We also thank God for his hand in making this book possible. Without the teaching and grace God provided through Jesus Christ, we would not be touched and moved to act as we have. It's often been Jesus's deep concern and care for the poor that has inspired missionaries to seek out and help the poor. As well, the prophetic writings and messages conveyed in Old Testament scripture have also led people to extend help to the poor. Jesus was adamant on issues of the poor. It is because he loves the poor, we love the poor too.

Warren and Todd

CONTENTS

PREFACE

The real power in life is not what happens to us, but rather how we respond to the circumstances we face… a choice of love or fear.

Wavers & Beggars is a heartfelt dive into the consciousness of poverty in our world today. It is both a personal and collective view of the mindset that perpetuates a struggling and suffering life or one that inspires a new and fresh breath of hope, dignity, and oneness. Imagine being able to envision beyond what's currently being seen, listen beyond what's currently being said, and choose beyond the catastrophic consequences that we as humankind are individually and globally facing. *Wavers & Beggars* is a loving and compassionate look in the mirror.

As people who share the economic resources of our water, sky, air, and land, we have reached a critical stage in our history: we must decide what kind of future to make for ourselves. Will it be a future that is derived from the values of fear, pessimism, greed, hunger, poverty, and war, or will it be formed from the liberating values of love, optimism, service, sustainability, abundance, and peace? It may seem like an obvious choice; however, where to begin? Even more, you may be asking yourself, "What could I possibly do to make a difference?"

Let's begin with a question.

If you were given the opportunity to create your life, a day, or even a moment in time, would you choose to create it feeling helpless or hopeless to change the outcome of the ravaging effects of poverty? Would you choose statistics like these to be a reality?

- At least 80% of humanity lives on less than $10 a day.
- The poorest 40% of the world's population accounts for 5% of global income. The richest 20% accounts for three-quarters of the world's income.
- Around 27-28% of all children in developing countries are estimated to be underweight or stunted. The two regions that account for the bulk of the deficit are South Asia and sub-Saharan Africa.
- Nearly a billion people entered the 21st century unable to read a book or sign their names.
- Less than 1% of what the world spent every year on weapons was needed to put every child into school by the year 2000, and yet it didn't happen.
- Some 1.1 billion people in developing countries have inadequate access to water, and 2.6 billion lack basic sanitation.

Would you choose this? If you had the ability to leave a legacy for our children's children, would this be the outcome you'd hope to come true? Of course not!

I'd like to propose a new perspective. What we know is this: *what isn't a choice or an action is a reaction*. In a state of reaction, we lack rational thinking, strategic planning, and creativity. When in a reactive state, the beliefs of the subconscious mind go on autopilot and take over for the way we perceive ourselves and the world, and even more, act as a magnetic attractor field bringing forward further circumstances that match the frequency of our beliefs. We do not perceive truth in life, rather we perceive what we believe.

Beliefs are learned, and not everything that we learn is true; or what may have been true at one point in time may not be relevant today. Questioning our beliefs and the status quo is necessary to create a portal for change. If left unquestioned, the reactive energy and emotion that is in motion will stay in motion until met by a force. Will that force be you?

Within your heart lies a truth that love is the answer to fear. What does your heart of love choose to feel? What does your heart of love choose to create? My hope in writing the forward to this epic book is to empower you with the knowing that you can make a difference.

When we place judgments on those who are the victims of limiting beliefs, as well as stressful generational and cultural patterns, it only further cements a reactive lens of separation and helplessness. Now is the time to act from your heart and courageously embrace what's possible. Acknowledging the immeasurable value of a single person being a reflection of the whole is a positive step on our journey of creating world peace through inner peace.

Dr. Warren Bruhl and Todd Love Ball, Jr. have created a platform for dialogue based on their own life journey, travels, and passion to make a positive impact on the world through service. May their vision inspire you to take an empathetic look at the mindset of poverty so that we can learn, heal, and evolve to be the authentic expression of love and light we are intended and destined to be. As the cultural anthropologist Margaret Mead is noted as saying, "A small group of thoughtful people could change the world. Indeed, it's the only thing that ever has." In this well-researched and compelling book, the inner-connected patterns of the human mind are woven together between *Wavers & Beggars*.

Keep shining bright!

With infinite love & gratitude,
Dr. Darren Weissman
Developer of The LifeLine Technique and best-selling author

Sources

2007 Human Development Report (HDR), United Nations Development Program, November 27, 2007, p. 25

The State of the World's Children, 1999, UNICEF

State of the World, Issue 287 – Feb 1997, *New International list*

2006 United Nations Human Development Report, pp. 6, 7, 35

Introduction

One of the most frequent questions Todd and I receive about our friendship is how we partnered to write Wavers & Beggars. People often ask, "How did you two meet? You seem like you come from such different backgrounds." While we're obviously different in easily identifiable ways—he's black and I'm white—we've discovered we are more alike than we originally realized. Moreover, our personal revelations and our friendship have helped us also realize that the more diversity we welcome into our lives, the stronger we can become. ***This is one of the basic themes of* Wavers & Beggars: *diversity helps make us stronger not weaker.***

As I began to write the early stages of the manuscript, a friend mentioned she'd read a book Todd published. She didn't know I was working on *Wavers & Beggars* at the time. But her mentioning Todd's book and, I believe, God's spirit speaking to me, led me to ask him if he'd be interested in co-authoring *Wavers & Beggars*.

Todd had recently begun working as a fitness educator at a local fitness complex I used. We had shared in passing some conversations about Kenya and other regions of the world. Todd expressed interest in learning more and seemed to have a quality of leadership and desire for knowledge to help create change in the racial barriers still dividing much of the world. Though our lives and backgrounds were from vastly different circumstances, I could see the perfection and opportunity to bring credence to our message by merging our diverse perspectives. Thus, we embarked on a journey writing *Wavers & Beggars*, finding our differences not a hindrance, but instead a strength and opportunity to reach a larger audience.

The information in this book is meant as a launching point for you to ponder poverty, scarcity, and resources in a new way.

In addition, our hope is the illumination we bring to issues involving poverty will awaken you to take the steps to act!

While there are vast resources available and many around the world who care about the needs of the poor, the abhorrent truth is the majority of people, *including us* for most of our lives, have given little more than a passing glance to the poor. We read about them or maybe saw a documentary on television, but often did little to help. We were not really interested in making our own lives uncomfortable to change our circumstances, or give our time and resources to help change the shocking needs around the world.

Awakened, Todd and I realized we could no longer sit back and do nothing for impoverished people, who are sometimes referred to as the 'voiceless' because we never see them or know their story because thousands of miles may separate us. In some instances, the unseen 'voiceless' people may only be a forty-five-minute trip away, as is the case in Chicago from the north side to the south side. But, we have been afraid to step out and make contact to lend a hand. Unwilling to roll up our sleeves and get dirty, we live our lives safely believing somehow that our ultimate measures of success are attained by living in larger mansions, driving expensive automobiles, and securing the prosperity Wall Street and Madison Avenue advertisers say are the medals of success. All when sadly both our neighbors within our own communities and people who live thousands of miles from us may have been dealt a deck that will never give them a chance to even complete sixth-grade education, drink clean water that doesn't infect their belly with parasites, or eat more than one meager meal of rice and beans daily.

However, as Todd and I came to grips with our own shallow, narrow, and small thinking toward the needs of the poor, we also recognized we did have the power to change things, starting with our own lives and then branching out slowly to lead a movement. This book is our message to start this movement and open the discussion. Our friends, the *wavers* and the *beggars*, are our teachers and as we waved at them and they waved back at us, we learned together from one another. Todd and I came to realize that we can do something meaningful but our first step was always awareness and then desire to change.

As you read this book, consider for yourself the *waver* and the *beggar* within yourself and how you may be changed to serve. ***As we have learned, the life that will be most touched by your transformation will not be the lives of the ones you serve but instead will be your own life.*** Touched and changed in your heart by the struggles and the triumphs of harrowing life circumstances, you will discover humanity has an amazing aptitude for survival and can claim victory even in the face of remarkable hurdles.

Though Todd and I have collaborated on all the material of this book, I have been the primary writer of most of the text. Todd has provided his own life experiences and reflections in a portion of the text. Thus, the majority of the book is written from the first person using 'I' to refer to me, Warren. However, Todd's insights and experiences as an African-American and the challenges he has faced because of the color of his skin were extremely valuable to my writing and the content of the entire book. I believe a significant stride in poverty alleviation around the world begins with active dialogue that occurs between people of differing backgrounds. Certainly, Todd and I discovered this was true in the writing this book. Our personal diversity gave us the perspective we needed to open up further and consider how other people live their lives and the way compassion, justice, and serving others plays a role in poverty alleviation strategies. As well, we discovered that even though we were different ethnically and in age, we were more alike than seemed obvious. Our own internal struggles as children had many similarities and these common experiences in feelings that came from adversity helped us shape our ideas and thoughts.

I am thankful to my brother and close friend, Todd, for his insight, love, and passion to learn and serve. This book is a blessing and I could not have written it without his help. We are a team and have a long-term perspective and plans to create materials that will help in poverty awareness around the world. If only we might see some progress in our lifetimes, I know both of us would feel enormously blessed by God to have been a part of such a change.

Dr. Warren Bruhl

WAVERS AND BEGGARS — WE ALL SHARE THIS COMMON BOND

"Never stand begging for that which
you have the power to earn."
– Miguel de Cervantes

Poverty's Impact: One out of every two children living today lives in poverty.

The A-ha Moment!

Stumbling upon the observation of *wavers and beggars* was not a quest I sought as an epiphany or an enlightening understanding of poverty. I wasn't trying to discover a new idea or a deep message lurking underneath an everyday social phenomenon. I had never contemplated the significance that could be ascribed to people who wave at passersby or who beg for money. But, as I noticed a simple yet profound social phenomenon unfolding in people I passed by on the road, I also began to recognize these two kinds of human expression had profound implications. But what, if any, significance is there when people wave happily or beg desperately? Why were people led to use these two expressions to either greet passersby or hope for a handout? As I researched poverty and the triumphs people accomplish to survive in the most desperate circumstances, I realized there were enormous problems I would only have limited ability to change. But, the *wavers* and *beggars* I first encountered along the roads in Kenya provided hope to me. Living in one of the most beautiful and picturesque places on the planet, a paradox existed. Social inequality, illiteracy, sickness, HIV, gender discrimination, and other powerfully paralyzing circumstances made it virtually impossible for people to survive and advance. But the contrasting paradox of beauty and poverty's epic challenges still offered hope, and often this was all people had to hold on to when prospects for a brighter future seemed impossible.

I questioned the circumstances that left millions around the world starving, persecuted, and forgotten. How undeniably slim the chance that anything will ever change on our planet with over seven billion people. But recorded history offers hope that miracles are still possible to change the circumstances of so many desperate people's lives. Great empires have risen and fallen. Ecological and geological changes have shaped our earth and continue today. Faith in many gods, and for most of the world a faith in one god, has taken place. Technology has advanced transportation, communication, finance, education, and health care solving thousands of challenges existing only a century ago. Yes, hope is evident and real! Change is constant and inevitable! Yet, the wheels of change and the pace seem to have ground to a stop for many I have met around the world. Though their spirits have not been destroyed.

Frequently, diversity, though uniquely special, has often served as a source of powerful discontent and struggle also. Factions of people have battled one another, shedding blood and hating each other. Religious differences, skin color, and ethnicity have been reasons for men to kill one another. ***Our inability to recognize diversity as something good and not bad has caused great harm to our world.*** But this struggle, though seemingly impossible to change, can become a new launching point for each of us to examine within ourselves how we can be a social catalyst for transformation, as well, becoming aware that *wavers* and *beggars* that live within poor communities are giving us an opportunity to discover something inside our own heart. As I encountered *wavers* and *beggars* in some of the poor regions I was visiting, I began to realize that human expression was giving me a gift. It was opening something inside my own heart that needed to be cracked open to encourage me to help further. If you've ever seen a poor, starving mother with little skeletally thin children crying and dressed in tattered and dirtied clothing, begging for some assistance to feed her kids, you know what this can do to your heart. It's really a hard feeling to describe. I just call it the 'this is unacceptable' moment. This wave rushes through my body and I feel the emotional welling of tears that come to the surface, and I shake inside with storms of anger and sadness all at once. It's as if at that very moment, something has changed inside my cellular DNA and my heart has been stretched and changed never to return to the smaller shallow way it was before my encounter. I have had this experience on so many occasions and I am certain it has done something to change me in ways I don't fully comprehend but know have been for my own good and desire to act to alleviate global poverty. As well, placing myself in communities where I have been uncomfortable and unknowing of the culture has further empowered me to recognize that diversity is not something to run from or be scared of.

No. Instead, every diverse opportunity can be a powerful magnet attracting us closer together to strengthen our character.

Perhaps in an ordained way, I was drawn to notice alongside the road *wavers* and *beggars*, who gave me a desire to understand this social phenomenon occurring around the world but never appreciated. I wanted to know why poverty was so horrific in parts of the world like Kenya. I wanted to understand why my life had been relatively comfortable compared to my brothers and sisters living in poverty. Why did I have opportunities that seemed virtually impossible for my friends in Africa and other areas of high-density poverty?

Beginning in 2011, I began to take frequent trips to under-resourced parts of the world to serve people with my chiropractic specialty and also provide youth with donated sports equipment. It was during these initial trips to the Dominican Republic and Kenya that the changes to my heart and consciousness I have spoken about began to unfold. The desperate poverty and lack of hope so many had with virtually no economic resources was something I had never witnessed. I had read about poverty, seen documentaries about it, and heard others tell the way it can be, but I had never allowed myself to ever get this close to it. At first, it was terribly uncomfortable to stand out because I was the only white person in a sea of dark-colored faces. I found myself unable to relax. It was very unsettling and felt deeply troubling to me. I felt unsafe; but why? Of course, the obvious answer would be I was in an unfamiliar place, but there had to be more to it than that. Perhaps my inner fears also came from the newly discovered recognition of just how bad it can be for so many people living in poverty.

Wrapped around the world, billions live with virtually no economic resources and struggle daily merely to survive on meager rations of water and food. Shelter is often in dilapidated buildings barely standing and frequently in tightly congested urban slums with hundreds of thousands of people packed into one square mile. Health care is either unavailable or severely handicapped by lack of medicine, chiropractic therapy, physical therapy, and prevention practices. People simply don't understand and have not been taught some the basic programs of health we take for granted in the United States. For many children, access to a complete education to grade twelve is still not possible because parents cannot afford school fees and public education is not available beyond the sixth or eighth grade. Political instability and corruption halt the advancement of reform in many places and have become the excuse too many people use for either not helping or citing as the reason it will never change. These realizations, and countless others I was beginning to process, frightened and discouraged me initially. But the epiphany and observation I made about *wavers* and *beggars* on my December 2012 trip to Kenya began an earnest quest to bring new hope and opportunity to millions who still live in poverty.

My initial observation of *wavers* and *beggars* occurred in the Kimana Rift Valley of Kenya, East Africa. Working with a medical team and giving chiropractic care to the local Maasai for the first time, we would take daily trips to remote villages. To travel to these locations, our bus would take a paved road for part of the trip and then turn onto a dirt road to drive into the more remote reaches of the countryside. Always in the shadows of the majestic Mt. Kilimanjaro, we cared for the indigenous Maasai, a people who had lived in this area for five centuries. The Maasai are a nomadic people who used to travel with the rains and thrived in this region. Proud and resourceful, they are recognized for their ability to survive in one of the harshest parts of the world. They live in huts made of cow dung and mud that attract thousands of flies and their main source of income is livestock. Because they have become accustomed to constant attack by flies, they don't even swat at them when the flies crawl on their faces and in their noses or eyes. Agriculture is possible for some who live in an area where rain is adequate, but for most rain is a luxury they are without. In fact, many of the places we visited on this trip, and have continued to work in, can go months and sometimes even years without rain. Many women walk a five- or even ten-mile roundtrip to supply the daily water needs of their family. Bathing, oral hygiene, and washing of clothing are nearly absent. Now unable to travel with the rains, the Maasai are forced to live within boundaries imposed by the Kenyan government and have suffered as a result. For most, lives and prayers often center on the simple need for water and rain.

Though their needs are often precariously in balance, the populations of Maasai share warmth and appreciation for the simplest needs met by God, which enable their survival. Many practice faith, worshiping God with ardent prayers in local churches. On Sundays, their beautiful voices and rhythmic drumming can be heard for miles streaming from the small wooden buildings with tin roofs constructed to be churches and school buildings. Virtually every member of the community attends church and prays together.

With our daily arrival, our Maasai friends thanked God for answers to prayers and blessings. They believed our arrival was an answer to their prayers. My perspective about poverty, prior to this time, was that it involved only a lack of material possessions. Instead, I now found poverty also caused deep emotional scars also. Yes, they were happy with the simplest of things and had made the best of their circumstances, but many felt a deeper sense of inadequacy. Though it may not be spoken, I could sense within their own country, they felt forgotten and betrayed by their leaders and other people of power who hoarded resources. As I became more familiar with their suffering, my desire to do something to ameliorate it was taking a hold of my heart. I began to rededicate my life to serving the desires of God over my own and discovered a profound inner peace.

My epiphany I called *wavers* and *beggars* occurred on these daily bus rides into the African bush as I started to notice a familiar trend. Alongside the paved road, near frequent automobile traffic and more mazungo (white people), beggars congregated with upturned hands, begging for money. Their looks of desperation, anxiety, and survival were communicated in their eyes. Looking for anything, the beggars' pleas were deeply moving and broke my heart. I wanted to help them but found myself feeling helpless. However, I also had a newfound desire to understand how their lives were so different than mine. How could God's promise to take care of His children go unfulfilled? I wanted to know more and see if there was a way I could do more.

But then I began to notice something, which at first seemed too simple but was a miracle in some way. When driving farther up the dusty, pothole-tracked roads only a quarter mile, and sometimes even less when we turned off the main roads, children and adults didn't greet us with outstretched begging hands. Hands were elevated high in the air and waving vigorously! The *wavers'* faces bore eyes bright with clarity and joyful welcome at our arrival. They didn't want anything from us, only a friendly wave in return. A stark contrast in human behavior was occurring only a quarter mile apart. Along the paved road, people had become accustomed to relying on begging. Yet only a quarter mile away people found no value in begging but instead waved in joyous celebration and greeting to strangers passing by.

As I encountered this phenomenon with more frequency, I asked others on our bus if they recognized it. My mother, who's lived in Kenya for twenty years, noticed the repeated behavior but had not appreciated the arrant contrast existing within such a short distance up the dirt roads leading to the surrounding villages in the Rift Valley. Other frequent travelers to this region also recognized the *wavers* and *beggars* too.

These *wavers* and *beggars* lived so close to one another and possibly even in the same villages. Yet, their communication and methods for accessing their needs were the antithesis of one another. The *wavers* didn't seem interested in receiving anything from us. Instead, they wanted to exchange greetings, smiles, and ultimately to be noticed, whereas the *beggars* were desperate, persistent, and unable to share nary a smile or a note of hope. *How had these two populations living with one another become so different?* As I soon learned, this question would lead me to discover that poverty is not complicated. The *wavers* and *beggars* illustrated this to all of us. Everyone has basic needs for survival. When our needs are fulfilled, we are capable of active exchange with our community and can wave proudly. However, if basic needs such as food, water, clothing, shelter, emotional support, being valued, and having hope are unmet, then an unfortunate transformation evolves.

Ultimately, for many the need to beg for basic survival and the consequences associated with it are usually the result.

Now determined and recognizing the sociological interplay at work in the Rift Valley of Kenya, I started examining other communities domestically and internationally to see if any parallels were evident. Were the *wavers* and *beggars* in Kenya similar to others around the world? Was there something to learn from the observation and the body language of the people cast into the streets and needing to beg compared to *wavers* who were not choosing or needing to beg? How could the resultant expression in neighbors be used to understand the mechanism of sociological factors unfolding along with their possible clue to poverty solutions? To discover answers to these questions, I read, watched countless documentaries, traveled to other under-resourced countries, and gleaned information from the vast Internet space to see if I could shed new light on poverty. I became determined to understand what was going on, so I could help and become part of the *solution* and not part of the *problem*.

What I realize from my journey is *wavers* are represented in all walks of life, not only among the poor or desperate, as I've focused on in the beginning of this book. Waving is a human expression representing character, experience, and the state of a man or woman. The ability and the desire to wave itself says something, not only about the feelings inside but also a person's willingness to actively engage in physical communication. In many of the villages, even where people live on meager earnings, *wavers* are enthusiastic. Sometimes they are farmers who are reaping a strong harvest or business people who operate a small business. Their circumstances, whatever they are, enable them to survive and have basic needs met, even if it is only sufficiency in terms of food, water, and shelter. The difference between the *waver* and the *beggar* lies in the proximity to survival and thriving at one end of the spectrum and despair and death at the other end. Survival and imminent death are the core difference between *wavers* and *beggars*.

Thus, *wavers* and *beggars* are real people who demonstrate their current relationship to survival, sufficiency, and abundance through their body language and the choices they make. As well, *wavers* and *beggars* also represent something deeper metaphorically that can connect us together with one another. I recognized from these observations and the self-examination of my own life that I was more like the *beggars* than I at first realized. Todd also discovered this same revelation about himself. We learned together that the characteristics, reasons for waving and begging, and what they said about humanity were ways we could explore connecting to one another. ***How many millions of times had people from different backgrounds and cultures waved at one another on roads like these in Kenya but not even known this was a message of deeper connection waiting to unfold?***

As I started to unpack this phenomenon and dig into poverty with a new fresh lens, it became apparent *wavers and beggars* was also a metaphor. Though the observation I initially made was in Kenya, a poor nation with many people living on less than $2.00 a day, the *wavers and beggars* metaphor also extends to people living in middle and upper-income social classes. Because Todd and I are able to feed our families, have a job, and feel valued and appreciated, we recognize our waving spirit. Each time we start our day, we approach the day with a sense of possibility and know we will not have to cup our hand and beg today for enough food to feed our family.

Like the wavers alongside the road in Kenya, the "what" that separates us from the beggar is our needs and purpose being fulfilled.

But another component is our desire to work and stay actively engaged in fruitful labor. Moreover, circumstances have also enabled work and fulfilled purpose to manifest. We live in a part of the world where opportunities are more plentiful and thus our ability to have a waving spirit is more attainable. The same could be said for some of the *wavers* who we see alongside the roads in Kenya. Their crops are growing because there have been rains. Their cattle have grass to graze on and are healthy so they have meat to eat and milk to drink. Tourism has been strong so there are buyers for necklaces and wooden figurines. The health of the children has been good so there have been no unexpected medical expenses and so on. When people live in cultures where resources are tight and their ability to earn money is difficult, small upsets like a child's illness or more major disruptions like tourism drying up can have grave consequences. When these consequences do unfold, in all likelihood some people have no other choice than to beg or die!

The metaphor of the *beggar* as we have stated thus far may seem obvious. But there is also something much deeper that deserves attention and is perhaps the more reflective opportunity for us to learn from. Begging is a depleted place that man turns to when hope is gone or seems invisible. It's a desperate emotional place probably first and then physically second. It cannot be easy to go from a place of self-reliance and being able to provide for one's self or family to now depending upon the kindness of a stranger and pleas for help. As both Todd and I discovered when we started to relive our childhood and into adulthood, we could see how begging and the need for a stranger's attention were present. Moreover, we both discovered the ability to recognize we tended to beg for things, praise, money, and fortune were not unlike the *beggars* in Kenya who needed a few shillings to buy food for the day.

Thus, *wavers and beggars* is a metaphor for a condition, a feeling, and a physical response we all relate to. It's a moniker to identify a sociological manifestation of humanity. *Wavers and beggars* is a fresh launching point for a new discussion on poverty that helps us identify our similarities with one another and not continue to place restrictive barriers in front of our connection because we are only aware of our differences. **Yes, wavers and beggars *is a powerful metaphor to see that there is a bond with every man or woman I meet or don't meet in my lifetime.*** I recognize when I see a *beggar* alongside the road, I am seeing a mirror of something inside myself I am afraid may happen to me. I am also seeing a hope that if this were to befall my life, a stranger would act in kindness and care enough to offer support. As well, when I see the boy smiling and waving enthusiastically as I pass by, I see the joy I have that my life has been blessed. I see his blessing and mine in the connection we share, even in that briefest of moments as we pass one another. Simple yet paradoxically complex, *Wavers & Beggars* should create a desire to question the status quo and help each of us to go deeper emotionally to ask the really hard questions about life: Why am I here? Is this what I am supposed to be doing at this time in my life? Is there something more I can do to make a difference? Am I showing up today as a *waver* or more like a *beggar*? Is waving better than begging? Is begging appropriate at this moment given the circumstances, and what is my responsibility at this moment to help the *beggar*?

Unfortunately, there are numerous consequences of poverty that help us to understand why the metaphor of *wavers and beggars* also reveals why it is so difficult to alleviate poverty. The physical cues we see in a *waver* or *beggar* tell us how his body is responding to life. If he is begging, and not already in declining health, the long or short fall into poor health is probably not far behind. As we detail later in chapter four, there are enormous tolls placed upon the nervous system of people living in poverty. The immune system is under assault constantly and the worry tears down the human body. Hormones shift into catabolism over growth while cognition and executive brain control are short-circuited. Moreover, there are long-lasting effects of poverty, which even change the genetics of entire populations for multiple generations and strangle progress in poverty alleviation for decades or even centuries.

The act of waving and begging is simple, and the information contained in this book is not intended to label people who are poor as *beggars* and people who have wealth as *wavers*. No, quite the opposite. Our intention is to help melt away social walls that may have divided men before from openly caring for one another with a compassionate heart. Compassion and love are two of the most profound emotions men were gifted by God, and yet our inability to fully access this gift has probably been one or our greatest downfalls. When men are compassionate toward one another with love, the murder, fighting, and hate don't happen in that same space. For this reason, our recognition of our own *waver* and *beggar* inside ourselves is a way for us to connect and not separate.

Characteristics and Circumstances of *Wavers and Beggars*

Wavers
Are working and or creating value in their life
Their basic needs are sufficiently provided for by their efforts
Desire active exchange with others
Are purposeful and feel valued
Their body language is enthusiastic; they smile, wave, are happy, have a
    strong voice, give good eye contact
Have high self-esteem

Circumstances that favor a waving spirit
Areas of strong trade and economy
Advanced education made available
Strong family and community connection

Food is plentiful or sufficient
Health care and personal health are strong
Family health is good

Beggars
Cannot work or have limited work opportunity
Are emotionally burdened
Their survival is in question
May require rehabilitation to return to the waving spirit
Their body language is sad, with head lowered, forward shoulders, lowered
 voice, poor eye contact
Have low self-esteem

Circumstances that often lead to a begging spirit
Weak economy and poor financial markets
Corrupt political leadership
Excessive greed
Illness and poor health care
Poor family connection and community support
War and civil unrest
Criminal activity that takes advantage of the person who must beg
Discrimination
Lack of education
Language barriers

The Embodiment of Waving and Begging

Perhaps no other gesture is recognized as universally as the wave. Whether you are living in the southern or northern hemisphere, in Asia or India, in the Americas or Europe, Australasia or Africa, virtually everyone knows the sign and intent of a wave. *Moreover, one of the most surprising neurological connections associated with a wave is our ability to smile while waving is much stronger than when begging.* It's true! Take a moment and place your book on the table so you can raise your hand to wave. Now, begin waving your hand enthusiastically and smile while waving. Do you notice how there is a natural ease to your smile and the muscles of the face seem to work with the waving hand? Although your smile may not be a natural smile because you think something is funny, the waving action submits a message to your mind that reminds you of happiness and connection with others. Connecting with people is necessary for our survival and when we wave, we welcome connection. Moreover, a smile is a welcome to people telling them you want to be friendly. This is why as I began to notice the *wavers* and *beggars* alongside the road in Kenya, I noticed their disparate body language. I never saw *beggars* smiling but virtually all the people waving smiled at us.

To contrast the natural way your brain organizes happiness with waving, now move your waving hand down and turn your palm up to beg with a cupped hand. Try and smile now. You will notice this does not feel natural. Smiling and begging don't go together. Why is this? Though you can manage a smile, it doesn't seem real. It seems feigned. Could this neurological embodiment be communicating something about *wavers and beggars*? Are we wired to learn how to connect with a wave and smile because these are universal cues we use to demonstrate our value and purposefulness? Does the requirement to beg signal sadness and despair? Is there an inherent pattern and hard wiring all humans share as *wavers* and *beggars* that can also become connecting points for us to develop new relationships with one another? Though a person who needs to beg for money to buy food may still have some happiness, the consistent need to turn the palm up and beg greatly overrides true happiness because of the imminent fear for survival begging is answering.

Embodied cognition is responsible for the phenomenon we feel in the smile muscles and the ease of this facial gesture with either the wave or the begging upturned palm. In the 1980s, a series of experiments by Fritz Strack at the University of Wurzburg in Germany revealed a link between facial gesture and value judgments. In the experiments, people were asked to hold pencils between their teeth to activate smile muscles or between their lips to register frowns. As Strack discovered when different facial muscles were activated by the placement of the pencil, individuals could be influenced in their choices based on either the frowning or the smiling placement of the pencil.[1]

Recognizing gesture and motion have significance and probably contribute in some part to survival; other research is discovering it may have more meaning than most people realize. As Daniel Kahneman describes in his bestselling book 'Thinking Fast and Slow,' our automatic thought processes and the ways that we interpret the actions of others are considered part of the fast responses of the brain. These are the modes of thought, which require little or no conscious effort but instead operate within the unconscious. As Kahneman points out, by being able to read body language, facial expressions, and make snap judgments, our ability to navigate our lives becomes more manageable. Apart from a very small number of people we may know very well, most people we interact with daily can often be strangers, and the likelihood of coming across their paths again can be remote. Therefore, we have to be able to assemble appropriate responses, for example to peg a waitress, a truck driver, or a business executive based only on the person's social place and our learned knowledge of how these people would probably act based on their social status.[2] The unconscious way we perceive them is more reflexive than willful, and any motivation to see beyond the automatic subconscious judgment only comes with determined intention. If negative associations are present, as we might have because someone is a *beggar*, we must look extraordinarily hard to see past his/her social status and engage the compassionate recesses within our brain to respond differently; whereas, if we pass a stranger who is waving instead of begging, our snap judgment may be completely different, based on our learned comprehension of the meaning of waving compared to begging.

Thus, our inclination toward the gesture of a wave or the act of begging not only activates meaning within our brain but also dictates an ongoing tapestry of communication experienced both on a conscious and unconscious level. If I see a child begging, I'm likely to stop to provide help if I feel I am able to help him. However, I could also fear the interaction and recognize my compassionate gesture, while genuine and desired consciously, could result in trouble and possibly lead to a threatening experience for me. Perhaps five, ten, or even a much larger number of begging people might see my act of kindness and rush toward me, engulfing my personal space and leaving me helpless to protect myself or my belongings. Perhaps there are predators lurking in hiding who are awaiting my kind response and will surround and rob me. Or none of these scenarios would occur and I might have an opportunity to just help a begging child with enough money to buy a meal or take care of a sick mother.

All at once, the various possibilities would resound within my unconscious and conscious, and if I am comfortable with poverty and begging, and familiar with the surroundings, I would probably be more likely to help. On the other hand, the constant barrage of poverty in my worldview and feeling helpless to do anything about the enormity of poverty may paralyze my response. I may end up looking away and ignoring the begging plea. This happens all the time in my hometown of Chicago on the exit ramps on the highway. It's very common for men and women to walk along the rows of stopped cars waiting for a light to turn with a cardboard sign reading, "Out of work, need food, can you help?" Or "Injured and can't work, can you spare some change?" Many motorists simply don't look at the *beggars* with the cardboard signs and choose to ignore them because they don't want to engage the *beggar*. Ignoring them and looking away is a safe way to avoid a possible exchange. Of course, the reason many motorists choose to not look toward the begging men/women on these exit ramps may be layered in belief systems about why they beg and what they might do with the money if given the handout.

In contrast, the exchange of a wave doesn't force us to get close or to engage further with a street *waver*. The wave is recognized by our subconscious as a friendly gesture and isn't asking for anything in return. However, a frantic wave with someone who is rapidly advancing towards us can ignite a threat in disguise to our subconscious. If we are already surrounded by unfamiliar people and enormous poverty, we can be guarded and not trust any advancing gestures even if they are energetic waves from a stranger. Once again, the complexity of language, meaning, and the surroundings becomes tantamount to the response I offer.

Other walks of life where waving of hands holds significance include religious settings. In many churches around the world, and especially in the African-American houses of worship in the south, congregants stand and wave elevated hands to celebrate and praise God. *Wavers* are often jubilant and appreciative when worshipping. Still, there are people who worship the Lord with their hands cupped as if begging or pleading for God to answer prayer. Though this act may be in desperation like a *beggar's* frantic plea when survival is precarious, a parallel meaning may simply be a believer's desire to give God a gesture of embodied cognition that demonstrates surrender of will.

Regardless of the intention, the custom of raising hands during worship can be traced to the early years of Israel. Aaron, brother to Moses and one of the high priests, raised his hands as he prayed and blessed the Israelites when the first sanctuary was established. Known as benediction, this form of prayer is often used in services but usually only the minister raises his hand. However, Aaron's ritual of the raised hand became a common ritual during prayer and worship and we can find it within scripture messages speaking of this practice. The book of Psalms speaks of raised hands regularly:

"Because your steadfast love is better than life, my lips will praise you. So I will bless you as long as I live; I will lift up my hands and call on your name." (Psalms 63.3-4)

"Come, bless the Lord, all you servants of the Lord... lift up your hands to the holy place, and bless the Lord." (Psalms 134.1-2)

Further, raising hands can also signify our attachment and need for one another. Like the hands of a child raised for a loving mother to pick him up and carry him while also comforting a wounded knee, raised hands are a signal the child gives to his mother. Outstretched raised hands may signal need or want in worship and prayer as in this psalm:

"I stretch out my hands to you; my soul thirsts for you like a parched land." (Psalm 143.6)

Our raised hands during worship are at times like Aaron's blessing of Israel in Psalm 63. There is at once a yearning for God's answer to our prayers while we joyfully give thanks for his blessings. A common refrain within the scriptures, the Psalms lend the words of hope in raised hands frequently to teach us there is a desire for us to come to God with the spirit of a *waver*.

Although, God loves us whether we are dispirited and left with no choice other than begging.

In the Bible, the word poor is mentioned 199 times and Jesus speaks of the poor throughout his ministry. ***Ironically, the word 'beggar' is only mentioned FOUR times.*** What does this contrast say about God's vision for our lives? Is his hope that we would find the life of a *beggar* our ultimate destiny? Or does he want us to rely upon his providence and his love? Does he desire for us to witness his love by the compassionate, loving care we provide to the sick, the poor, and the weak? I believe he wants us to know his love by being his hands and demonstrating love through our compassion for one another.[3]

The Waving Spirit in Nigeria (The Delta Boys)

Following the lives of a band of militant youth captained by Ateke Tom, 'the Godfather,' documentary filmmaker Andrew Berends takes us inside the camps and lives of Nigerian youth taking injustice into their own hands. As we have shared, it is our belief there are two spirits of humanity, which unfold and are seen with clarity in the most under-resourced and poverty-stricken places on the planet. One such place is the Nigerian Delta, nestled within the vast oil reserves of the region. Although enormous profits from expansive oil reserves reside in the Delta, only a small fraction of the capital and profit finds its way to the most needy. As is all too common in the continent of Africa, there are large tracts of land and millions of people who live in poverty. Adequate clean drinking water, food, shelter, clothing, chiropractic and medical care, education, the arts, recreation, sport, and safety from military conflict are all strangled and disturbingly plagued.

In the Delta, local Nigerians have suffered through hardships for centuries but have still managed to sustain a life rich with culture, love, and loving family connections. However, the discovery of oil and development of this large-scale operation further damaged what little hope many held for brighter tomorrows. As oil companies began to establish operations taking the prized black fuel from the land and beneath the murky brown sediment-filled water of the Delta, extremely troublesome signs began to emerge within the region. Environmental disregard, callous actions, and selfish motives became clear on the part of the multinational oil companies who were now working to feed the hungry oil consumption practices of much of the industrialized world, including the United States, which counts Nigeria as its fifth largest supplier of oil.

No longer willing to allow outside interests that seemed to disregard the needs of local Nigerian citizens, this band of misfits and action-driven youth took it upon themselves to change local oil company behavior and policy. Though their responses were often truculent and highly destructive to the personal property of the multinational companies, their motives seemed appropriate. When people are dismissed and their livelihood is taken in the form of killing the fisheries, polluting the landscape, and stealing a resource that should share wealth evenly, sabotaging oil rigs, hijacking supplies, and destroying company property may seem like the only answer. As I began to examine the plights of the impoverished around the globe with a new lens and applying our metaphors of the *wavers and beggars*, I also understood with more compassion militant actions like those of the Delta Boys. Not willing to sink into the despair and begging for survival, Chima, a fitful young Nigerian youth featured in the documentary, signifies in his courage and perhaps immaturity the *waver* as he summons a newfound purpose wanting to do something that has meaning and significance for his family and the many other despondent Nigerian people living in the Delta. His willingness to leave his family and join Ateke Tom's band was a clear intention to take action and not remain silent in voice and response. Though troubled by his choices to leave and exercise bellicose response to the oil companies, he nonetheless gained stature and self-esteem through his action over inaction.[4]

Though I would not choose personally to regard militant action as the first choice in the Delta or any other conflict, the deeper meaning and context from which these actions arise must be considered purposeful, even if the end result may leave long trails of property destruction, and in some cases loss of life. The desire to survive, retain purpose, and have lasting meaning in life is an imperative that is found in the spirit of the *waver* and the sociological manifestations of each waving farmer, child, or mother working along the dirt roads we traveled in Kenya who waved enthusiastically as we passed. Their waving and connected purpose were in some ways not unlike the spirit living inside Chima, Ateke, or those other youths choosing to change their circumstances with a warring stratagem.

Thus, I could now see the breadth and the deeper ribbons surrounding the hearts of men and women when willing to see how each motive, action, or feeling could be explained in the metaphor of the *waver* and the *beggar*. The struggle the Delta Boys have to secure basic necessities is an example of choices billions must make around the world to survive. Moreover, the courage to fight for their resources and the needs of their neighbors is further testament to the powerful desire to maintain a *waver* spirit. But I also realized as I researched poverty with a closer lens that there are long histories behind most impoverished regions of the world. Each country has its own story. Every struggle is unique, and, though there are similarities between regions and countries, giving time and discovery to understanding each challenge is critical at this juncture to solve poverty.

In my travels and personal experiences I have also learned *wavers and beggars* are found close to home. My story has some of the trials of life characteristic of the *beggar* metaphor. But I also learned as I wrote this book that I am a survivor, and this has led me to want to help under-resourced people around the world who have no voice and are unable to even be given a chance at a better life. As Todd and I further collaborated in the writing and he traveled with me to Kenya, he also got in touch with the feelings of a *beggar*. He came to understand that his poverty was unlike anything he experienced when he traveled to Kenya and saw the poverty there for the first time.

His feelings are expressed in this excerpt from his reflection on what his childhood was like and how it shaped him…

As I reflect back on my life, the motivations and thoughts I felt in my heart never seemed to spread past my own needs, and selfishly I often cared more for just the things which existed in my immediate surroundings. I wasn't a selfish person or narcissistic, but my heart and mind weren't open to things different. My mother, father, brother, sister, and closest friends, along with my material desires as well as the things just in front of me, seemed to be all I cared about.

I tried to tell myself that I was a good person because I wasn't being mean to people and I wasn't getting in trouble. I figured not only was I a good kid but I was black and did okay in school so I was better than the stereotypes. But just that selfish thought said a lot about me and my mirror evaluation, and the true loss was my connection to God. I prayed on a regular basis, but my prayers were for riches and money and to get out of hard work to go through life the easy way. Nothing brings self-reflection like being in the middle of the bush in Kenya and seeing such desperation and sadness. My dreams about being a superstar ballplayer seemed silly standing in front of a girl who had nothing yet dreamed of being a lawyer. My lust for a big house and packed bank account seemed laughable sitting next to a little boy who has no water, electricity, food, or education yet dreamed of being a pilot one day. I still fight the thoughts of having extreme riches, but now my thoughts are plastered with a mindset of giving back and doing God's work. I am a spiritual guy, but I wouldn't call myself a religious guy, yet my heart was moved and my body was pushed to places I had never seen. I had to get out of my comfort zone to open my surroundings…

Thus, I came to recognize my spirit to wave was clouded and I harbored a deep river of grief and discouragement that I had begged for so long in my life. My begging for acknowledgment, recognition, and stardom had been tantamount to my self-worth. However, like so many wavers *we had come to know, my* wavers *spirit breathed deeply and had a profound sense of purpose that grew stronger when I began to focus not only on the needs of myself or my immediate family but also on the desperate lives of millions domestically and internationally. A turning point in my discovery and moving from the* beggar *who needed recognition came in large part through education.*

Education: How Does a *Waver* Show Up in the Classroom?

In classrooms around the world, it's fairly common to see children raising hands when they want to ask a question or have the answer to a teacher's question. Students are encouraged to raise hands to ask questions. Questions and answers, the active exchange of ideas, are initiated and shared through the signal of a raised hand, often waving in small cycles of movement side to side. When children answer a question successfully, they often beam with pride. Raising a hand and knowing the answer to a question sends a message of preparation and a willingness to stand out. In some ways, there is a parallel with children who are waving alongside the road in Kenya. The children I have seen dotting the road also feel a sense of joy, wanting to stand out and be seen. The commonality *wavers* in classrooms and *wavers* alongside the road have is a desire to connect and be seen. The gesture of waving signifies 'Notice me, I matter.'

Even though every human matters to God and should to each of us, it's not always evident that people feel as though they matter or their lives are important. ***It may not be possible to know the feelings men hold about themselves, but the messages many who live in poverty communicate about their self-esteem and self-respect is evident.*** Fredrick is a man living in Chicago who has lived on the streets for several years. He is also a patient at the free clinic where I work. Fredrick was a star athlete in high school and had hopes of one day making it to the National Football League. But drugs and alcohol and poor parental support led him astray from his dreams and his education. Eventually, he ended up in trouble with the law and landed in prison for a short time. His on-and-off-again struggle with his addictions caused havoc with his health and his mind. Eventually, he lost friends and family. And he lost hope.

His feelings about himself and the way he postures his body indicate his strong sadness. He has trouble looking people in the eyes. He hangs his head down and his body language of sloped shoulders and rounded back tell of his sadness and despair. His words are soft and he seems to have very little to live for. He doesn't feel as though his life matters. Fredrick is an example of how many feel they don't have a purpose anymore and their lives don't matter. His posture, attitude, and emotions are similar to the *beggars* alongside the road. The distinction and clear demarcation between the *waver* and the *beggar* is evident in Fredrick and many other people like him. How many people in America feel just like Fredrick? How many worldwide? How many have lost hope and sunk to a low and despondent place with no clear way to dig themselves out of the emotional hole of poverty?

The millions of people who teeter on the edge of survival come from every nation—poverty knows no ethnic, color, gender, or religious barrier. Poverty is everywhere! But, this is not a stumbling block to change the circumstances of millions. As we will discuss in chapter eight, there is incredible promise and there are willing leaders who are taking on poverty challenges. Meanwhile, we also have to be realistic and derive expectations that come alongside the painful reality that many we want to help today may not receive the blessing and resources we are attempting to provide. The best possible scenario may be a gradual transformation of the youngest generation, or even their children or grandchildren.

Children raising a hand in a classroom and asking questions is also like an active parallel dialogue between the impoverished and the people who have resources and can help. Imagine them asking questions like, "Why doesn't anything seem to change in our lives?" "Why do you seem to have so much while we have so little?" "Will it rain and if there isn't any, what are we going to do so we can eat and feed our families?" "How come it seems like the politicians are corrupted and don't care about us?" "Why do the police not protect us and demand bribes or pay to do their job and investigate crimes like robbery?"

Many of the impoverished people around the world ask these questions and wonder when their lives will change. Asking questions and actively seeking ways to change the circumstances causing poverty is another indication of a *waving* spirit.

Wavers and beggars as a metaphor for humanity demonstrates relevance on many levels of consciousness. Though our notion that *waving* is a preferred option over *begging* is important to dispel and assume a non-judgmental view; there are clearly times that the 'best' and perhaps the 'only' option a woman with hungry children may have is begging! Moreover, the courage and the humanity a *beggar* who is truly confronted with no other choice but begging cannot be seen with a disparaging view or be shunned as a degenerate of society. ***No. Instead, we believe the culture that has created a world so desperate and unbalanced must examine the individual motives and ideals of each citizen and take a hard look at the success of that generation.***

Each of us lives within this time of responsibility in the 21ˢᵗ century, and acknowledging the interconnected lives we share helps develop a framework for changing poverty. If I can recognize there are limited differences between the man begging on the side of the road and myself, I am apt to have greater compassion and empathy with him. Then, I am more likely to look upon our world together as a shared experience like a beautiful blanket and we are weavers together in its tapestry. Sharing the experiences of poverty with my brother and doing my part with him to change the circumstances that have led to the tragedy of poverty is the beginning of total transformation.

But transforming poverty together is not easy, nor is there a blueprint for the success of this venture. Even in viewing scripture and seeking God's wisdom on this matter, the struggle a wealthy man has in letting his possessions go for the poor was clear. In the Gospel of Mark, Jesus answers a man's request to understand what he must do to have presence with the Lord.

In response to the man's request to know what he must do to have eternal life, Jesus lovingly looks upon him and answers, "Go, sell everything you have and give to the poor, and you will have treasure in heaven. Then come, follow me." At this choice, the man's face falls and he goes away saddened because he had great wealth. To which Jesus looked around and said to his disciples, "How hard it is for the rich to enter the kingdom of God."[5]

But the poor widow in Mark, Chapter 12 is an example of how beautiful a compassionate heart for service despite one's circumstances can manifest.

"He sat down opposite the treasury and watched the crowd putting money into the treasury. Many rich people put in large sums. A poor widow came and put in two small copper coins, which are worth a penny. Them he called his disciples and said to them, 'Truly I tell you, this poor widow has put in more than all those who are contributing to the treasury. For all of them have contributed out of their abundance; but she out of her poverty has put in everything she had, all she had to live on.'" [6]

Within these two examples, we can imagine the souls and hearts of these two whom Jesus used as examples to teach humanity how to care for the poor and more importantly how we regard our own poverty. Though struggling and probably hungry, the poor widow did not allow her condition to shift her role in life into that of a *beggar*, but instead chose to be needed, valued, and thus retain the giving spirit of a *waver*, while the wealthy man, though comfortable and secure, was unable to trust in the providence of the most magnanimous human to have ever lived and the son of God who told him what he must do to find peace and enter the kingdom of God.

Thus, we must acknowledge our inner struggle; that begins with our own soul, our compassionate heart, and our willingness to act from a place of cooperation and to consider the needs of others possibly greater than our own. Moreover, the quiddity of life may be wrapped into this one single province: *that to give is greater than to receive and to regard another as higher than self may be the ultimate ascent a soul can know.*

Certainly the foundation for much of Jesus's teaching affirmed what has now become known as the golden rule: *"Do unto others as you would have them do unto you."*

Our wisdom, when set in motion around compassion, justice, and service, is capable of prodigious change, and we believe the world is asking for this change today. At no other time in the history of civilization have we been at such a perilous precipice of possible destruction and the end of human civilization from war, depletion of the earth's resources, and human suffering. And yet we are also in the midst of one of the greatest awakenings and available resources in the world of communications. Information organized and digitized passes at billions and trillions of information units per second over airwaves and wired tethers. Our ability to share in the human drama and write a parallel story with our farthest human brother and sister halfway around the world is now possible.

Inspiring and fueling the spirit of the *waver* and changing the world so no one will ever have to sink into the despair of the *beggar* is a challenge we must aspire to accomplish. As you consider your life and the possible ways you can make a difference, the interconnectedness you allow yourself to experience with everyone around the world will be a key to success.

This book will help you unlock your potential to make a difference and to feel compassion and love for people living in challenged lives.

Summary Questions for Discussion

1. As you have observed people begging alongside a road or in a public place, what judgments did you create in your mind about them?
2. If you have traveled to areas of high-density poverty, how did it make you feel to see people living there? To see dilapidated buildings?
3. *Wavers and beggars* is a metaphor for an expression we all feel inside and embody. How have you felt like the *beggars* alongside the road? How have you also been like the *wavers*?
4. As you consider blessings in your life, how do you see yourself helping others with your time, talent, or resources?
5. The Bible mentions the word poor 199 times but begging only four times. Why do you believe the writers of the scripture were more focused on the care of the poor and not on the act of begging?

CHAPTER 2

OUR OWN STORY OF WAVING AND BEGGING

"Human progress is neither automatic nor inevitable. We are faced now with the fact that tomorrow is today. We are confronted with the fierce urgency of now. In this unfolding conundrum of life and history there is such a thing as being too late...We may cry out desperately for time to pause in her passage, but time is deaf to every plea and rushes on. Over the bleached bones and jumbled residues of numerous civilizations are written the pathetic words: too late."
– Martin Luther King Jr. *Where do we go from here: chaos or community?'*

Poverty's Impact: one in three children today lives without adequate shelter.

The remarkable hope and desperate depravity I observed in *wavers* and *beggars* was something I could identify with, in large part because inside my heart I knew God created me in the same way he had made them. The saddened, terrified, and desperate eyes of the *beggars* reminded me of my own frailty, how circumstance and luck of the draw being born in America, with more opportunity, was the only relevant difference separating my existence and theirs. If I was truly honest with myself, I could connect to the times when my desire to hold out a hand either for real or metaphorically was a connecting point of my humanity with people living the most horrible circumstances. My own defeated life and feeling like I wanted to quit and giving up my dream was something I knew personally. I discovered virtually everyone could relate to cupped begging hands and what this means to the human spirit. At the same time, I also recognized the spirit of the *beggars and wavers* was a characteristic we shared humanly. They signal victory or defeat in our consciousness and people anywhere in the world can relate to the feelings of victory or the sadness of defeat.

My co-author Todd grew up with immense challenges in his life. His parents never married; he was 'an accident,' as society sometimes refers to unwanted pregnancies. Still, he was fortunate his father provided a stable home, even though his birth mother never wanted him. His struggles to be affirmed and secure recognition haunted him through most of his childhood and into young adulthood. Eventually, he found peace, but his story as the 'football hero' and the hopes other people had in his success was difficult for him. His football hero story is similar to some of the stereotypes people have about young black men in America and what they are or are not capable of doing.

Todd's Story

Begging to Wave

Have you ever truly looked at yourself in the mirror and questioned your role in the world? Yes, raising a family, having a career, leaving a legacy for your kids are all self-defining accolades in life. But that is just bubble-minded thinking. I mean making an impact in the world that would make a lasting difference beyond your life here on earth. If the very thought of that is overwhelming, you are not alone. There is only a small percentage of people who are willing to embark on something that they know from the start they won't finish in their lifetime. I can name a few: Martin Luther King, Abraham Lincoln, and Albert Einstein. The enormity of what they did still affects our lives today. Yet at the time they were making a difference, they had no idea where their journey would lead them. Of course, there will never be another Rosa Parks, but we all have a little bit of those heroes in us. The questions we need to ask ourselves in the mirror should be, "Am I willing to start my journey? Can I look past my bubble called now and sow seeds that can be called miracles in the future? Is my heart open enough to question whether I am doing enough?"

My journey began with the question: Am I a *waver* or a *beggar*? Let's put it in the context of a worldview. I will be the first to admit, I swore I was a *waver*. I thought I was doing my part in making the world a better place. I was sure I was staring life in the eye and saying hello to the blessings of life. I figured I was doing enough. I was waving my hand high enough to be seen. But the truth is I had to take a look in the mirror before my journey to Kenya to try and understand the perilous grips of poverty, and what I saw in myself was a *beggar*. As a matter of fact, Warren and I were noticing more *beggars* than *wavers*. To come to that point, we had to go back in our lives to see how our own *beggar* mentality began.

So I took a look in the mirror and there I saw myself as a *beggar*. I was not a beggar in the sense of health or monetary terms. I was a beggar in my soul. From the time I could remember, I clamored for money, power, and, sadly, mostly popularity and fame. Born in Long Beach California, raised in the southern suburbs in a city called Rowland Heights, I was an athlete out of the womb. My father raised me as a single dad—statistically uncommon for a black man. We moved around the towns of Los Angeles until he met my stepmother and we settled in the suburbs. We lived a middle-class life; I like to call it a black blue-collar family life. My dad was the head of the household, but my stepmom laid down the rules and kept us in line at home. My father owned his own termite company and my mom worked logistics for a big corporation. I felt like I never begged for anything and I lived an okay lifestyle. My sister lived with her mom, so mostly it was just my stepbrother and I growing up. My parents both worked long hours, so it was pretty much the two of us taking care of each other during the week. But sports and a wild imagination were my vices growing up. I played basketball, baseball, and my aunt even tried me in tennis for a few sessions, but my God-given talent was in football. Football would shape my entire childhood and create paths that have shaped who I am today. From the time I could say the word football, I was walking around with one in my hand. My first shirt was a football shirt. My first and favorite video game was John Madden and my first female attractions were cheerleaders. From my first practice, I was a step ahead of everyone. My speed, hunger, and just a mental knack for the game were stronger than anyone else my age. So much so that my father moved me up a year to play with kids older after my first year. I took a beating and pounding, but it made me better and stronger as a player. Everything I did growing up revolved around football. My social life, my friends on our team, and my personality came with a running back's ferocity.

Sadly my education was also tied to football. Instead of wanting to learn or get smarter, I just wanted to pass so I could play football. There was no emphasis on a strong education because a 2.0 grade point average was acceptable to my parents, coaches, and teachers. That 2.0 mark was accepted all the way to high school and college. My acceptance of mediocrity in education started there, the mentality for just getting by. I was terrible at reading, math, and social studies. Pretty much everything that didn't involve P.E. or music and arts I was average or below average. I didn't even grasp basic concepts. My parents tried to get me help with tutors, but as they were busy trying to provide a roof over my head I did a good job of acting like I had everything in order.

By the time I got to high school, my respect for education had turned more positive and I took more of an interest in learning. But I was so behind and my mental fortitude was down. It took extra teachers and tutors just to get me to a C+ average. Yet, while my education struggled, my football stardom was rising.

All the years of playing with older kids had finally paid off in my freshman high school year. My team went undefeated that year and we dominated opponents. My stat sheet was also starting to fill as well. I was still, after all these years, a step faster, so much so that it caught the attention of the varsity coaches and I was named starting running back for varsity before the summer of my sophomore year even started. The football legend around my town had been born. My sophomore year just kept my status climbing. My life was in good standing. My social life was picking up. I had never had as many friends. I had a main girlfriend and my grades were getting better. Sophomore year was also when my affection for education picked up as well and I started to get more interested in the arts, music, and acting.

But as I look back, I know all of it seemed to come together because I didn't disappoint on the football field. I was exceeding all expectations. I was already starting to get college letters—big-time schools just letting me know they were watching from afar. We had a pretty good year and made a playoff run. My first year in varsity would end up being my best. The problem was, and I didn't know this at the time, my football celebrity was starting to overshadow my other interests and my education. I couldn't just be Todd the student or the artist. I was being typecast as only an athlete rather than someone who could do anything in life. My friends around me were being told they could be anything they wanted: teachers, firemen, or a CPA—anything they wanted to be. But my career had already been picked out for me and it involved football. It got to the point where I couldn't detach myself from it. I knew I had been working hard at studying and doing my school work, but still I was just not smart enough and there was no way I could have been better than a C- average. But I was getting B+ and A- grades. And they weren't because of my work. It wasn't lost on me that I was given the benefit of the doubt because of my football stardom.

My junior year is when I realized my love for football was more about hanging with my friends and playing a game rather than a tool to get into college or the pros. Football had become a job now, a stressor in life. Instead of being about my boys and I going out there and having fun while pounding someone, the game became about college letters and trips. When I jumped to varsity sophomore year, I also jumped away from my friends, and by the time senior year came around my entire close friend base had quit playing football. While my football love was subsiding, my love for the arts and music was becoming more serious. I was accepted into a class called VAPA (Visual and Performing Arts). It was in this class that I first believed I could do something other than sports. At the time, VAPA was a new-age learning approach to learning history and English through music and acting. Instead of your typical brick and mortar style learning of reading books, watching movies, taking tests, we would learn English comprehension and historical facts by singing them out or acting them out through films that we made. I was finally able to express myself without feeling the athlete label. I could remember we would put on shows for the school and I would get the same butterflies pre-show as I would pre-game. The sad part was I had to hide my love for the arts because my football status was still peaking and no one wanted to hear about me wanting to be a singer, an actor, or a writer. My *beggar* was starting to creep out. I begged to be seen as something other because it was becoming more apparent that football would not be the tool for me to make an impact in life.

But no one knew at the time. And, I will admit, including me. But it wasn't just begging to make a small difference. I wanted to have the kind of effect and stature of an NFL player. I didn't know what I wanted to do, but I wanted to make a difference. At first, it boiled as selfish lust for attention. I wanted to show everyone that I wasn't just some dumb jock. My steam boiled over so much so that I would eventually give back a full-ride scholarship to Boise State, a college football powerhouse. This fire that started would change the landscape for the rest of my life.

Warren's Story

Needing to Feel Safe and Wanted

Similar to Todd's experiences growing up, I had my own struggles to find security and feel safe. Never really able to settle anywhere for too long and feel like I belonged, I tried to make people like me so I would be accepted. In many ways, my need to feel safe and belong thrust me into the feelings of sorrow *beggars* may feel every time the cupped begging hands extend and hope a stranger will accept and give something. I struggled with the insecurity of not knowing whether we were going to move or whether I was going to have a place I could call home. I learned what it felt like to be on the edge of survival by American standards, though I never became homeless. My lessons I learned through my struggles helped me understand with certainty I could end up on the side of the road like any beggar who has to beg to survive. I also learned the remarkable grace in

God's provision to care for the poor, the weak, and the people in need. As life teachers along the way helped me to understand, God has a plan and he cares and loves all of us.

While growing up, I learned fear that told me the world was unsafe and I couldn't trust the behavior of adults who were supposed to be taking care of me. Though my childhood was unmarked by the atrocities so often befalling a child growing up with sexual abuse or chronic mental and physical abuse, I suffered from a disorder of security. Unsafe is perhaps not even the correct word to describe what I felt. I grew up like many young middle-class white American children in a suburban home near a metropolitan city. Born in Detroit in 1964 during the era of the civil rights movement, post-Kennedy assassination, and predating the Vietnam War, my parents were young and excited, set to live the American Dream. My father was a young engineer entering into the professional world working for the Ford motor company and my mother a stay-at-home mom. My parents met while my mother was still in high school and my dad attended Purdue University. They eventually fell in love and were married young. My dad was only twenty, my mother eighteen. My mother didn't complete her high school education but instead left school two weeks before graduation to get married.

As a toddler, I had the usual friendships and playmates while living in Detroit. Around aged two, my father was transferred and took a new job in Pittsburgh. My family purchased a suburban home and my younger brother, Tim, was born when I was about three and a half. I have fond memories of Pittsburgh's rolling hills, of afternoon naps and watching my favorite television shows, Mr. Rogers and Captain Kangaroo. Life seemed idyllic. However, my father was transferred again and took another job when I was around four and a half. This time, we made a large move all the way to the west coast of Northern California. For the second time in my young life, we moved.

I made new friends quickly and my parents started me in kindergarten classes in a nearby school. One of the familiar memories I recall beginning around this time were evening fights that I could hear my parents having as I attempted to drift off to sleep. Muffled yelling and shouting echoing up the stairway and down the hall, the anger and hurt in the voice of my parents became a regular signal the evening was upon us and now was our bedtime and they could talk. Although their fighting frightened me, I don't recall talking with either of them about their arguments or any mention of assurance from them. The fighting was just something that became a part of my memory.

Living in Walnut Creek, California, I developed a close group of friends in the neighborhood. Kids gravitated towards me, enjoying my aggressiveness and my fun-loving personality. At this same time, I also began to notice a small demon growing inside me. I became a bully and started to fight regularly with other children. I also became a daredevil, pushing limits and testing boundaries. One of my most regretful memories, where I acted out in an irresponsible manner, occurred when I broke into a neighbor's house with some friends to raid their refrigerator and just look around. On another occasion, I betrayed my parents' trust, and instead of taking the school bus in the morning as I was supposed to, I ran home from the bus stop and ditched the bus to ride my bike instead. I always wanted to ride my bike as other children in the neighborhood were allowed, but my parents had expressly forbidden it due to safety. While this was not the first rebellion I had conjured, it was a further progression of dissidence. A series of other acts followed over the ensuing months, including injuring a child with a large stone I threw at him after leaving the bus. On another occasion, I was asked by our bus driver to bring a sweater home to a girl who was my neighbor. But my rebellious spirit growing inside led me to make another poor choice… Instead, I led my group of friends to the backyard of an empty home for sale with a pool to dump the sweater in the pool.

From where was all this anger and negative rebellion coming? As I matured, I recognized I was a troubled child not unlike many of our youth today who commit crimes of destruction and malice. As my parents' lives began to come unglued, my actions were a mirror of their unrest.

It wasn't long before they divorced and we moved out with our mother. The day we moved is memorable. I can still recall the words my younger two-year-old brother Tim said as I played next door with neighbors: "Mom wanted me to come and get you and tell you to come home!" My only response being, "Why?" He replied, "Because she said we are leaving!"

Not really fully comprehending the enormity of his statement or belief in its accuracy coming from my barely two-year-old younger brother, I followed him home to discover my mother frantically packing our belongings. Questioning her regarding the statement Tim had just conveyed, she confirmed we were leaving for a new home. Memories fade with time and the convergence of new experiences, but when I sit in silence focused on that day and access the feeling of separation that befell me, I only remember deep sadness. Seeing my yard, our home, and the bright early sun on a March spring day, I recall the engine of the car igniting with a roar and the car backing down the driveway, and then my home fading in the distance as we pulled away.

I remember on that day, time seemed to almost stand still. We drove for what seemed like hours but was probably not more than an hour, maybe two at the most. Driving up and up into the hills outside the beautiful and picturesque San Francisco Bay, my mother had carefully arranged for us to stay at a type of halfway house with a kind older woman who owned a furry cat. As we traversed the winding roads loftily perched above the scenic San Francisco Bay, I recall the angelic songs of the early 1970s streaming from the radio. "On the day that you were born the angels got together and decided to create a dream come true," were the words I remember the most. The Carpenters' music painted hope for me. They sang the promise that angels were present and caring for all of us. The verse from this song will always take me back to those moments when I first learned the meaning of separation and how leaving home can be frightening and painfully sad to a child.

Slowly, my mother began to sort out her life and how she would take care of two small boys on her own. Our lives became routine and the furry cat and the older women were a comfort to my brother and me. I loved to feel the cat's fur by my chest as I held her close to the place where the sadness was strongest in my body, my heart. Many years later, I realized how important bonding with that cat had been in helping me learn to trust again after my family had crumbled.

Eventually, my mother moved my brother and me to her own small two-bedroom apartment in nearby Walnut Creek, California. I enrolled in school and we began to learn a new life and have a set of new experiences. This would begin a long period I call 'apartment living.' Apartment living was different and wonderful for me. I had access to a swimming pool, new friends, and all-day play through the entire summer. It was a time when we experimented with life, leadership, disappointment, and testing limits.

My memories of living in that first apartment complex are positive and those days were instrumental in growing my leadership and adventuring spirit. Days were often filled with activities like swimming, playing by a nearby creek, riding Big Wheels down the hill and jumping the creek, building forts, and trespassing into the nearby farmer's cornfield to steal corn and eat it raw. Every day, we had unplanned creative play and worked together to create our experiences. Because we lived in a complex with hundreds of apartment units, there were always new children moving in and some leaving. I became accustomed to the rhythm of friends coming and going in life, accepting this as normal without regret.

My mother continued to work hard to make our life normal. We paid visits to our elderly friend in the hills with the furry cat. I always looked forward to seeing my furry friend, and on one of our visits I remember an experience that marked a turning point in my life because of a statement our kind elderly friend made in response to a miracle that day. For the second time in my life, I had the opportunity to see the birth of life when the cat I adored gave birth to kittens. As I witnessed this amazing miracle, standing by my side, the elderly women described the event and shared the detail of God's plan for birth and life. She continued, telling me my little furry friend had waited for me to come. She knew I would be visiting soon. It was a miracle and to think my furry cat friend had waited and only then when we arrived did she determine it was safe to give birth to her litter. The feelings of belonging, making a difference, and being someone who mattered began to come together with that single gesture of birth that day.

This cat had comforted me in my time of need and given me hope that tomorrow would hold a brighter future. Moreover, she communicated that I mattered and was important. I was important enough to wait for, to hold back the natural course of labor and birth till I could witness her miracle. As a young child, the impact and enormity were immense, and only many years later did I realize how this event shaped my life.

As is often the case in our lives, early life experiences are indelibly imprinted upon our hearts. Some hold lasting joy while others can leave long or deep scars. The sadness and loneliness that had harbored inside my tender heart had a soothing answer in the cat. As life continued to take shape in our apartment living, it was not long before my mother decided it was time to move on again. Although there was no surprise announcement from my younger brother this time, the move and the magnitude of this event would provide one of the most lasting and deepest scars in my heart. Unbeknownst to me, my mother had decided it was time to move far away from our California home and head east toward the Midwest. On a sunny Friday morning, we packed her 1971 green Maverick full, completely loading the trunk and back seat with as many belongings as the car would hold. I remember how absurd it seemed to have piles of clothes, books, and personal effects overflowing in such a disorganized manner. Clothes were taken right from the closet and left on the hanger, while various personal items were put in boxes and loaded. At the time, we even had a bird and dog, which were packed along for the sojourn east.

As we neared the ready for our journey out of state, my mother needed to make one more stop so we would have enough money to pay for gas, food, and other incidentals needed for a long journey. I recall as we headed toward San Francisco to cross the Bay Bridge my mother sharing some of the details of our upcoming journey and the inclusion of a trip to see our grandmother in the tiny town of Attica, Indiana. Unknown to my brother and I, once again my mother had intended to vacate the area without telling our father. This time she would be taking us across several state lines, thousands of miles away from our California home. As we slowed down in the traffic congestion near the toll booths of the bridge, my mother realized going through her purse she did not have the money needed to pay the toll operator fifty cents to cross the bridge. She had spent every last cent she had from the meager alimony and child support check sent from our father the last month. Now, she was on her way to pick up a check from our dad in downtown San Francisco at his Bechtel offices where he worked. Although she did not panic when she rolled her window down to tell the toll operator she didn't have even fifty cents to cross the bridge, she did plea for asylum and leniency to be allowed to cross the bridge. Her case pleaded without success, I recall the tollbooth operator telling her he could not allow her to cross without the toll. She would have to pay the money to pass. This represented a strong roadblock to my mother's plans to leave the state that day. But she was not going to let this small amount of money or slight aggravation deter her exit.

She carefully pulled the car over across six lanes of car traffic to the edge of the roadway and stopped the car on the safety lane. She told my brother and me that we had to find fifty cents in the car and she knew there had to be enough money under seats and in the cracks and creases of the interior design elements of the car. Quickly, we sprang into action, pulling out gum wrappers, old burger bags, hardened French fries, and sticky, dirty food wraps from under the seats, floor mats, glove box, and in between the seat crevices. Each penny we discovered seemed like a victory and our excitement propelled us further to see if we could find the fifty cents needed to cross the Bay Bridge. As our thirty-minute search came to a conclusion and thousands of rush-hour commuters passed by gawking at our open doors with stacks of clothes, I felt a mild embarrassment from the attention drawn to our poverty on the side of the road. Here we were, practically penniless and unable to get to the city where we could get some help. I remember feeling as though I wanted to hide, but there was nowhere I could, other than to keep my head down at the floor in front of the passenger seat in search of more coins.

As I reflect how I felt that day, I imagine the shame and the desire to hide is not unlike how beggars feel when people pass them without offering to help. "Doesn't anyone care?" "Is anyone going to help me?" "Why me?" are only some of the questions that raced through my mind that day on the bridge, and probably also tear at the heart and mind of beggars alongside the road.

It's ironic thinking back. There were no commuters willing to slow down or inconvenience themselves to offer assistance to a young mother with two little children obviously in some need. Maybe no one stopped because we didn't raise the hood on the car or maybe it's because my mother did not signal for help out of fear she may not have been able to trust a commuter's intentions with two little children and herself. Whatever the reasons, no one came to our aid and when our final money count was complete, we were short thirteen cents toward our goal. With only thirty-seven cents, our efforts, while noteworthy, were a failure in securing passage on the bridge. However, my mother, as I have come to know time and again, would not be deterred in her quest to cross the bridge. She took the thirty-seven cents in hand and walked across six lanes of heavy congested traffic to the tollbooth operator who had stopped our passage only a short time before. As she showed him the results of her search and once again pleaded her case, he provided a thirteen-cent random act of kindness to pay the remaining shortage and allowed us to cross the bridge.

I recall my mother sharing with us how happy she was that he was willing to help her out and that there are good people in the world. My trust in things working out was strengthened. Our short visit to San Francisco was the first stop on our way to the Midwest, and with an alimony and child-support check now in hand, we were ready to leave California for the Midwest.

After cashing the check, gassing up the car, and stopping by the grocery store, we headed east toward Indiana. Though many of the details of the trip, I've forgotten, one very distinct detail of our journey has always troubled me. What was my mother thinking when she picked up a young male hitchhiker heading back home to see his family in Indiana? Though the 1970s viewed hitchhiking with more acceptance, picking up a hitchhiking stranger on our journey has always seemed out of place. Though, when I consider the compassionate ways of my mother and her enormous ability to give, serve, and trust, the explanation seems far more elementary. As she drove along the highway, she may have heard a whisper from God in her quiet prayers she was saying to herself on an empty stretch of highway in the high desert of Nevada. It's possible she felt this young man needed support and she was attempting to be a Good Samaritan like the parable Jesus shared in Matthew.

Several days on the road and sleeping in the car at rest stops to save money, we eventually arrived in the Midwest and dropped off our new friend, the hitchhiker. Then we headed for Attica, Indiana, my mother's hometown. Since my mother did not have a firm action plan, this short stay would be a good way to take some time and gather her thoughts about what would follow next. Ultimately, she wanted to move to the Quad Cities to attend Palmer College of Chiropractic in Davenport, Iowa. In the preceding year leading up to this cross-country trip, her healing under chiropractic care had given her a desire to become a chiropractor.

In Attica, we settled into a familiar routine with my grandmother, great uncle, and great grandmother. Attica is a small town with simple values. Everyone knows one another and calls them neighbor. People take things at a slower pace and extend a hand just a little further.

We lived there for only a short time and moved once again in an abrupt manner. One of the things I began to notice in myself as a result of these frequent moves was an unexplained fear that I hadn't felt before. It wasn't consuming but I had less trust that things were going to be okay. I missed my old home in California and my friends.

Our move had been hastened by an argument between my mother and my great grandmother. Though my mother had no plan for her arrival and where to stay in the Quad Cities, she left anyway and trusted things would work out. Her resolve and faith often prompted her dramatic moves without fully knowing how it would work out and she relied upon her tenacity and grit to prevail. I suppose, reflecting back, I can say I learned some difficult but important lessons through these sad exits and farewells.

When we finally arrived in downtown Davenport after our long ten-hour car ride, it was nearing five o'clock and we were hungry. My mother spotted a Dairy Queen and was intrigued because a car parked in front had California license plates. Since Iowa is over two thousand miles away from California, this is unusual and it got my mother's attention. As we entered the small, sparsely furnished restaurant, I remember feeling the stares of strangers and uncomfortable feelings welling up inside. Though I was young, I can still remember the uneasy feelings I had. Another new surrounding and leaving a familiar place gave me insecurities and fear. In only two months, I had been moved across the United States and displaced twice in a short time, almost like a refugee.

My mother made an announcement as we stood there in the Dairy Queen. "Hey, I just moved here from California and I noticed there was a car in the parking lot with California plates. Whose car is that?" A man minding his own business looked up suddenly volunteered, "That's my car lady." And with that, we were introduced to Mark, a total stranger. My mother sat down and gathered information, discovering he had a sister who needed a roommate. His sister had recently divorced, too, and had a three-bedroom home in Moline, Illinois. She was looking to share some of the expenses, and so it was settled: we would be moving in with his sister and her three kids in Moline that evening.

Driving to a stranger's house and spending the night was not an unknown for my brother Tim and me. However, this new arrangement represented something entirely different. Our new home had three children we had never met before, and now we were going to be sleeping in beds right next to them. It was kind of like going to overnight camp when total strangers are suddenly thrust upon one another into cabins and bunk beds. But this was not overnight camp; it felt awkward and frightening to me. As I reflect now, it seems there had to be a divine presence for us to find shelter that first night so easily. Time and again, I remember the serendipitous circumstances following my mother's life. Perhaps it was only because she was willing to trust that things would work out, or she really had no other choice. While I may have felt uneasy and unsettled by the whole thing, I can honestly say at no time was I ever in any danger. This is a credit to the tenacity, drive, and faith of my mother.

Our lives began to take shape in Moline, and we enrolled in school. I became the 'new kid,' and so began a series of new-kid-in-school experiences. These were the days when new students were ushered into a classroom and introduced to all the students from the front of the class. Of course, this introductory formality could have been passed on as far as I was concerned. Not only was it scary, but also I found it humbling and shaming as I could hear the whispers around the room and the thirty sets of eyes staring at me. This event would become something I would get used to as we moved frequently over the next few years. Eventually, I would end up living in twenty different homes from age five to young adulthood. Being settled was not something I ever knew as a child.

As I reflect on the way these moves affected me as it relates to my *beggar* inside, I sit with sadness if I choose to see what I did not have. I was not afforded an opportunity to know a community well and have lifelong friends. Instead, I had a series of shorter, but perhaps no less meaningful, relationships. But I learned how to adapt and be flexible, and this gave me a strong sense of how it feels to be an outsider looking in. Many beggars would admit this is also how they feel. Begging can make a child feel like an outsider.

The frequent moves and fear gave me a small appreciation for how some beggars may feel as a result of their circumstances. Probably my saving grace in my own life was the eventual settling my mother found in the Quad Cities and marrying my stepfather. Our lives took on a comfortable balance, and we lived in Davenport for a number of years. I eventually had a group of friends and felt like I fit in. Fitting in is vital and important to all people. We want to know we fit in and matter. We want to know we are needed and valued. *Beggars* often don't feel any of these qualities.

I believe through my childhood experiences that I've touched some of the ways true beggars can feel. I rarely felt like I belonged or mattered. I felt insecure and afraid, not knowing how or if we would survive when my mother didn't have enough money for food or the monthly child support checks were late. I even had to beg my father on the phone to send the monthly checks on time when the money would arrive a couple of days late in the mail. Security, confidence in a safe future, and feeling a sense of connection to our community were all experiences I lacked—similar inadequate feelings for beggars.

While my life never stood as precariously in the balance as many *beggars* around the world, the feelings I had were helpful for me to connect with the humanity of men and women who struggle to survive. Their lives and the ways they feel matter more to me because I have allowed myself to explore how I have a *beggar* inside of me. At the same time, I'm also able to relate to the *wavers* of the world by accessing my feelings of purpose and desire to connect with others. I have many close bonds and feel confident in new surroundings because I have strong self-esteem. This confidence and desire to seek out new experiences I believe parallels the *waving* spirit of men and women. *Wavers* have more security in their survival than *beggars*.

The two extremes in my life were helpful in giving me perspective and compassion toward men and women in different aspects of their lives. Recognizing the feelings I share in common with *beggars* like fear, insecurity, shame, and depravity helps me gain empathy. While also having confidence, wanting to be seen, feeling valued, and engaging purposeful life creates more connection with *wavers*. Viewing *wavers and beggars* around the world as people just like myself and seeing the ways they navigate life as I do is a strong place to begin a journey of global change.

Summary Questions for Discussion

1. Everyone has a story to share about their life. As you consider your childhood, how have you felt like the *waver* and the *beggar*? What feelings does this bring to you?
2. In many instances, people can recall turning points in their life, when a decision to do something, take a new job, go to school, get married, etc. changed their lives. What decisions have you made that were turning points in your life? Did any of these decisions also create emotional healing or wounding for you?
3. Do you think as you pass by *beggars* cupping their hands or holding a cup out for change, your attitude and thoughts about them will be different now? Do you recognize in yourself the way we are all connected?

CHAPTER 3

THE ORIGINS OF POVERTY AND THE ENORMITY OF THE PROBLEM

"The greatest disease in the West today is not TB or leprosy; it is being unwanted, unloved, and uncared for. We can cure physical diseases with medicine, but the only cure for loneliness, despair, and hopelessness is love. There are many in the world who are dying for a piece of bread but there are many more dying for a little love. The poverty in the West is a different kind of poverty – it is not only a poverty of loneliness but also of spirituality. There's a hunger for love, as there is a hunger for God."
– Mother Teresa. *A Simple Path: Mother Teresa*

Poverty's Impact: One billion people entered the 21st century unable to read a book or sign their name. Two-thirds of them are women.

Columbus and Other Explorers

In preparation for this chapter, I realized tackling the origins of poverty was a monumental task. How do you begin to write about poverty? How did so many people's lives become so desperate? Why does it all seem so unfair? Some have enough, or more than enough, while billions are teetering on the edge of survival. Poverty is a symptom of many problems. It is emotional, physical, and varies depending on location. The squalor, lack of opportunity, and hopelessness that millions experience is so widespread that the breadth of the problem defies description.

The seeds of poverty were cast hundreds of years ago and are still being sown throughout the world. Colonial exploitation marks the beginning for most of the tragic poverty we are writing about through this book. But incomprehensible political corruption, capitalistic greed, failed socialistic ideals, geography, and social barriers have also lent fuel to the tragic circumstances of billions of people and the plight many *beggars* are in today.

In the documentary *The End of Poverty*, the haunting details leading up to the majority of the poverty people must endure and tragically still grips them is explained with clarity. Seeking wealth, fame, and riches, vast numbers of early European settlers left their motherlands in search of commodities in Africa and the Americas. Their greedy desires were the domination of the untapped markets and exploitation of the native people to enrich the European powers. Spain, France, England, Belgium, and Portugal were among the most notorious. But later the United States, Japan, and other Asian powers would also follow a similar path of deceit and greed to achieve monopolistic economic control over weaker nations.[1]

One of the earliest and perhaps most famed explorers was Christopher Columbus. Setting out to discover a new trade route to India and explore new markets, Columbus mistakenly landed on the tiny island of Hispaniola, now known as the Dominican Republic, on its east side and Haiti on the west side. Thwarted by his mistake but recognizing landing on the island among the indigenous Taino tribe that lived there could be an opportunity, Columbus quickly began to take advantage of the peaceful Taino. From the beginning, Columbus, and others who followed, showed little if any regard for the inherent rights of the native Taino people of this small island, but instead enslaved, tortured, and murdered them. As the Spanish powers and Columbus conquered and stole the Taino's natural island resources, they would eventually massacre and destroy the entire civilization of the Taino. It is estimated the bloody genocide would eventually claim nearly three million lives.

Columbus's duties for the Spanish would include four trips to the Americas. While his historical significance and heroic merit are often hailed as great leadership and courageous endeavor, I regard his role in the murder and exploitation of millions in the Americas as abhorrent. His brutal torture of tribal people who lived in relative peace for centuries doesn't deserve the reverence we pay him in historical literature. His disregard and destructive greed, along with others who also set out to tap the wealth of the Americas and Africa, would dramatically alter the course of life for billions of people throughout the Caribbean, the Americas, and Africa. The period of exploration set into motion by European leaders would lead many to seek their wealth and fame in new lands. In vast tracts of land, abundantly filled with resources unimaginable to the new settlers and vast numbers of obedient people vulnerable to enslavement, colonies were formed for the enrichment of powerful motherlands to the North and East.

Early settlers in new lands forbade many native people from practicing their traditional faiths, from living in the harmony of their cultural rites, and thrust the European Christian beliefs on them. The loss of culture, historical record, and the death of millions of the colonized people is a cavernous and sad hole in the hearts of many people living in these nations today. Though slavery and immigration to many of the poorest nations of the world have also changed their cultures and influenced the way people live their lives in them, the disconnection from the original natives still haunts these countries today.[2]

Taking hold of natural resources, restricting trade, and heavily taxing people, European countries were able to create vast wealth. By enslaving people and forcing them to work on plantations, in mines, on ships, and in factories, the ownership interests in European nations were able to install the needed engine that drives capitalism—cheap labor! Whereas in these tribal economies before there was a communal understanding about the fair use and distribution of resources, the Europeans dashed the cooperative communal ways of the native people in favor of a greedy, capitalist model built on the backs of indentured slaves. Countries that had produced their own finished products including coffee, tea, textiles, and precious metal objects now had to export all their materials to the European countries to create finished products. Then European companies exported the processed materials back into the colony economies, forcing high tariffs and costs on them.

As colonized countries began developing structured economies, large multinational companies and banking interests created laws and debt repayment terms, which made it impossible for these poor countries to repay their debts taken to build their infrastructure. Some countries were buried under enormous debt as they gained independence because the system of taxation and investment that had been operating under colonial rule was inadequate to shift so abruptly to independent state status. New leaders who had never tasted power or had a sense of the true essence of leadership were given opportunities to also exploit their own people. Treating the reserve currency and banking system as their own piggy bank, many leaders in African nations have continued, and even deepened, their country's poverty by placing their selfish interests in front of the needs of the people they are supposed to serve. Often, colonial powers created taxation models and legislation that favored their interests and limited the ability of the colony to grow its own economy or improve the lives of the local native residents. In the same way, having learned the self-centered methods of the motherland powers, independent country leaders would also install laws and taxation methods that would favor themselves. The tragic result of this greed and unwillingness to grasp the bigger picture has caused hardships that will likely take decades and perhaps centuries to reverse.

Prior to the arrival of European explorers, ancient cultures of the colonized countries had little contact with others. They learned a life of independence from outside influences. Needs of the community for shelter and food were shared by everyone in the tribe. Farming, hunting, and foraging provided sustenance. Water was available in streams, lakes, and rivers. Crucial in ancient cultures as today, water and fertile soil allowed tribal people of pre-colonial period to flourish.

Many of the thriving cultures living in communal tribal villages were successful, surviving thousands of years because they shared resources and recognized the requirements to move when environmental circumstances changed. Mostly agrarian with survival depending on rains for crops and water for animals, there are still archeological ruins and clues that help us understand their lives. Many of the ruins seem to point to dramatic climate change being a determinant in the eventual survival and the paths that large numbers of tribal people took. Dwellings in Arizona, sub-Saharan Africa, and Central and South America are examples of the resourcefulness and creativity tribal cultures had long before European explorers came to 'civilize' them.

The history of colonization and the timetable when it took place varies depending on the region of the world. In Africa, colonial empires divided the regions to avoid conflict with one another. African colonization occurred in the latter half of the 19th century and the early 20th century. However, a European presence existed for several centuries prior with the Portuguese being among the first to settle and lay claim to lands of Africa. The Americas were colonized in the 16th century following the successful exploration of regions beginning with Columbus's voyage from Spain. In the ensuing years, through most of the 16th century, Spain seized control of most of the Americas and Caribbean. In 1519, Cortez subjected the Aztec empire of Mexico to his control. Further expansion continued to the north and the south with Coronado invading northward through New Mexico and California. The Spaniards took the most southern lands of the Americas, Peru, and Chile.[3]

The Araucanians' Struggle to Survive

Without fail, virtually every culture settled by the colonials adopted the rituals and traditions of the European powers. Often by power and bloody persecution, native people were tortured, enslaved, and had little or no choice to change—or die. However, some courageous exceptions of hope did stand firm and made valiant efforts to retain their ceremonial and cultural ways. One of these nations that held a secure position for nearly 350 years were the Araucanians, a group of South American Indians concentrated in the fertile valleys and basins of south-central Chile. The Araucanians' will to live as their ancestors did for thousands of years is powerful testimony to the fact that people should be afforded cultural freedom. Moreover, it represents a strong signal of the waving spirit found within *wavers* alongside the road and within every person.

The Araucanians, like many tribal people of various regions, had sub-tribes within their larger tribal nation. Not all were able to resist the force thrust upon them by Spain. The first of the Araucanians to fall were the Picunche in 1536, who were willing to accept colonization, even growing accustomed to outside rule. A peaceful people, they provided little resistance to the Spaniards as many ancient cultures did during the rapid rise of the colonization of the Americas. Following their fall, dominion, and assimilation by the end of the 17th century, the Huilliche tribes also succumbed to the dominant powers of Spain. But far less tolerant and more aggressive, the Mapuche did not lend their cooperation or willingness to Spain.

Living in the central portion of what is now the country of Chile, the Mapuche were mostly farmers growing corn (maize), beans, squash, potatoes, and other vegetables. They hunted and fished, and guinea pigs were raised for meat while llamas were used as pack animals and for wool production. The Mapuche were also excellent metalsmiths and pottery artists. To resist the Spanish conquest, the Mapuche formed widespread alliances above the village level and adopted the strategic use of horses in battle. For 350 years, they successfully defended their culture, land, and ideals. Eventually, their successful stand would end in the latter half of the 19th century during the War of the Pacific, when Chilean forces subdued them. But, the Mapuche had demonstrated incredible courage, resolve, and will standing firm against Spain, Spanish-influenced Chileans, and other settlers who attempted to displace or lay claim to their native lands. After their defeat, they signed treaties with the Chilean government and were settled to reservations farther to the south. Their 350-year stand is remarkable when considering how rapid and complete the total domination of Spain became in the Americas.

Like the American Indians of North America, valor and courage sought to protect the land and cultural heritage. But colonial expansion in North America was also more than they were able to resist.

Understanding the significance of the Mapuche's cultural demise and how it has paralleled other cultures also helps to clarify why modern poverty in the 21st century has become complicated and seemingly unsolvable. In the 1980s, the Chilean government established reservations for the Mapuche. However, rather than providing the land without cost like the United States offered, the Chileans saddled the Mapuche with debt to have the right to their individual ownership. Similarly, like the United States' American-Indian tribal nations, the Mapuche were forced to live on reservations. But the Mapuche's burden of the debt limited virtually any ability they had to exercise personal freedom or succeed economically.

Throughout many previously colonized independent nations, the burden of debt has also stunted or completely paralyzed economic growth. Countries have been forced to take on debt for a variety of reasons. Lack of infrastructure, no roads or poor roads, inadequate educational systems, immature banking and financial systems, no public buildings, and other programs that were not in place for an independent nation to thrive have all led to burdensome debt obligations. [4, 5]

The IMF (International Monetary Fund), a multinational finance cooperative created in 1945, has the duty of analysis and support of a stabilized global economic system. Originally begun with twenty-nine member countries, the Fund has expanded to over 188 partner countries. To support the Fund's objectives, partner countries agree to provide money to the Fund in a quota system. The IMF monitors the global economy, recognizing imbalances, and provides stabilizing loans and capital infusions.

However, in many cases the loans provided by the Fund have been a burden many nations struggle to repay. While the debt obligation may have originally been provided for social need such as education or roads, it's likely not all of the funding has been used to fund the original intent of the loans. While this system of loan dissemination was successful after the Second World War to rebuild European nations that had been destroyed, the resultant objective in impoverished nations has not met with the same success. Consequently, billions of people on every continent feel an ongoing crush from their country's national debt.

To help emerging nations, the IMF began disseminating loans aggressively in the early 1970s. Over a seventeen-year period, the IMF made a valiant effort to give the necessary loans to impoverished countries in the hope that this would bolster their economies and help them join the economically strong. But this would not be the case: the debt burden grew from a manageable 9.8% of average GDP to over 47.5%. ***What this meant, in essence, was already cash-strapped nations would be paying back almost one out of every two dollars to satisfy the interest on debt obligations.*** In less than two decades, the debt interest grew over 1,300%! How could any nation's people with inexperienced leaders and lack of infrastructure be expected to repay debt of this magnitude? The trickledown effect would stifle growth and hinder any real significant expansion in any meaningful way. In the ensuing years, debt obligations would continue to escalate.[6]

The expanding debt did not rest solely on the declining infrastructure of the developing nations but also on global increases in oil prices and the supply and demand associated with this valuable commodity. Prior to the oil price escalation of the early 1970s, much of the debt of developing nations was financed by public agencies such as the World Bank, presumably provided as a mechanism toward the genuine promise of economic viability and success to the recipient countries. However, after the oil crisis of 1973-74, many private banks raised substantial capital from higher prices and were looking for ways to invest their abundant cash stores. The private banks sought ways to lend to emerging economies in the hope this would further bolster the profits of the private banks. Countries like Nigeria who supplied oil saw the boon in oil pricing along with the desire of banks to court them and offer loans as a way to advance their economy rapidly. Private banks loaned the money, willingly believing this represented sound investment and seeking a high rate of return. Oil-producing nations believed high oil pricing would support their debt program and made agreements believing the prices would never drop. However, when pricing changed, reflecting a dramatic deflationary pattern in the price of oil, these same nations who had depended on oil as a marketable commodity for their economy were shattered and overwhelmed with a debt burden they were unable to satisfy.

Further complicating the debt picture for nations who had benefitted from loans made by the IMF were staggering interest rate spikes, which resulted during the worldwide recessionary period of 1981-82. At this time, a confluence of economic struggles was present that led to bank rates climbing well into the teens and sometimes as high as 20%. With the interest payments burgeoning and growing beyond the capability of indebted nations, the crushing blow of debt repayment became a hardship indebted countries could not fulfill and they sunk deeper into poverty and hopelessness. It became evident with debt obligations consuming a higher proportion of GNP than is fiscally healthy there was little many of the nations who borrowed to support their infrastructure and normal operating expenses could do to dig their way back to economic prosperity. Moreover, with the additional strain placed on some nations by corrupted government policy along with few economic commodities, the seeds for a catastrophic plummet into a fiscal black hole were created, possibly for generations to come. ***Thus today the effects from the borrowing programs of the 1970s, coupled with the centuries of oppression brought by colonialism, have led to the dismal conditions existing for most of the poorest nations today.*** Even in the most economically advantaged and resourced nations, there are stark and cavernous gaps between the wealthiest and the poor. Moreover, while there are more safety nets present in nations such as the United States designed to catch the poor, these programs are limited or do not exist in poor nations; the chasm that has opened is outrageously wide.

Poverty in America

Poverty in America, is not unlike that of other regions of the world. While there are programs for the poor in America including free food kitchens, homeless shelters, and Medicaid, the disparate gap between the wealthiest and the poor has grown catastrophically. The evolution of the emerging middle class with plentiful jobs was a boon to the growth of the US economy during the early half of the 20th century. Abundant fossil fuels coupled with ingenuity and technological prowess rocketed the United States into rapid expansion in regards to the standard of living. The phrase 'The American Dream' was born. Industries, including automotive, oil, media, and textiles, generated enormous wealth for the entrepreneurs of this early era of the 20th century, while in the latter half technology and financial services would lead the American economy. But a gradual erosion of jobs created by changes in economic strategy and policies would take center stage beginning during the 1970s and continuing through the present.

When coupled with other global economic changes, including the emergence of a greater reliance on imported fossil fuels and economic growth rising in Asia and other countries, which had lagged behind our admired system for decades, a transition in wealth and opportunity began. Many of the middle-income jobs that workers had thrived in were transferred overseas and to economies that offered lower wages to corporations interested in ballooning profits to spur Wall Street investor expectations. Moreover, labor unions systematically were broken by organized business to erode benefits and cost of living adjustments that had previously allowed lower and middle-income families the ability to keep pace with rising costs and economic expansion within the US.

In urban areas and small towns, this tragic loss is evident today in all walks of life but is no more plainly seen than in the heart of New York on Fifth Avenue. Opulent condominium homes rising thousands of feet and ultra-luxury merchandisers make this one of the most concentrated regions of wealth and power in the entire world, with the pinnacle being 740 Park Avenue. Built in 1929 by James T Lee, grandfather of Jackie Kennedy Onassis, 740 Park Avenue is home to some of the most powerful and influential titans of commerce; they boast billions in economic wealth, but even, more importantly, wield enormous political weight shaping the economic futures for millions. The unmitigated contrast between the corporate billionaires in 740 Park Avenue and the lives of thousands living in poverty only ten minutes away in the South Bronx is stunning.

In the documentary *Park Avenue: Money, Power, and the American Dream*, Academy Award-winning director Alex Gibney presents a startling examination of how the gap between the wealthiest elite and the poor has grown. Only ten minutes separating the two extremes of life, the 700,000 residents of the South Bronx represent the poorest congressional district in the United States. As Gibney elaborates, the past thirty years have produced unprecedented wealth never seen before in the history of mankind while simultaneously the extreme poverty now experienced by so many in the Bronx and other stricken areas of the United States has become an epidemic. Nearly 40% of the residents in the South Bronx live at or below the poverty line earning less than forty dollars a day. However, the 'American Dream,' as Gibney says, should be available to everyone if they are willing to work hard and apply themselves. Gibney exposes a different story, a radically unfair opportunity which has tipped in favor of the ultra-rich and left so many out of the possibility of achieving the American Dream. As he questions: "What went wrong?"

Using an experimental game of Monopoly, social psychologist Paul Piff, explains how the rich have rigged the odds in their favor. As he explains in *Park Avenue*, imagine a game of Monopoly where you arrive to play and discover all the properties have already been divided up amongst other players before you even arrived. Moreover, the money and the Community Chest and Chance cards have also been divided. But you are going to get a chance to play and make an attempt to win with these limited odds.

To test his theories, Piff developed a Monopoly game with unfair advantages tipped in one player's favor. As he elaborates, some have far more upward mobility to access resources than others. They have opportunities unavailable to some, and as a result with weighted odds shifted in their favor, they have far greater economic success. To demonstrate his theory, players flip a coin to decide which one receives the favorable odds. As Piff points out, this is kind of like the randomness of our birth—how some are born into families with far more resources and opportunities than others.

The players then begin playing the game with one player enjoying more opportunity. He will be able to roll two die instead of only one. He will collect two hundred dollars each time he passes go, instead of only one hundred for the disadvantaged player. He will start the game with twice as much money. As the game progresses, the predictable result begins to develop. The player with the unfair advantages begins to pull away from the under-resourced player, and, even more startlingly, develops a sort of entitlement showing little concern for the player who has been given an unfair stake.

Piff explains the Monopoly experiment is not unlike the real world where some people have a distinctly unfair opportunity. Large segments of the population are unable to access the American Dream. The common misconception is that all you have to do is play the game and be willing to work hard. However, this is not the case. As Piff says, "All the rules have been decided, all the properties have been divided up, and the opportunity is not there." [7]

For some, the bane of poverty and the egregious disparity in opportunity and access to material needs are not tied to the good fortune related to birth or social class but instead an equally troubling cause. Millions of Americans live with addiction and mental-health problems and the attendant consequences that result from these challenges. It can be a dark and frightening place for these people and mental health disease often leads to catastrophic economic outcomes. For many who walk into this horrific place of uncertainty, the road to recovery can be as ominous as the attempt to wrestle an aggressive man-eating lion in the African Serengeti. Often, people use drugs, alcohol, or other addictive behaviors to escape life's hardships; those who find themselves trying to break the grip that has ahold of their body and mind say that this is unlike anything anyone could ever imagine. Moreover, they would not wish this affliction on anyone. The struggle with and victory over addiction are something I've witnessed firsthand, working with victims of addiction in Chicago.

Perhaps nowhere are the ravages of poverty, addiction, and mental illness seen with more clarity than the health clinics and centers around America caring for the poor. I have been honored and often humbled by the stories of men and women I have spoken with, who tell stories of dreams and aspirations of something better for themselves. They recount memories of great joy when they were employed or had a decent life. Yet, their addiction to drugs robbed them of all they had hoped for.

The Heartland Clinic, founded in 1993, is a progressive, comprehensive clinic system employing medical, dental, and chiropractic services and other therapeutic services.[8] My association with the clinic system began in 2011 when I left my practice to devote time to charity and mission work and instantly fell in love with the experience and people who came for care. But at the same time, I was often troubled and saddened when I heard the commonality of the stories shared. "I had a good job and then I lost my job and couldn't find work!" "Losing my job was the beginning of my fall and my deep depression along with my alcoholism taking a grip on my soul!" "I don't know why I couldn't stop once I started, but man I tell you that stuff [crack cocaine] will trick you and consume you like nothing else I've ever known. You will steal, cheat, and do whatever is needed to get your next fix!"

The repeated refrain is almost always some variation of words like these. It becomes evident that tragic addiction and mental health can often play in the cinema of poverty and its ultimate toll.

However, I have also discovered the incredible hope and perseverance many have to beat their addictions, face the demons, and crawl back to life. When I recollect the lives I have been blessed to care for at Heartland and around the globe, it is overwhelming to me. There are moments when I wept internally alongside a man who is suffering, and I find it difficult to sometimes hold back my tears. Sometimes all I have to offer is a listening ear and caring heart. Yet, I have also realized that the immense appreciation and satisfaction the people I visit and care for at the Heartland Clinic, along with other places around the world, are cultivating a hopeful transcendence. Many of the patients report victories, report their newfound strength, and welcome the healing they've received through chiropractic care and the other ways we help them piece their lives back together. It's as if the life pieced back together is the beginning of fitting the broken pieces of the planet back together to once again make it whole.

Similarly when I travel abroad to the Dominican Republic with our compassion partner, ChiroMission, I have discovered providing chiropractic care is one of the most powerful ways to connect and heal many of the physical pains people suffer with living in extreme hardship. But even more importantly, the improvements in mental health and hope that results from chiropractic care and a group of committed chiropractors have been awe inspiring. ChiroMission began as a vision of Dr. Jean-Claude Doornick and Dr. Todd Herold. They wanted to bring the natural healing of chiropractic to people who have no access to conservative drugless healing. As well, they wanted to engage more doctors and volunteers in acts of service to under resourced people. My experience partnering with them provides hope in the possibility people have to heal physically and emotionally to alleviate poverty's chains on humanity.

Still, further compelling, and not surprising, is that mental-health disorders plague the poor twice as frequently as the rich, with the uneducated and unemployed carrying the burden of mental-health disease at the highest levels of all populations. As a subset and deeply ensconced in this domain, the staggering number of people suffering from schizophrenia are eight times more prevalent among the lowest socioeconomic class in America. The likelihood that mental illness will lead to begging and the fall from the spirit of the *waver* is extremely strong. It is common to find *beggars* who are suffering from mental illness and often there is limited or no treatment available to them. The complicated nature of mental health, coupled with the variety of extenuating circumstances that are often involved, provide few easy answers.

The Psychology of Money and its Influence on Poverty

Additionally perplexing and cogent in the analysis of poverty, author Lynne Twist examines the role our man-made relationship to money plays in our minds and the complex attachments it can foster creating poverty or the antithetical wealth some wield. Lynne Twist is a remarkable force in the world of charitable work, providing leadership and response to one of the largest and perhaps most perplexing problems in the world, hunger.

Beginning in 1977, Twist founded the Hunger Project in response to monumental challenges recognized internationally, hoping to end a scourge that had taken too many innocent lives prematurely. Though hunger projects had been undertaken before and others were also answering the call, the immense problem of hunger was gaining the needed attention it deserved as a global crisis. Twist wanted to answer this call; in the process she discovered the resources to end hunger were unquestionably available, but hurdles and psychological blindness loomed for many who could help, but were unwilling to jump in and join the effort.

Recognizing money as a resource like time and talent, Twist began to unlock a code of conduct America and other industrialized nations had systematized their lives around. Though in essence nothing more than a symbol of value and holding little real worth in terms of sustenance of life, our affliction to monitor everything in our lives around the lack of money or the accumulation of this currency vehicle was consuming psychologically and spiritually. It was as if money had a soul. Twist came to appreciate the very nature of how we bartered with money and how the psychology of exchange held the key to unlocking poverty's gates and probably had driven much of the diseased behavior leading to poverty's existence.

As Twist explains in her seminal book *The Soul of Money*, the concept and application of money is a man-made entity, not occurring naturally like other forces of nature. Wind, rain, sun, wood, stone, water, precious metals, and other organic and inorganic matter are naturally occurring. Money, in contrast, was created within the past 2500 to 3500 years to augment the exchange of goods and services among individuals and groups of people. Twist explains that the power we have given money has "outstripped its original utilitarian role. Now, rather than relating to money as a tool we created and control, we have come to relate to money as if it is a fact of nature, a force with which to be reckoned. This stuff called money, mass-produced tokens or paper bills with no more inherent power than a notepad or a Kleenex has become the single controlling force in our lives."

As a result of our inordinate attention to the power of money beyond a vehicle of trade and its simple characteristics, Twist further believes we have come to give it "almost a final authority... If we look only at behavior, it tells us that we have made money more important than we are, given it more meaning than human life. Humans have done and will do terrible things in the name of money. They have killed for it, enslaved other people for it, and enslaved themselves to joyless lives in pursuit of it." She continues the point: "In the name of money, humankind has done immense damage to Mother Earth. We've destroyed rain forests, dammed and decimated rivers, clear-cut redwoods, overfished rivers and lakes, and poisoned our soil with chemical wastes from industry and agriculture. We've marginalized whole segments of our society, forced the poor into housing projects, allowed urban ghettos to form, exploited whole nations to get cheap labor, and witnessed the fall of thousands—in fact, millions—of people, many of them young caught up in selling drugs for money, hurting others and wasting their own promise in a life of crime, enslavement, or incarceration. We've perpetuated age-old traditions that assign men and women different and unequal access to money and the power we place in it, subjugating women and distorting men's expectations and obligation with their privileged access to it." [9]

The affliction money has imposed on our lives has further created a canyon beyond the cooperation and sustained efforts to share equally with others who have significantly fewer resources. And yet we must ask and try to imagine how our planet would be more fulfilled and richer if only our relationship to money were different.

How Poverty Is Expressed in the Bush of Kenya

In a remote area of Kenya four hours outside of Nairobi, where I travel frequently, is one of the most picturesque places on the planet. Our Dreamweaver offices are stationed on a ten-acre campus in the heart of one of the poorest indigenous populations alive today. The Maasai tribes of Eastern Africa have a long history of living off the lands and the animals they herd. Their nomadic traditions are still practiced to the best of their ability within the confines of their land allotments provided by the Kenyan government.

The countryside is magnificent in grandeur and scale, with blue sky that seems to reach fully toward heaven and open savannah that stretches beyond the eye's vision; it seems like the perfect place for economic prosperity to have showered its blessing. However, these tribes live shut out from the industrialized world's resource-rich providence. Driving along the lone stretches of road—both dirt and paved—ramshackle housing structures dot the landscape, with adults and children standing or sitting outside their homes. They have little opportunity to enter the global economy and contribute beyond their own meager survival. The eye of any outside passerby recognizes the unmistakable curse poverty has left on this region. Similar to the South Bronx and New York's Fifth Avenue, these poverty stricken areas often reside in close proximity to those where people live in paradoxical abundance. Some have opulent homes, as measured for this part of the world, while their nearby neighbors live in hovel that looks like a strong windstorm would destroy it.

What is gravely troubling is the number of children affected by the weight of poverty.

The harrowing fact is that 50% of all children alive today live in poverty; many will not live to see old age— in fact, many are probably going to die before the age of five.

Dreams and productive lives will not be realized for millions of children who are consumed by the travail of poverty. With families unable to provide food, potable water, shelter, clothing, education, safety, health care, and the basic necessities of life, their chances of survival and meaningful contributions to humanity will never come to fruition. It is a waste of the brain trust of the human species that such a high percentage will die, robbed of the chance to become part of the solution to the ills of the world. Perhaps one of these individuals would unlock the riddle of cancer, discovering a promising cure, or develop a breakthrough technology for water purification.

Climate Influence on Poverty

One of the consistent concerns in the field of meteorology is the effect that greenhouse gasses have on weather and the warming of the planet. A greenhouse gas is a carbon-based emission that flows from the combustion of the fuels we use for our automobiles, power plants, planes, boats, and for heating our homes. Typically, greenhouse gasses are commonly found as carbon dioxide, but other gasses also exist, including water vapor, methane, and nitrous oxide. As the sun warms the earth's surface, these gasses create an increased warming of the earth's perimeter and augment life. Without the natural heating mechanism created by greenhouse gasses, of course, the earth could not sustain life; we would suffer frigid temperatures making it uninhabitable. Thus, greenhouse gasses are a necessary adjuvant to life on earth. But the concern many experts hold today is the rapid increase in population on the planet coupled with the prodigious application and use of carbon-based fuels over the last century seems to be elevating the temperatures on the planet more rapidly than the natural cooling systems can dissipate them.

The Environmental Protection Agency (EPA) of the United States reports the overall effect of these increases in temperature has led to the decade between 2000 and 2010 being the warmest decade on record in the United States, and global temperature increases have risen nearly 1.4 degrees Fahrenheit over the past century. The EPA goes on to report that the oceans are warming and becoming more acidic while polar ice caps are melting at alarmingly rapid rates. EPA reporting is further supported by other national organizations, including the National Aeronautics and Space Administration (NASA) and the National Oceanic and Atmospheric Association (NOAA).

As we consider the relevance of global climate change to the discussion of poverty and its possible role in creating it and sustaining it, the EPA further elaborates on why this condition, which affects every living structure, is critically involved. The EPA concludes that a two-degree Fahrenheit temperature increase of the earth's temperature would have the following effects:

- 5–15% reduction in the yields of crops as currently grown
- 3–10% increase in the amount of rain falling during the heaviest precipitation events, which can increase flooding risks
- 5–10% decrease in stream flow in some river basins, including the Arkansas and the Rio Grande
- 200%–400% increase in the area burned by wildfire in parts of the western United States[6]

The EPA goes further, elaborating that the possibility for even more dramatic increases could be felt over the next hundred years with increases rising an additional 2–12 °F. Troubling and alarming, the impact of this consequence of greenhouse-gas warming would be cataclysmic drops in human population and the dramatic movement of millions, and possibly billions, of people who would have to leave uninhabitable land for more sustainable terra. Already, the tragic theater of this consequence is beginning to play in areas of sub-Saharan Africa, where droughts of two to five years have become common while other parts of the globe are experiencing shocking and torrential flooding rains destroying structures, agriculture, and consuming human life.[10]

This is the impact of such violent weather extremes, and while it is not felt as sharply by most of the economically strong nations of the world, in under-resourced countries depending on agriculture for survival, the repercussions are lethal. Thousands lose their lives in locations when violent tsunamis, tidal waves, floods, and scorching heat dry up and wither food supplies and wipe out animal, plant, and human existence. As a result, any meaningful attempts to shift economic and opportunistic change in the most poverty-stricken places in the world today can be fraught with ruination. Hence, the impact climate has in both causing and sustaining the fatal grip of poverty globally must be considered as one of the most important determinants in the matters of poverty in all parts of the world, and even more so in the most under-resourced and developing nations.

The magnitude of factors leading to poverty around the world is an enormous topic with many complex layers. Hundreds of years of oppressive policies coupled with deplorable mismanagement and greed have crippled nations. Generations of people have lived and died while never realizing economic stability, and many such deep-seated situations around the world seem hopeless. However, understanding the longevity of the problem helps grasp the necessity of a long-range view toward solutions. It became apparent in researching material for this book that I would have to adopt a willingness to see change happen slowly, and possibly accept that I will witness very little progress in my lifetime. With this book, I hope to provide readers with a launching point to understand the causes of poverty and begin the process of poverty alleviation.

In the next chapter, we will take a hard look at poverty from a perspective few authors have considered and begin to unpack this issue from a fresh viewpoint.

Summary Questions for Discussion

1. Though Christopher Columbus is often recognized as a great explorer, his exploitation along with others set the stage for the demise of entire civilizations. If the European elite had not sought to enslave the people of the Americas, what do you imagine nations would be like today?

2. In the documentary *Park Avenue*, the Monopoly game example sheds light on how human nature tends to move people toward a sense of entitlement when the odds for success are stacked in their favor. Have you noticed this tendency in your community, or on the national and international level? What steps could be taken to help people consider a different approach to living in community and the distribution of wealth?

3. Lynne Twist speaks about sufficiency rather than accumulation as a goal to strive for in her book, *The Soul of Money*. Are there situations in your own life when you have felt the tendency to accumulate things, money, and are less inclined to recognize sufficiency as a goal to strive for?

---

4. Carbon-based emissions are gradually warming our planet by disrupting our atmosphere. The scale and the damage are enormous, and it will require tremendous cooperation from many of the most industrialized nations to change our energy uses to save the atmosphere. Do you believe we can come together as nations and people and cooperate with one another so that we can save our planet and the futures of generations to come? What steps would you take to bring people together?

5. There are many factors which have led to modern poverty gripping billions today. How long do you believe it will take to unravel the tangled predicament we have around the world and do you feel there is any hope for a solution?

CHAPTER 4

POVERTY IS A DISEASE

*"If poverty is a disease that infects an entire community
in the form of unemployment and violence, failing schools
and broken homes, then we can't just treat those symptoms
in isolation. We have to heal that entire community.
And we have to focus on what actually works."*
— Barack Obama

Poverty's Impact: There are fifteen million orphaned children worldwide due to HIV/Aids. This is equivalent to all the children living in Germany and the UK.

In the human body, billions of regulatory functions operate simultaneously. Seamless with almost no conscious thought, we breathe, move, talk, smell, see, hear, and are incredible wonders of nature. We take for granted good health and the elaborate systems residing within our body that keep us alive. Like small universes, humans are organized similarly to our vast solar system. There is an order and a predictability that functions according to the natural laws of our universe. As we have a night and a day because the earth rotates, there are also cycles in the body. The sleep–wake and the digestive cycle are examples of regulatory systems in the human body. But thoughts also play a role in the homeostasis of our bodies. Humans coexist and share a plethora of thoughts and ideas. When ideas are in agreement, forward progress takes place. Agreement leads to growth and harmony in relationships, giving men the ability to build foundational change in the world. However, chronic incompatible thinking in communities often leads to pain and destruction. Thoughts become actions and actions become destinies. It may seem our one idea or act may not matter when there are so many troubling issues to tackle in the world, but they do.

As experts have discovered, our thoughts and actions are more powerful than many realize. Thoughts and prayers carry energy and have been demonstrated to hold incredible strength to influence life events. Thoughts also connect us in a shared experience, even if we don't speak the same language or even personally know one another. The connection is a launching point for people who live with abundant resources to extend help to those living in poverty.

We are all created with a purpose or plan to give something unique and special to the world. When poverty and begging are the only options for a child, their opportunity for anything hopeful, possibly meaningful in life is shattered. Sure the possibility for moments of joy, laughter, and play can still exist? Yet, the need to survive snuffs out any possibility of a higher purpose and drive towards a more fulfilling life. Even the body language of *begging* compared to *waving* accesses emotionally dark places of sadness, despair, and fear. The cognition the brain attaches to the body in the act of *begging* and of *waving* model emotional circuitry in disparate ways.

How Does Begging Make People Feel on the Inside?

Take a moment and place this book on the table or chair next to you and do an experiment. Hold your hand in front of you in a cupped position as if you were begging. Close your eyes. Imagine you're standing along a busy intersection. Cars stop then move on. You're hungry and begging! Feel your fear and pain… You have two small children who haven't had more than a few ounces of mashed cornmeal and rice everyday for a month. There's no job, no crops to cultivate, no opportunity in the foreseeable future for any of the circumstances in your life to change. No one appears to cares if you and your children live or die. Sink into the feeling for a moment. Picture and feel how desperate your life would be if your survival today depended on the gracious care of a stranger to simply reach into his or her pocket and give you some spare change so you can feed your family.

As you stand on the roadside, imagine people in cars who don't bother even looking your way or acknowledge you exist. Some look your way out of the corner of their eyes but fail to take a good look or even acknowledge your standing on the corner with your desperate outstretched cupped hands. You know their glances, stares, or averted gaze signal disdain for you, judging your competency and ability. You make up in your mind that maybe their thoughts about you are correct, that you have been a failure, that your life means nothing and your value in this world is inconsequential.

While still holding onto your feelings with your hand cupped and in front of you, furrow your lips and the muscles of your face taking on those feelings. Do you feel sadness welling inside? Your shoulders slouching forward, you may feel weakness move through your body. You may also feel sorrowful tears behind your eyes and something shift in your chest. Your breathing becomes shallow and feelings of anguish rise. Once you have a clear image and you can feel those feelings associated with your poverty and begging in this exercise, shift one feature of your body language. Instead of frowning and holding onto the solemn face, turn the corners of your mouth up and smile while still holding onto the feelings you had before with your cupped hands.

Though your smile appears somewhat normal to an onlooker, the authenticity is feigned; inside your own heart, notice it doesn't feel real. ***It's unnatural to smile and feel a sense of peace and wellbeing when begging.*** Instead, devastating, dark, and shameful sadness steeped in despair and hopelessness take center stage in the heart of a *beggar*. Moreover, poverty and the incipient changes that occur to anyone forced into begging become a dis-ease. I've written disease with a hyphen to illustrate the true uneasiness and damage. The prefix 'dis' means without, so dis-ease is a state within the body of uneasiness, discord, even chaos. Harmonious function is discarded and true health is impossible in a state of dis-ease.

The Consequences of Poverty on the Brain

In studies conducted at the University of Pittsburgh, researchers have found dramatic changes occur in the brains of children raised under the duress of poverty. The inability to focus, concentrate, and formulate healthy patterns of sustainable learning have surfaced from the research. As well, emotional stability is further challenged when a constant barrage of stressors play out in the homes of the extremely poor.

Dr. Farah and her colleagues found that kindergartners from low-income families showed poorer function than their middle-class peers in the parts of their brains used for reading and language and for 'executive control.' Executive control includes such skills as working memory (remembering a phone number long enough to dial it correctly) and quashing impulsive behavior (holding your tongue instead of lashing out with an angry response).[1]

In a study conducted to examine the impact of poverty on children, University of Pittsburgh researcher Peter Gianaros and his colleagues found that college freshmen and sophomores who ranked their families lower on the socioeconomic scale had stronger emotional reactions to photos of threatening faces than students who ranked themselves higher. The students were asked to look at three photos at a time and find the two that matched, so they weren't aware of what the researchers were measuring. They performed the task while lying in a functional magnetic resonance imaging scanner, which can measure what parts of the brain are active at a given moment.

The students with lower socioeconomic rankings showed more activity in the amygdala, a part of the brain that processes negative emotions and stress. In another study, Dr. Gianaros' team found that students from lower socioeconomic backgrounds also had less brain tissue in the anterior cingulate cortex, a frontal region that controls emotional impulses.

Why would these students react that way to the angry faces?

He doesn't know for sure but speculates that there not only may have been more physical punishment in their households but more arguments over such issues as money. "Fights over bills can sensitize the development of these brain systems that are responsive to stress and uncertainty and unpredictability," he said. [2]

Poverty is not only an affliction of an individual but can also permeate the consciousness of a community, an entire country, and even worse a whole continent. Rampant scarcity coupled with extenuating circumstances wires the brain to perceive lack and paucity as the accepted norm triggering 'fight or flight' and hijacking the higher forms of reasoning. Without full attention to upward mobility, peaceful cooperation, and communal coexistence, people living in the most troubled areas of poverty struggle against enormous odds to make any progress. The strands of these findings are further revealed and supported by research in genetics.

Epigenetics May Explain Poverty of the Mind

Genetics holds enormous promise to understand why each of us has many of the same needs, and how we are similar and yet also each uniquely special. Wrapped in the intricate protein matrix of every single cell are individualized sequences of biochemical mediators that make every human a distinct individual. Every one of us is a one-of-a-kind creation, all 6.5 billion people alive today. Genes are responsible for determining hair and eye color, height, skin color, male, female, the ability to sing, to perform athletically, and every single specialized trait that makes us each uniquely special. Within sequencing of genes, familial traits of height, nose, and facial features are determined. Made of proteins called nucleotides, DNA (deoxyribonucleic acid) is the foundation of all living matter. Structurally oriented in a long cylindrical helix, the DNA matrix of guanine, adenine, thymine, and cytosine come together in a remarkably elaborate theatrical science. Though considerable volumes of knowledge have unlocked many mysteries, confusion still remains in fully understanding the codes and sequencing of DNA and how variegated genetic dispositions originate.

One of the most confounding questions that perplexes scientists today is the role environmental factors play in the gene expression of individuals and their offspring. This area of genetic science is called epigenetics. Epigenetics is the study of changes in the gene expression of cellular phenotypes caused by mechanisms other than changes in the underlying DNA sequence. For many years, scientists have questioned whether genes or environment are the focal points predicting the outcomes of disease and destiny in our lives. Long thought to be the strongest predictor of success or failure, genes were believed to be the only informational signals that mattered in the human experience. If you had healthy genes, you were likely to stay fairly healthy, avoiding many common diseases. However, if you were unfortunate enough to acquire genes expressing significant disease markers, you were doomed to a short lifespan and possibly a life of suffering. In other words, medical thinking predicted if your mother had breast cancer and your father had cancer, you were extremely likely to get cancer. However, the emergence of epigenetic science is now helping us to discover there are far more intricate biological mechanisms acting on our human experience and gene expression.

As we age, our genes are the building blocks that will express our individual characteristics down to the tiniest detail. As cells grow, die, and replace one another, it is our genes that will send the coding and blueprints that continue to make us uniquely special. However, our genetic code is altered by diet, environment, emotional stress, and trauma. Environmental influences are significant factors in slowly evolving the genetic expression of every human being and, moreover, for future generations. When a significant dietary influence—emotional stress, for example, or the environmental factor—is strong enough, the genes can lapse and fragment in their ability to replicate strongly and in the proper sequence. Broken links and chains in the double helix structure occur and a cascade of dysfunctional sequencing follows. Eventually, this incorrect sequencing causes disease if the proper repair of the genetic material does not take place. Now thought to understand many of the mechanisms behind cancer and other chronic, life-threatening diseases, epigenetic science is one of the most promising medical research venues.

At Duke University, Dr. Randy Jirtil has been uncovering some of the possible ways we could influence our genes positively and possibly change our destiny. He has discovered using laboratory rats of identical genetic material, the ability to influence epigenetic expression with diet and nurturing signals. Using rats that have a gene marker called the Agouti gene, he's discovered that when environment favors a methylated diet or a stronger-loving environment, identical genetic rats grow dramatically differently. The Agouti gene marker seems to weaken the ability of rats to contain their appetites and drives them toward cancers and diabetes as they grow fatter and more lethargic with age. However, when identically birthed rats are fed a diet high in nutrients called methyl donors, they seem to resist the scourge of obesity and disease. Moreover, he has also discovered when rats are given love and affection, this same Agouti gene seems to turn off and thinner rats with brown coats instead of obese rats with yellow coats are born. By placing the identical rats in different cages where the mothers either constantly lick and give attention to their young or only occasionally provide nurturing licks, Jirtil is making a remarkable discovery. The constant licking some mothers provide offers reassurance to the newborn rat of safety and comfort, leading to a change in gene expression.

The epigenetic differences in both of the rat populations are found in the ability of loved and well-fed rats to methylate their DNA sequencing in their genes. Methylation is a biochemical process occurring at the chromosomal level of cell function, where methyl groups of carbon and hydrogen atoms attach to genetic links in the DNA structure. Nutrients, which drive methylation, are vitamin B12, folic acid, homocysteine, methionine, and choline. Food sources like eggs, vegetables, fresh fruits, and complete proteins serve as strong catalysts for favorable methylation. In Jirtil's research, he altered the diet toward stronger methylation in the rats that maintained lower body weight and browner coats. [3]

The significance of this research is dramatic because it means our genes are playing a stronger role in our lives than we knew. As we examine *wavers and beggars* and the precarious lifecycle of many children and adults in poverty, there are stark contrasts to the comfortable lives wealthier populations live. The absence of adequate food, water, combined with the constant barrage of viral, fungal, and bacterial assault are weighty elements in the evolution of the poverty cycle. Moreover, the stressors that a pregnant mother surrounded by strife and inadequate resources encode into the genetic material of a female fetus the same destructive epigenetic patterning bombarding her body. A developing female fetus will carry the genetic expression of the mother's lifestyle forming inside her ova. Because a baby girl born to a mother in poverty has developed inside the womb of a mother tragically afflicted by poverty's gloom, she is likely to carry the exact genetic expression the mother had on to the next generation in her eggs residing in her ova. ***Considering the ramifications, it's plausible to understand why the poverty cycle continues and the inability of people to progress economically eludes our best efforts.***

Further support for the hypothesis that poverty leads to disease has been reported in a landmark study published in the journal *Epidemiology* in 2011. Researcher Moshe Szyf, a professor of pharmacology at McGill University, who co-authored the study with colleagues at the University of British Columbia and UCL Institute of Child Health in London, elaborates on the significance of their finding. Szyf explains that researchers have known genes are programmed to turn on and off for various disease pathways. But the findings in this study were the first to show an actual link between a person's early economic circumstances and the biochemistry of that person's DNA.

Szyf and his colleagues examined the DNA substrate of a large group of 40–45-year-old British citizens since birth. As a result, researchers were able to determine the economic status of the subjects. Szyf and his colleagues were looking for a chemical marker in the genes called a methyl group. Similar to the Duke University study, they were interested in the ability of the test subjects to methylate DNA and therefore exercise a natural protective ability of gene preservation from damage. Remarkably, their findings discovered test subjects raised under economic duress gravitated toward epigenetic expression favoring more aggressive immune response and body fat preservation. Szyf concluded this finding was indicative of a signal that there is "going to be a harsh world, there's going to be a lot of bacteria around, prepare yourself." However, the aggressive immune response found may trigger autoimmunity in some because the environment many poor live in today is often different than one or two generations prior. As Szyf further elaborates on this finding, "Essentially you have an immune system that's programmed to deal with something that was anticipated but never happens. And now that immune system starts working against itself." [4]

The findings of Szyf and Gertil tell us that poverty can no longer be looked on as a problem that will plague our current generation only. We must also consider the long-term damage that poverty causes. As our population swells over the coming decades and the economic disparity between the rich and the poorest on the planet grow, the imbalance will require a natural rebalance. Nature always acts in this way. The laws of physics deem that for every action there is a reaction and energy is neither created nor destroyed but only changed. *As the DNA substrate of the poorest people of the planet continues to drag on the world, there will become increasingly fewer available consumers, intelligent & creative minds, and an overall damage to inspiration and opportunity.* Already accounting for one-third of the world's population, the poorest and least healthy will clamor for survival through fighting, procreation, and the necessary means to stay alive. But as this population grows from one-third to two-fifths, and eventually reaches half the world's people, a tipping point will develop that has the seeds for catastrophic disaster. Former President Jimmy Carter echoed these grave concerns in 2002 when he was awarded the Nobel Peace Prize for his dedication to the poor, healing disease, and the growth of democracy.

"At the beginning of this new millennium I was asked to discuss, here in Oslo, the greatest challenge that the world faces. Among the all the possible choices, I decided that the most serious and universal problem is the growing chasm between the richest and poorest people on earth. Citizens of the ten wealthiest countries are now seventy-five times richer than those who live in the ten poorest ones, and the separation is increasing every year, not only between nations but also within them. The results of this disparity are root causes of most of the world's unresolved problems, including starvation, illiteracy, environmental degradation, violent conflict, and unnecessary illnesses that range from Guinea worm to HIV/AIDS." [5]

As we have seen from past civilizations, when large populations are undervalued and plainly ignored, the basic necessities of life, such as adequate food, clean drinking water, sanitary living conditions, and economic opportunity, lead to civil war and political upheaval. The American Revolution and French Revolution are two more recent examples that have taken place over the past three centuries. All great empires fall and new ones rise. Newly formed leadership takes ahold to hopefully give people what they had fought to rightfully gain from their battle.

Without a call to act on behalf of the growing poor around the world, our great civilization will likely not survive. Considering the response to poverty, begging, and the difficulties coexisting without adequate solutions, it might be helpful to look at poverty from an immunological response. Viewing poverty as a viral infection gripping the human body and knowing our bodies have adaptive mechanisms to recognize, initiate, assemble, deflect, and remember for future predatory invasion, our understanding of possible ways we can respond as a global culture can be summarized in this way.

Man has always encountered catastrophic illnesses caused by viruses, bacteria, fungi, and other pathogenic perpetrators. Plagues, famines, and sweeping disease have ravaged entire societies. Today, cancer, HIV/AIDS, heart disease, diabetes, and chronic illness take the center stage of our health-care resources. Often, our cures are only partially successful, and many times focus on symptom alleviation and less on the prevention and the cause. The unfortunate result: many of the current disease scourges we struggle with continue to kill millions annually, possibly with preventable disease.

But there is hope if we consider a more holistic view of disease. *As well, a fresh perspective can also help us seek new approaches for poverty alleviation using the body's adaptive immune capacity as a metaphor.* Utilizing a vast array of complex biological markers and coordinated biochemical pathways, the human body boasts remarkable adaptation to infection and disease, which protects and strengthens it. Under the control of the brain and the nervous system, all functions of the human body assemble and process to grow, respond, repair, and regenerate the body throughout a lifetime. From the moment of conception until death, there is an elaborate symphony of actions that operate in unison and harmony when function is normal and in homeostasis. Moreover, the impressive immune system stands out as a stunning feat in intelligent design of man.

Encompassing a vast network that touches every single cell of the human body, the immune system is trained to respond and recognize foreign antigens that may harm the body. Using white blood cells that have the ability to distinguish, respond, and destroy infectious agents, the immune system is the agent of safety and conservation for the body. Furthermore, it has the ability to learn and thereby develop a strategy for passing on this knowledge through acquired immunity passed on through genes. ***The immune system is ultimately responsible for the preservation of man.***

When we consider the parallels of the immune system to adapt, respond, and strengthen itself against infectious agents, we can use a similar line of thinking to address poverty and challenges befalling man around the world. Within our intelligence is the ability to solve the varied crises we encounter as a global culture. But in order to operate a reflective and cohesive response, we must first recognize that, just like in the human body, no part of the body can operate alone without the connected circuitry of the nervous system and cellular communication networks of the body.

Our bodies are not unlike our cultural need to be connected and work together. When we place a priority on the needs of others—on the poor, on the weak, on the afflicted, as Jesus taught—we find the very real possibility for transformation can occur.

Like our body's need for rest, nutrition, a balanced nerve system, health, exercise, prayer, and meditation to implore a strong immune system, our response to poverty must also take the same holistic action plan, recognizing that our needs—whether poor and under-resourced, or rich and blessed with abundance—have a commonality that does not separate us but links us like a chain. Then when we acknowledge this connection, as white blood cells recognize infectious agents, we are quicker to respond to the needs of others and also to co-create strategies for changing the social hardships that still afflict far too many today.

As the immune system notices, responds, and then destroys, we can also take on the corruption, greed, inequality, lack of opportunity and education, health-care inadequacy, and lack of opportunity billions of people around the world still cope with courageously. But we must move away from thinking that teaches it is from something outside moving in that will change the ultimate health of the planet and mirror the organization God already installed in all of us. It is from within moving outward that we will ultimately change the course of social injustices and inequalities around the world. As we continue to explore poverty as a disease and provide additional insights, new ways of engaging in cooperative efforts will begin to take shape.

Equally plaguing, the antithesis of the under-resourced people of the world is our industrialized consumer-driven wasteful habits and carefree excessive lifestyle that disregards the needs of others. We forget it is on the backs of the poorest people alive we are able to enjoy a lifestyle that gives comfort, convenience, and little worry. This disease, affecting millions of over-zealous consumers, demonstrates itself as a need to over-consume and gorge on material possessions. Like the disease of poverty that afflicts billions and leads to the emerging population of *beggars*, overindulgent hoarding and consumption are filling another void. People are begging for recognition, to find meaning in their lives, and sometimes this deep need ends up filling our lives with *stuff*!

Garbology: the Symptom of an Impoverished Mind

In the book *Garbology*, Pulitzer Prize-winning author Edward Humes brings to light a startling discovery. Humes uncovers the love affair we passionately embrace with our garbage and indulgence in waste. As he points out vividly, Americans have become the most wasteful nation of people the earth has ever known. No civilization has been more distracted, unconscious, and unaware of the damage we are making on the planet and the futures of generations to come.

Humes begins his book by sharing a story of a South Side Chicago home that rescuers entered in 2010 to save a couple from the mountains of trash they had hoarded over the years. Donning hazardous waste-material suits, rescuers pulled Jesse Gaston, a seventy-six-year-old chemist, and his wife Thelma, a retired schoolteacher, to safety from a home of trash threatening to engulf them and take their lives. Over the years, every surface of the Gastons' home had become covered by layers of newspapers, empty plastic jars, pieces of broken furniture, garden tools, soda bottles, cans, clothing, broken lamps, old magazines, piles of junk mail, and garbage bags filled with every imaginable piece of rubbish and debris.

The Gastons were hoarders, unable to part with their trash. Though not immediate, they had found themselves trapped by their repulsion against disposing of anything, and instead their home became a one-way depository for everything they consumed or owned. They were simply unable to part with their trash! As the piles grew to heights above the cupboards in the kitchen and the garage became packed floor to ceiling, Thelma became trapped by falling debris one day and Jesse, in an effort to rescue her, became pinned in the mountains of trash consuming every square inch of their home.

The Gastons' lives and their consumer addiction to hoarding trash unfortunately do not stand as an isolated instance according to Humes. "Although most of us tend to view extreme hoarding as an aberration, it's a surprisingly common occurrence. Variations of the Gaston household are found around the country more or less on a daily basis, although most often after the hoarder's demise. Somewhere between 3 and 6 million Americans are thought to be compulsive junk hoarders with living spaces that, to varying degrees, resemble the Gastons'."[5]

While these numbers still represent a small segment of the US population, our attention should turn to the symptom and how it has spawned. As well, we must further examine the therapeutic approach therapists and coaches attempt to remedy this phenomenon, and look at the larger view of how we interface with our trash. Finally, we must consider the symptoms of hoarding and how it mirrors a far more troubling problem in our society. The fascination with the freakish images of hoarding lifestyles have spawned network television blockbusters sensationalizing the lifestyle in the most vulnerable and personal detail. While hoarding is not considered a disease in the Diagnostic and Statistical Manual of Mental Disorders, it is categorized as an obsessive compulsive disorder.

Humes elaborates further on the Gastons' lifestyle as a possible microcosm of a much larger problem we have as an American society. While we may eventually take the single small space of a gravesite at the time of our death, our footprint of garbage and the trail left behind is staggering. "Consuming nearly 7.1 pounds of trash daily, 365 days a year, our legacy of trash consumption over our entire lifetime will tally over 102 tons or 1,100 graves." Moreover, the tragedy of this consumption is most of this trash will probably outlive the grave marker, Pharaoh's pyramid, and many of our modern skyscrapers. [6]

Knowing we are prone to waste, consume, and indulge in this way should motivate each of us to consider our motives. Our addiction to ease, comfort, and the consumer lifestyle leads us to rely on our plastic bags, disposable toiletries, and single-use throw away containers, and much more. Permeating every facet of American consumerism, garbage and waste creation has become an unconscious way of life for all of us. We are accustomed to the ease and comfort that manufacturers advertise and persuade us to adopt. Sadly, we are not the only culture who wastes with reckless disregard. Other industrialized countries also waste and so do under-resourced countries. Garbage is becoming an epidemic everywhere.

But what does this addiction say about our mind, our hearts, and a need to fill us with more? Is there possibly a poverty we feel inside our soul from a lack of something missing in our lives? Is this same poverty mindset also felt by other nations, rich and poor? ***Moreover, have our DNA and the epigenetic influences known to change the poorest people's genetic expression also become a factor in our addiction to trash?***

What is our addiction to consumption and trash doing to our environment? Located in the Pacific, caught in the currents between the west coast of North America, Australia, and the Asian continent, a massive watery dump of plastic garbage and debris floats in the Pacific Ocean. Known as the Great Pacific Garbage Dump, the murky, plastic-laced, dumpsite has grown in size over the past two decades from our carefree waste disposal habit and stratospheric growth of plastic materials. By some estimates, the dumpsite is estimated to be nearly the size of North America and approximately one hundred feet deep. The trash collectively unites in an ever-changing oceanic submarine, trapping sea life and dumping potentially hazardous plastic bisphenol-A (BPA) sediment into the aquatic food chain.

First discovered in 1997 by Captain Charles Moore, the enormous patch of garbage vacillates in the currents of the North Pacific Gyre, a series of currents several thousand miles wide that create a circular effect. Moore discovered the garbage patch while competing in the Transpacific Yacht Race and has since become passionate about investigating it and bringing awareness about its significance. What Moore has discovered is startling and extremely troubling. "In the North Pacific Gyre, pieces of plastic outweigh surface zooplankton by a factor of 6 to 1." According to a report citing Moore's research, "Ninety percent of the Laysan albatross chick carcasses and regurgitated stomach contents contain plastics. Fish and seabirds mistake plastic for food. Plastic debris releases chemical additives and plasticizers into the ocean. Plastic also absorbs hydrophobic pollutants like PCBs and pesticides like DDT. These pollutants bioaccumulate in the tissues of marine organisms, biomagnify up the food chain, and find their way into the foods we eat." [7]

The catastrophic consequences of this finding and the rate of growth of the dumpsite should be an alarm for us to look at our indulgence, and our hazardous and wasteful lives. As researchers studying the garbage dump site have noted, the density of garbage in this site has increased one 100% in only six years. Perhaps this can be traced to the stratospheric growth of the plastics industry, and the desire the most industrialized people on the planet have to consume beyond our needs and seek convenience over conservation. ***The Pacific Ocean garbage dump is a symptom of our consumer-driven society, our depravity of the soul, and the poverty of the spirit we have internalized. But would this poverty and depravity exist if our intent was not focused only on our own needs, but instead examined the need of everyone and the use of resources with attention to care and conservation? Moreover, would this extreme of waste and depletion of resources exist if we considered the need for excess or beyond our needs irrelevant and unbalanced?*** Later in this book, I will examine some of the possible ways our consumption and excess can be healed through expression and devotion to sharing and service. As we further consider the seeds of poverty as disease, Mr. Geoffrey Canada's Harlem Children Zone will further elucidate the deep furrows of historical impression poverty has laid in the minds and hearts of our children. But as you will find in Canada's research in education, when a compendious set of programs along with patient dedication to stay the course is followed, success and positive results are possible.

Whatever it Takes

Geoffrey Canada is a maverick educator focused on transforming young people in one of the poorest areas in the United States: Harlem. Uniquely capable for the role as educator, coach, and disciplinarian, Canada grew up in difficult circumstances himself. As a child in the South Bronx, Canada was raised by his mother, Mary Elizabeth, along with three brothers. His father provided virtually no financial or emotional support. Raised among chaos, violence, and crime, he learned lessons in life that have served him and the thousands of children his work influences.

Canada's most intriguing and influential accomplishment has been his Harlem Children's Zone. Recognizing education in Harlem was a dismal failure and poor children growing up in the chaos and crime of Harlem had few possibilities to step out of the mire of poverty with the skills and system in place, he set out to create a new way of educating the poor. At first, the focus of the Harlem Children Zone set out to encourage two sets of students to begin a process toward graduation and eventually college degrees. Beginning first with students in the sixth grade and then adding students from lower levels with each additional class year, the plans were to gradually build a school from kindergarten to grade twelve. Canada had a far-reaching, but yet untested, model he wanted to explore to break the cycle of poverty suffocating thousands in Harlem. Many methods had preceded the Harlem Children Zone and were working to save a few children in isolated circumstances. But a large-scale impact to lift and educate thousands and break the cycle of poverty was non-existent.

Canada was asking new questions. What would it take to change the lives of poor children, not one by one through heroic intervention or occasional miracles as other programs had accomplished? But what would it really take to build a program that could be standardized and easily replicated nationwide to break the cycle of poverty strangling our urban cities? With the first group of students enrolled in classes, his team set out on a mission to see that every child was educated and mentored in a new way previously untried. Daily and rigorous tutoring sessions coupled with longer school days would be a significant part of the curriculum. Focused attention to raising the test scores achieved by students would also be required since many, or in some cases a majority, were testing far below the required grade levels.

With hopeful aspirations, gleaming new facilities, and competent educators, Harlem Children's Zone embarked on a quest in 1990 to set a new standard of education. However, what Canada and his team discovered within a short time was their task ahead was more substantial and provided far more obstacles than originally anticipated. Beginning an education process with students in the sixth grade and then hoping to raise their academic standards in a year or even two or three was going to pose problems they did not anticipate.

Many of the students enrolled through the lottery program were deficient in basic skills to succeed academically. They also harbored emotional strain and overwhelming lack of support from safe and reliable homes. Many students were living in homes without adequate parental supervision, and at times their survival was in jeopardy. Moreover, what Canada discovered and was unaware of when he embarked on this journey to rewrite the educational ladder of education within the inner city was very troubling.

By the sixth grade, and even earlier, youngsters growing up in Harlem and other poverty-stricken areas were falling behind their counterparts in middle-class and wealthy homes rapidly, and earlier than first realized. For many years, Canada was under the impression—and he was not alone—that children in poor neighborhoods were stricken with poverty mostly out of the guns, violence, and drugs that filled their neighborhoods. Then Canada began to ask different questions to answer the dilemma of poverty and the terrible consequence: ***"Why are poor people poor and why do they stay poor? And what would it take for them to get out of poverty?"***

Covering Canada's quest and strategic interventions to stem poverty, author Paul Tough also began to ask these same questions while writing about the efforts of Geoffrey Canada. Tough discovered the thoughts surrounding the why and what to do about poverty had evolved since the depression. Powerful and economic forces beyond the control of the individuals stopped many from moving beyond the poverty they lived in. If there was to be any hope of stopping the cycle, an early and regular intervention would be the answer. Utilizing Baby College, preschool and pre-kindergarten class programs, prior to elementary education would formulate the evolutionary process necessary to radically shift the horrific outcomes within this community. Calling this process Project Pipeline, Canada and his team would use a system closely paralleling the success found in many middle-class and upper-class segments of the population.

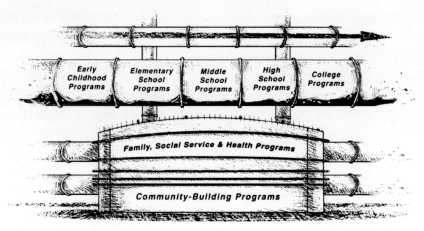

Diagram: Harlem Children's Zone educational process, Project Pipeline

While not revolutionary in more affluent educational systems, using a comprehensive program from birth to college was untested in poor communities. Moreover, it was necessary if poverty's hold on the community was going to stop. The disease of poverty would not respond to Band-Aid approaches but would require a systematic and a complete ladder of remedy. Often the care and prevention of disease parallel this requirement in poverty alleviation in the same way. In order to cure a disease, it has to be prevented from developing in the first place. As a result, the Harlem Children's Zone discovered when they implemented a comprehensive holistic model using an inside-out approach and a sustainable model in which the students who entered the programs as soon-to-be parents or even parents with toddlers, an indelible impression was made. Young sixteen-year-old mothers and fathers who had no true compass to know what being a parent was really supposed to be or how they were even going to survive now had a system, a program in place to encourage their success. They could now break a cycle befalling the poor.

What Canada had done to promote an inside-out series of programs was similar to the way the human body tackles infectious agents and learns to recognize, respond, and eliminate disease. Demonstrating results previously unheard of in the inner cities and among the poorest in America, Canada's Harlem Children's Zone could proudly boast a 95% rate of young people entering colleges to go on and inspire, contribute, and maintain the spirit of *waving* instead of *begging*. Likewise, Canada's project was addressing the disease of poverty as preventative medical measures would, with both physical cost savings and, perhaps even more importantly, emotional cost savings. As Canada and others who work intimately with the most challenged children in America in the inner cities know, the true cost to society of abandoning children and providing no reference or pipeline of possibility often takes on catastrophic consequences.

The actual cost of incarcerating and tending to a young man or woman who falls through the social net into crime and chaos can cost over a hundred thousand dollars a year, with the average individual serving time in America in a typical prison system costing over thirty-five thousand yearly. Canada, and others who have initiated programs to stop this deadly and poisonous disease ending hopeful lives, found that for three to four thousand dollars they could assist a child at the start—when all children deserve the real chance to succeed. They could take them through to the end and then deliver a leader and a servant to society who will make a difference. Children once thought to be need*y* now became need*ed* and had value. His experience and results mirrored our findings and hypothesis of poverty. In order to solve this problem, a thorough and exhaustive series of programs have to be in place like the complexity and the brilliant orchestral symphony of biochemical actions that take place every moment in the body to eliminate disease and retain a healthy homeostasis.[8]

Taking the context of poverty one step further and recognizing this condition and its symptoms is not one we can ignore any longer but is one we must tend to like a patient visiting a doctor because he has debilitating back pain and sciatica, high blood pressure, or is having trouble breathing means understanding that poverty is not an isolated problem which the poor burden alone. It is a worry we all share as a body, a planet, and a society that must cooperate or perish.

Summary Questions for Discussion

1. In this chapter, you were asked to imagine yourself as a *beggar* on a busy road, hoping for a stranger to give you money to feed yourself or your family. Explain how it feels to take on the body image of a *beggar*.

2. Since we know poverty is a consequence of children receiving inadequate intellectual attention early in life and often-negative messages, how would you create a program to help change this devastating reality for children? What positive messages would you want to share with children to encourage their future success?

3. The plastic garbage dump discovered in the Pacific Ocean and the other great oceans of the world is a symptom of our wasteful nature. What other messages do you believe this symptom is saying about people today? Do you feel responsible in some way for the dump and also the effort to clean it up? What personal changes can you make to be more socially responsible with waste and conservation?

4. As Geoffrey Canada has realized in education, when we begin teaching values, character, and the basics of education later in life, it is more challenging to help children become successful and happy. Have you attempted later in life to learn how to play an instrument or learn a new language and found it extremely difficult to learn? What did it feel like to struggle to learn something so many people find easy, like speaking multiple languages or playing multiple instruments?

5. Dis-ease is hyphenated because it means without ease. What are some of the ways you would help bring ease and health back into our world to alleviate the suffering and dis-ease of poverty? Are you discovering new insight about poverty you did not realize before? Are you becoming more willing to seek out more knowledge to help people living in poverty?

CHAPTER 5

POVERTY IS EVERYONE'S PROBLEM

*"There is no need for temples, no need for
complicated philosophies. My brain and my heart
are my temples; my philosophy is kindness."*
— Dalai Lama

Poverty's Impact: 121 million children worldwide will never have an
opportunity to receive an education.

The Plan is Simple

When you aren't forced to see poverty every day, it's easy to believe it's
not your problem! Your personal problems seem large enough already
without taking on more burden to notice or care if a woman living forty-
five minutes away has a job, if a child is growing up without a father, or if
a mother is a victim of domestic violence. ***However, if we stop noticing
and caring about the tragic circumstances of others, an opportunity
for something more fulfilling, far more rewarding is stolen from our
hearts—the opportunity to feel the power of compassionate love.*** Living
in a vacuum, not appreciating the terror caused by the pain of hunger, lack
of water, or ravages of disease is stealing the greatest opportunity we have
to connect with humanity and God's gift to us. Even more disappointing
and painful is not the millions of lost opportunities to create transformative
bonds between us, it's the deeply agonizing loss of the meaningful happiness
we could achieve by helping other people in need. We remain blinded and

don't even realize that the efforts we could make to improve the lives of large numbers of suffering people can help us psychologically, emotionally, and spiritually, and give our lives profound meaning.

In *The Hole in the Gospel*, author Richard Stern provides the simplest reason why we were designed by God to provide assistance and help to people who are suffering. There are some who question if there is a God and if so, "Why did he forget the poor? Why is there all of this suffering? Why are people killing one another and don't seem to care?"

As Stern points out, God has not forgotten the poor! He sees their suffering and is aware that men with their free will choose to murder, harm, and hurt one another. In fact, He sees everything we do and has provided the seeds for transforming our lives. He has given the ability of those blessed with abundance the opportunity to lavish this blessing on those who hunger. God has given this legacy as a way to bring the giver and the receiver together as a strongly bonded magnet. When people who have been blessed with more than enough seek and help people in blighted poverty and fulfill God's plan, they mirror the sincere love of Jesus in their giving, teaching, and mentoring. God's essential nature is demonstrated in this achievement. The moral acts of kindness to the poor are not confined to Christian theology, of course, they permeate Judaism and other faiths as well.

God didn't intend it to end there; he wanted us to nurture and assist the poor. Renouncing this responsibility ultimately causes a gap between God and us. It's like God has offered us a gift with the opportunity to care for the poor, and our reward will be a transformative communion with Him. But we are unwilling to unwrap His gift to us. *As anyone who has volunteered and helped feed the hungry in a food kitchen program or provided Christmas gifts to children through a program like Toys for Tots knows, the act of giving always feels more satisfying and edifying than receiving.*

The essence of the problem according to Stern is that too many people aren't helping. God has a plan for the world, but we aren't following his plan. The people who have the means, the ability, and the resources to help are supposed to connect with the other half of the world that has little or nothing and whose lives are precariously holding on for survival. The world is organized like a two-piece jigsaw puzzle and when the two pieces come together, **those who have** help **those who don't have** and the world is complete and suffering ceases. Stern believes it's simple but we complicate the edict and shun the responsibility.[1]

Taking this one step further, our mission statement at Dreamweaver International is, *"We help the needy become the needed"* Every person wants to be needed, valued, and appreciated. Poverty strips the dignity from people and leaves them feeling needy and devalued. *If we first notice them, then help them, and finally provide the path for value and need to return, poverty ends!*

Ethnography Can Help Us Understand

It's difficult comprehending the challenges people living in extreme poverty encounter simply to survive. While seeing a picture, a video, or even hearing a speaker from a native country tell his story is compelling, the limitation of a secondhand message compared to going and seeing poverty's devastation firsthand limits feeling the enormity of it. Certainly this was my personal experience when I encountered the dark empty hole of hopelessness children and families are living in every day that so often goes unnoticed. Their stories were waiting to be told and celebrated as measures of human achievement despite unimaginable odds for survival. The firsthand experience of interacting, teaching, and playing with local children in Kenya and other centers of poverty was inestimable toward gaining a deeper compassion for their struggles and victories of life. Seeing life from their perspective and trying to experience what it feels like through the experiences of the poor gave me humbling perspective. Moreover, others who have taken the time and the expense to travel to the poorest regions of the world and spend time with these people also report similar connections developing. Seeing the hopelessness firsthand helps them want to do something to help. Comments like, "I had no idea people lived like this!" or "I cannot imagine how terrible it must feel to wake up and know you can't feed your children today!" and

"I am completely overwhelmed with the thoughts of where to start to help them" are common refrains visitors echo.

Living among other populations and making a careful study of their lives is one of the most promising methodologies for transforming global poverty. This branch of science is called ethnography, and it's helping people gain a deeper understanding and compassion for the most impoverished. To execute an ethnographic study, analysis is careful to examine the natural lives of people capturing the social meaning and activities 'as they are,' not how an observer perceives them. ***Of course, the challenge in all personal experience is that we each see the world metaphorically through our own set of framed glasses. Our experience, feelings, judgments, and conclusions are formed from the resultant impressions we make in our lives and an attempt to assimilate incoming information.*** Every moment and interaction we have with the world comes through a personal filter and is processed based on our understanding and past experience of the social interpretation the event means to us. Therefore, personal experience, moving toward and experiencing life among people is always preferable to gain compassion.

Beginning in the early 1980s, researchers Baxter and Hopper began studying the homeless of America using ethnography. Studying the homelessness crisis emerging in New York City, they began to untangle and carefully tried to understand the circumstances of this growing epidemic. They wanted to get to know the people who had become homeless. If given the choice, they would certainly not have chosen to live this way—sleeping on subways, under boxes in alleys, and in bus stations on hard plastic or wooden benches. But there were often no other choices, as many recanted when given an opportunity to share their story. Gaining insight into their research, this excerpt from their book, *Reckoning With Homelessness* provides a haunting reflection of how the poor forced to live on the streets feel.

"It must be some kind of experiment or something, to see how long people can live without food, without shelter, without security." – Homeless Woman in Grand Central Station

"Homelessness is a routine fact of life on the margins. Materially, it emerges out of a tangled but un-mysterious mix of factors: scarce housing, poorly planned and badly implemented policies of relocation and support, dismal prospects of work, exhausted or alienated kin.... Any outreach worker could tell you that list would be incomplete without one more: how misery can come to prefer its own company." [2] Anonymous Homeless Person

Their work also inspired others in cities across America to learn how the homeless were able to eke out a survival despite tremendous odds. Though heeding the growing epidemic and responding appropriately has still been a daunting challenge in America and other countries. As we have detailed, millions of under-resourced people live hanging from the thinnest of lifelines and die every day from preventable disease, hunger, thirst, and war that rips their countries apart. In America, some safety nets exist to catch the poor from falling all the way to the ground, but they are still not plentiful enough or structured in a way to stop the steep slide into economic ruin and blighted existence. Countering this sad reality, in the majority of the poorest nations around the globe far fewer government-sponsored programs exist. The majority of the aid, programs, and renaissance needing to occur are borne by the non-governmental organizations (NGO), churches, and charities. In fact, the resources provided by private entities and individuals bear a large burden and deserve substantial thanks for propelling compassionate change around the globe. *The World Giving Index published by the Charities Aid Foundation found in a survey of people in 153 nations that nearly a quarter of all people in these nations had volunteered to help in a charitable way.* Further, it was discovered that over a third had donated money for a needed cause, and almost half reported participating in the act of being a 'good Samaritan.' Indeed, these are notable overtures toward feeling the needs of others and connecting with a desire to help.[3]

Promising and hopeful, the charity that people have demonstrated to millions who are suffering and in need reveals that humans do care for one another and have the ability to show great compassion. Charity is one of the markers we can measure in our response to need and it's also a demonstrable vehicle to show the love of God, as Stern points out in *The Hole in the Gospel*.

When a caring stranger who may have traveled halfway around the world to participate in a collective effort feeds starving children, Stern believes this may be the demonstrable way that God's love is revealed to humanity. Moreover, when sustainable efforts are created to help local farmers improve crop yields, address deteriorating weather issues leading to drought, or standardize a program for entrepreneurship, our endeavor is connecting need with resources. As these collective efforts multiply and local communities discover their own ways of managing sustainable economic health, global change is possible.[4]

However, despite the favorable data demonstrating global charity efforts, we are still far from a global call to all the people who can help to act and change the circumstances that will alleviate poverty forever. Perhaps this is why the real *beggars* of the world are still staggeringly plentiful. Even more salient is each of us must consider these statistics as not merely *numbers* but as ***people***—for that is what they are. These are the people who suffer, yet the suffering they must endure could end. Sometimes, the only remedy needed to end suffering is a phone call or an email asking leadership to act in a more humane manner. Sometimes, it is a collective of people coming together who share a common bond to change the circumstances.

In November 2013, the World Economic Forum released its outlook on the Global Agenda 2014. The report revealed alarming data and a warning that the continually growing disparity in income between the wealthiest and the poorest was one of the greatest worldwide risks. The words sound hauntingly familiar to the ones spoken by former President Jimmy Carter when he received the Nobel Peace Prize in 2002:

"Some economic inequality is essential to drive growth and progress, rewarding those with talent, hard-earned skills, and the ambition to innovate and take entrepreneurial risks. However, the extreme levels of wealth concentration occurring today threaten to exclude hundreds of millions of people from realizing the benefits of their talents and hard work.... Extreme economic inequality is damaging and worrying for many reasons: it is morally questionable; it can have negative impacts on economic growth and poverty reduction; and it can multiply social problems. It compounds other inequalities, such as those between women and men. In many countries, extreme economic inequality is worrying because of the pernicious impact that wealth concentrations can have on equal political representation. When wealth captures government policymaking, the rules bend to favor the rich, often to the detriment of everyone else. The consequences include the erosion of democratic governance, the pulling apart of social cohesion, and the vanishing of equal opportunities for all. Unless bold political solutions are instituted to curb the influence of wealth on politics, governments will work for the interests of the rich, while economic and political inequalities continue to rise. As US Supreme Court Justice Louis Brandeis famously said, 'We may have democracy, or we may have wealth concentrated in the hands of the few, but we cannot have both.'" [6]

As you contemplate our world and how God would really want us to care for one another, it's seems evident that Gandhi's words, the "Earth provides enough to satisfy every man's need, but not every man's greed," are staring back at us.[7] If we are willing to walk through a door that leads men to share, to act in more egalitarian way toward one another, we can change the course of human history. But the desire to accumulate great wealth sadly speaks to the words of Brazilian businessman and leader, Ricardo Semler, from his 2014 Ted Talk: "If you find yourself looking for ways to give back in your life when you have achieved financial freedom, you've probably taken too much!" ***Yes, the richest eighty-five billionaires control as much wealth as half the world's population—3.5 billion people globally.***[7]

The statistics contained within this chapter are meant as signposts for each of us to examine whether we are satisfied with the present circumstances. Seeing the people who comprise the *haves* and *have nots* not as statistics but as opportunities is part of the beginning to change. Indeed, the philanthropic passions of Bill and Melinda Gates and Warren Buffet have spurred a new direction in the use of the massive wealth accumulated by the elite. Called The Giving Pledge, the purpose of this special organization is to encourage the wealthiest to make a pledge to give half of their wealth away. By July 2013, already 115 billionaires had signed up to share over half a trillion dollars.[8] The leadership and direction are encouraging, speaking to the roles we have outlined in this book. We are all connected,

Dr. Warren Bruhl, Todd Love Ball, Jr.

and within each of us is a *waver* and a *beggar*. Perhaps this connection is partially responsible for the inspiration the wealthiest participating in The Giving Pledge have connected to in their spirit and soul.

The Wealthiest are Becoming Wealthier – the Poor are Becoming Poorer

In the US, the ***wealthiest 1% captured 95%*** of the post-financial crisis growth since 2009, while the ***bottom 90% became poorer.***[9]

There are ***1,636 billionaires*** who control a net worth of ***$5.4 trillion as of 2014***.[10]

The wealth of the ***top 1% in the world amounts to $110 trillion***, a staggering ***65 times the wealth of the bottom half of the world's population***.[11]

The Majority of the World's People is Poor!

50% of the world's population ***lives on less than $2.50 day***.[12]

80% of the world's population ***lives on less than $10/day***.[13]

The Wealth Disparity is Becoming Dangerously Imbalanced

Here is an analysis of the long-term increases in wealth of the richest people in terms of wealth, income, and GDP relative to the poorest. In 1820, the wealthiest earned only three times more than the poorest people. Today, the wealthiest people and the wealthiest countries control 88 times the wealth of the poorest.[14]

3 to 1 in 1820	11 to 1 in 1913	35 to 1 in 1950
	44 to 1 in 1973	72 to 1 in 1997

88 to 1 in 2013

92

WISDOM PRINCIPLE:

In the book of Luke, Jesus shares this parable, elaborating the accumulation of wealth is not for man to store for himself alone. To gather, accumulate, hoard, and take more than is needed would ultimately cost us our spiritual lives and possibly our earthly lives.

Someone in the crowd said to him, "Teacher, tell my brother to divide the inheritance with me." Jesus replied, "Man, who appointed me a judge or an arbiter between you?" Then he said to them, "Watch out! Be on your guard against all kinds of greed; a man's life does not consist in the abundance of his possessions." And he told them this parable: "The ground of a certain rich man produced a good crop. [17] He thought to himself, 'What shall I do? I have no place to store my crops.' Then he said, "This is what I'll do. I will tear down my barns and build bigger ones, and there I will store all my grain and my goods. And I'll say to myself, "You have plenty of good things laid up for many years. Take life easy; eat, drink and be merry." But God said to him, "You fool! This very night your life will be demanded from you. Then who will get what you have prepared for yourself?" This is how it will be with anyone who stores up things for himself but is not rich toward God." Luke 12:13-21

Water's Impact on People Living in Poverty

1.1 billion people do not have access to adequate water for drinking, bathing, and agricultural needs.[15]

400 million children lack access to safe drinking water and *1.4 million die every year as a result.*[16]

80% of all illness in the world is *caused by waterborne* illnesses.[17]

In Africa, 5–10 times more people die from diarrhea than war.[18]

443 million lost school days every year because of waterborne illness.[19]

A child dies from a waterborne illness every 15 seconds. By this time tomorrow, 2,500 more will be dead.[20]

Half the world's schools do not have access to clean water, nor adequate sanitation.[21]

On average, a woman in Asia and Africa *has to walk 3.7 miles* to collect water.[22]

Reality Check: $8 billion was spent on cosmetics in the US

Only $9 billion would provide *water and sanitation* for all people in developing nations.[23]

A five-minute shower in the United States
*will use more water than a person living in a
developing world slum will use all day.*[27]

To make *ONE Sunday paper requires 300 liters of water.*[24]

People are Hungry

870 million people suffer from *chronic hunger and malnourishment* (1 in 8).[25]

Reality Check: Americans throw away between 160 and 295 billion lbs. of food annually. This is enough food to fill 90,000 football stadiums to the brim with food.[26]

Globally, 1/3 of the food produced for human consumption (1.3 billion tons) is lost or thrown away.[27]

Climate change is expected to add 20% more hungry people by 2050 and population is expected to be 9 billion worldwide. Rising food costs, the inability to earn a living, food security, and war are likely to result from the effects of global climate change on the food supply.[28]

Children & Adults Never Learn to Read

Over 785 million adults cannot read worldwide. Two-thirds are women.

In the US, over 93 million have basic or below literacy skills.

Africa as a whole has less than a 60% literacy rate.[29]

Reality Check: Only $6 billion would provide *basic education for all people* in developing nations.

$780 billion is spent on military worldwide.[30]

Too Many Children Still Die Too Young

The United States has the *highest first-day infant mortality rate* among all industrialized nations of the world. Inadequate prenatal care and low birth weight of children being born to the poor were pointed out as the probable reason.[31]

Sub-Sahara Africa has the *largest concentration of high infant mortality rates* (# of infant deaths per 1000 live births in the 1st year of life) in the world. Sierra Leone and Angola have infant mortality rates over 100. *ONE out of every 10 CHILDREN BORN DIES before AGE ONE!* [32]

Reality Check: Only $12 billion would provide prenatal and reproductive health care to all women in developing countries. **THIS IS THE SAME AMOUNT SPENT ON PERFUMES IN EUROPE AND THE US.**[33]

It's startlingly somber when the money spent internationally on cosmetics and perfumes could provide enough resources to dramatically end a significant portion of poverty's strangling grip. Moreover, recognizing the distances in comparative use of resources between the most economically advantaged nations and the poorest, we have to seek new answers to questions that have not been answered. Furthermore, if we heed the words of Jesus when he said, "Love your neighbor as yourself," we have the ability to recognize that matters in another region of the world are ours to be concerned with. We are created to be compassionate, to pay attention, and be engaged to take the steps to change so we can help the poor.

When we ask the hypothetical questions like, "If I were dying, starving, wasting away, and parched with thirst living thousands of miles away in Sub-Sahara Africa, would I want my brother in America to help me?"

On some level of spiritual consciousness, we have to consider why we are alive at this time in history.

Moreover, why are others we know or have not met alive also at this time? There has to be an order to the universe that aligns us in some manner. But is God leaving it up to us to figure out the 'why' and 'what' we are supposed to be doing with our time, talent, and resources? Additionally, is it all right that I personally don't accept responsibility for doing what I can to improve the lives of people I don't even know or may never meet? These are questions we individually must ask ourselves and consider the markers of time that have brought us together at this time in history. Like the billions of people who have passed before and are likely to follow, the same questions and thoughtful answer seeking probably occurred and must continue to bring us together. What is the purpose in God's plan that some should need so desperately while others have more than enough and don't share their abundance adequately? How can we believe we don't have a moral responsibility to help change the path of humanity to align more with God's plan?

God's purpose is simple. If I have plenty, more than enough, I need to share with my brother who has little or none. As well, we need to consider our present lives and our spiritual lives. If we examine Jesus's words, "Many who are first will be last and many who were last will be first," Jesus taught it is not our earthly bodies that will live for eternity but our spirit, which moves onward toward our heavenly home. The poor are not forgotten, and though they may live with meager sustenance in this brief earthly life, there is an afterlife in which the promise of no more suffering will be fulfilled. As well, we need to consider the man we didn't help because we were too busy or more self-absorbed in our own wants and desires as a soul who may be first in heaven, while we may be last.

The Global Economy Connects Us

Every person on the planet has a consequential role in the global economy. Rich or poor, the interconnected framework of the world's economies has become bonded in ways economists never predicted a century ago. There is a constant flux of economic capital investment and spending taking place to push forward the remunerative engine of the industrially developed countries. Banks, corporations, and governments monitor and depend on one another for trade and purchase. The United States is dependent on a healthy economy in other countries, and they depend on our solvency. The Middle East's vast oil reserves supply the bulk of the energy needs for the world. Their oil gives them enormous power and responsibility to help sustain economies that depend on fuel for manufacturing and transportation. Asia's prodigious population gives multinational companies a large consumer pool to grow financial returns and reward stockholders. The cheap labor of many of the under-resourced nations aids economic expansion and profit. Simply accepting and embracing this economic system is the status quo, and declaring capitalism is the best way disregards the people who are left out. Words of business leaders echo the thoughts, "Show me a better way than this!" or "Surely you don't want us to be a socialist nation?" But accepting this social order and the financial structure we've created as the healthiest system of governance gives us little reason to change. And this is all right as long as you're the benefactor of the blessed life and the abundant resources.

However, as the distance between the poor and the super-wealthy grows, a vast strata of people occupying the middle is falling further behind. The true center, the middle class, is being swallowed, becoming extinct. As a result, fewer domestic and international consumers are able to fuel the growth machine in America turning our mammoth gross domestic product (GDP).

When American and foreign citizens riddled with poverty cannot afford the purchase of the items we produce, our economy stalls. In many ways, we are at a crossroads in the global economy as we see a period when the methods to propel economic expansion favor debt creation. The United States flounders under a mountain of debt, which our nation will likely never pay, and other industrially affluent nations around the world, including European commonwealths, are following our lead.

In 2013, the United States harbored a debt of $12.312 trillion, 73% of the total GDP of the nation. While a staggering figure, the United States debt has at one time topped this ratio of debt to GDP. Prior to World War

II, debt obligations to GDP were 113%. However, the national debt was gradually paid down over the ensuing thirty years. But the trouble with the present debt ratio in America is the actual dollars are significantly higher and the middle class that can fuel healthy economic expansion is dwindling.[34]

A Pew Center Research Report found the share of income the middle class receives has fallen over 17% since 1971, while the preponderance of income has shifted to the wealthiest in America. In 1971, the middle class was responsible for earning over 62% of GDP while the wealthiest garnered 29%. But since then, the middle class only claims 45% of the total wages earned in America while the select wealthy now tally a staggering 46% of the total income earned. The trouble with this finding is the wealthiest consumers don't need to purchase more than five pairs of pants a year, buy more than a dozen pair of undergarments or take more than a couple of vacations annually. As fewer people control more resources, the ability for purchasing power to grow shrinks. And this is the unfortunate state America is in today.[35]

While the United States still claims dominance as an economic power with the number one GDP in the world ($16.8 trillion), China ($9.2 trillion) and Japan ($4.9 trillion) are rapidly vying for a larger percentage of the of the global GDP.[36] As well, Brazil, Mexico, India, and Korea, are also growing their economies, in part as a benefactor of inexpensive labor and massive increases in manufacturing of finished goods. Much of the manufacturing previously done in the United States and Europe has gradually shipped overseas to increase profits for multinational companies and shareholder stakes. Though capitalism has created dramatic innovation, there is an imbalance tipping towards a global economic collapse if steps are not taken to create more equality. Furthermore, as our global economies continue to enmesh, if a catastrophic collapse of the world economy occurs, the poorest and most vulnerable will certainly be the hardest hit and the first to feel the volcanic wave of chaos that will follow. This means we need to take notice when a country or an entire continent falters or is unable to keep up. The race to economic power will not be won by only a few nations with so many held back only hoping to receive an invitation to watch from the stands, or maybe listen from the outside while the games go on inside.

If we consider all the nations of the world in a metaphorical running race that some nations are allowed to run while others are not invited, this is the unfortunate scenario for the poorest countries. Strong and wealthy countries are invited to the race and weaker poorer ones are unwelcome. Surely, this is not God's intention for His remarkable creation, man! Unifying as God's people and sharing our resources makes us stronger. Helping the impoverished people to the starting line of the race and giving them encouragement along the course will give an accelerated global economic boost in unimaginable ways.

The Small-World Problem: We Are All Connected More Closely than We Realize

In the book *Six Degrees*, Duncan Watts theorizes that people are connected in closer proximity to one another than we realize. It's easy to forget, not offering a passing thought or a real hard look at the struggles billions of humans endure while we peacefully enjoy comfort and security knowing our head is covered, our mouths fed, and our thirsts quenched. But Duncan challenges us to take a look at the way in which we can, through only a few channels of connection, influence the lives of others who we may not even know.

Duncan writes of a 1967 experiment conducted by social psychologist Stanley Milgram. Milgram was interested in the resolution of the hypothesis circulating in the sociological community of the day, which viewed the world as a vast social network with enormous connectivity but in a sense really only a small network by actual standards of connection. Sociology experts theorized that while the world had billions of people dotting continents in distant and far places, there were only a few distinct connection points between one person and another who don't personally know one another. The experiment Milgram devised became known as the 'small-world problem' after the cocktail banter in which two strangers discover they share mutual acquaintances. Their humorous discovery leads to their determination that they live in a world actually smaller than they realize.

To devise a system of testing the interconnected relationships people share and determine just how closely we are all connected, Milgram created a simple experiment. Residing in the Boston area and teaching at Harvard, he surmised his conclusions could be drawn by providing several hundred letters to distant populations and asking them to follow a carefully detailed instruction. In his experiment, he asked the participants to send their letters to people they knew personally by first name only. Participants were chosen from Boston and Omaha to offer seemingly distant and non-existent connection. Participants were given clear instructions to send their letters to people they believed could move their letter closer to a stockbroker in Sharon, Massachusetts. If the participants knew the stockbroker personally, they could send their letter directly to him. However, if they didn't know him, they were required to send the letter to someone they believed moved the letter closer to the experimental control, the stockbroker, in Massachusetts.

As the experiment began, Milgram asked participants to estimate how many hands it would take for the envelope to finally reach the stockbroker. As you would expect, most people believed it would probably require the letter to pass through the hands of hundreds of people before actually finding the postal box of the final delivery point in Sharon. However, Milgram discovered the majority of the envelopes required no more than passing through six individual hands before delivery. The result was a remarkable surprise at the time. It eventually led to the phrase 'six degrees of separation.' Six degrees of separation would eventually become a play written by John Guare in 1990 and spawned a number of parlor games and extensive fodder for cocktail party banter. Later, it would become a hit movie in 1993 starring Will Smith, further immortalizing the uniquely interconnected lives we lead with one another regardless of the distance separating our physical address.

Milgram's discovery, while unique, is not all that amazing, as Duncan shares in *Six Degrees*. If you consider each of us individually and our connections to our core group of friends, I may know five friends with whom I can share a message. My five friends know five, and their friends know five more. This endless cascade moves from me as the center of the message in only a few short links in the circular chain and grows exponentially. Within only three links, my five has grown to 105.

Duncan hypothesizes further if I were to know one hundred people and they each know one hundred, and this chain continues by the fourth and fifth link in the chain, our connections have eclipsed the one million and four million marks. By five steps, the connections have already surpassed the nine billion mark. Duncan brings to light this important takeaway for the purpose of understanding just how interwoven our lives are. Though my life in a Chicago suburb may seem distant and somehow unaffected by an unknown person in Cambodia, Africa, or India, we are connected in relationships by no more than only six links in a chain of relationship.[37]

The significance of our interconnected relationships is a beacon of hope and mustn't be forgotten in our call to act to alleviate the suffering of the world coming from distant places. As we know from the human body, every part of the body is interdependent for health. If I hold my hand up and wave, which finger would I be willing to sacrifice and say I don't require that one anymore? While I may be able to adapt and operate mechanical functions missing a thumb or a finger, the more fingers I lose, the harder it becomes to operate fine-detailed hand-motor operations. If I cut off all of my fingers, I am left with a palm that is crippled, unable to grasp, and can only push or nudge.

In some ways, our inability to recognize our connections to our brothers and sisters in distant lands is no different than the hypothetical severing of fingers from my hand. The more disconnected I choose to stay, leads to a more crippled ability to fully realize the potential grace, passion, and opportunity I have to be fully whole. My five or six degrees of separation between myself and another human being is really only a stone's throw away. If I choose to wave with my full hand of fingers at a distant brother or sister, I am likely to receive a full wave back. However, in many cultures without opportunity and only fractional hope, the fingers of the children and the many men and women living there are cut off almost immediately from birth. Economic suppression, famine, lack of resource, and few mechanisms for support weaken the hand of far too many in distant lands. *Waving* becomes difficult when the hand does not have fingers and is only a palm or worse yet maybe a stump cut off at the wrist, elbow, or even the shoulder. Metaphorically, this is the unfortunate circumstance many brethren are faced with when they're birthed into a culture of chaos, disease, and hardship.

The Shared Narrative of Life

In the studies of math, science, and physics, scientists are constantly attempting to understand and entertain new ways of looking at our universe. Collectively, from the very first recorded observations to the present, we have assembled a vast network of knowledge. The experience of men and women who have passed before has allowed a shared experience of knowledge propelling our inventive opportunities. From the dawn of time, man has used devices and expertise to survive and improve the nature of the human experience. From the discovery of fire and the wheel to the super computer and microchip, our discoveries have collectively grown and gathered significance to propel industry, communication, and consciousness.

Our ongoing tapestry of thought, science, and art is a narrative. Like a long-running play, this narrative has evolved from the earliest known life and the far-reaching galaxies. We know there is a universe, which seems almost infinite—and our existence when compared to the enormity of it seems rather small and insignificant. We coexist on our planet, in our solar system, and our galaxy. Our lives are part of this continuum and are creating history every day. New discoveries made today will become the seeds fueling the great breakthroughs of tomorrow.

One of the most intriguing elements is our information age. Information travels in byte-size pieces in milliseconds along lines or in waves from land to space and back again. Instantaneously, a thought, a message, a picture, a film, or a song travels a distance that is faster than ancient man could have ever imagined possible. We live in a time when our ability to connect has never been more definite or possible. *Literally, every day we share a collective consciousness of thought, art, and nature that we propel forward with each passing twenty-four-hour period. This time is unlike no other in man's history!*

Collectively telling about our lives to the world and the world telling us their stories has become one of the most undeniable needs humans share. The emergence of Facebook is no accident. Why? *Humans have a need to be noticed, heard, and to relate in special ways to gain meaning and knowledge and to exercise our abilities to love and be loved.* In essence, we must create a 'shared narrative' every day, and we find ourselves hopelessly fascinated with the ongoing pursuit of connecting our narrative to the world. This is Facebook! Facebook is a shared narrative of experiences for which we post, write, share, and watch the lives, pictures, thoughts, and drama of our 'friends.' Even the phrase 'Friend Me' has become a lexicon of our language in only a few short years. Speed, information, and narrative move at a pace unseen before and perhaps will move even faster. It was not more than 150 years ago, a small timetable by the comparison of the billions of years we know the earth has history, that the fastest object known to exist was a railroad engine at full throttle with no cars behind, and a few years before that, a horse at full gallop. Man simply could not have known that the collective consciousness and narrative would have arrived a mere century and a half later, where we are capable of such incredible connectivity.

The shared narrative also holds meaning to teach and give life to the experiences others have halfway around the world or even in our own backyard. Using online forums, blogs, videos, and social sites creates a vehicle for people living in poverty to connect with men and women who can help them. These opportunities, along with other real-life scenarios, can bring us closer to feeling and realizing the way it might be for us to live a life of a person in Africa, India, or some other place where dire straits exist.

Puzzles May Help Organize our Reality and Connect Us

We live in a world with ordered events. The sun rises and sets every day on the horizon as the earth rotates away from the sun's brilliant light. Animals and plants live in symbiosis, exchanging gasses we both require to live. Unfathomable organization resides in the genetic code of every living structure. Everywhere, the pulse and rhythm of life are observable, even palpable. Becoming familiar with the world around us and recognizing it helps us to survive and to feel safe and connected. Everything in the world fits together like a puzzle. Even looking around yourself right now, as you're reading, you'll notice the objects in the room are geometrical. Tables have square, rectangular, or rounded surfaces. Windows are various shapes and dimensions. Doors, chairs, appliances, homes, cars, and everything we use or see is geometric. Even the air, though we cannot see it with the naked eye, has a geometry that can be seen with special viewing equipment. Our brains connect our observations and experiences of the world like a puzzle. *As informational images, sounds, smells, and experiences are processed in our brain, the memories and wiring of our central nervous system possess the ability to recognize the familiar from the unfamiliar and piece these multi-factual inputs together to make sense or be incongruent.*

To illustrate this premise, let's use puzzle pieces known as polyominos to illustrate a composition that can help us understand our interrelationships with one another. A polyomino is a sequence of squares arranged in a pattern that can fit together like pieces in a puzzle in two- or three-dimensional spheres. Starting with a monomino and expanding upward to a domino, triomino, tetromino, pentomino, and so on, these geometric shapes can help us to better understand some of the reasons we create the lives we lead and trust the people we welcome to our worlds and the ones we disallow or choose to avoid.

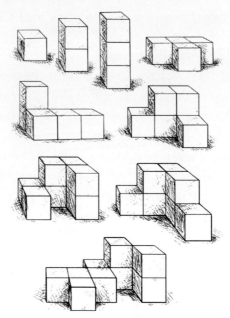

Polyominos are arranged as multilayered block-like shapes in varying numbers and arrangements.

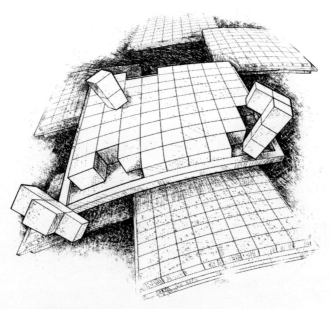

Polyomino puzzles are created in two- or three-dimensional methods by piecing together the various-shaped polyomino blocks into an interconnected pattern.

In order to understand the way our brain wires experiences with the familiar and unfamiliar, imagine our daily views of the world as energy patterns stored in the brain for immediate and future reference, like files stored in a file cabinet. All experiences since conception until our deaths are stored in our brain and available for access and use. But for most of us, the ability to use this stored information is limited even though it exists in storage. Every sound, image, object touched, emotion felt, and smell sensed takes a place in the massive architectural divisions of the human brain. As we become familiar with the input, we recognize patterns and can recall them. Our mother's voice, the taste of the foods we enjoy or dislike, and the people we know all begin to take shape in the brain of a human, and possibly all living animals. Familiar with our environment and knowing what to expect, we feel safe, connected, and comforted in knowing the people and the surroundings we inhabit regularly.

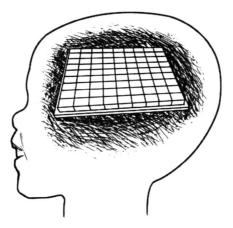

The brain organizes experiences and information like a puzzle.

Using polyomino puzzle sequencing as a visual geometric metaphor, we can understand our own human behavior and others by replacing individual processes within the brain with polyomino puzzle pieces as symbolic elements. Our brains are processors designed to crunch large amounts of data and create symmetry and order to our experience of the world. For simplicity, we could say our world is like a puzzle! ***In our minds when we awaken, there's an idea of how all the pieces will come together to make our experiential puzzle fit together and make sense.*** We even use words like, "All the pieces are coming together," "It feels like I'm trying to put a square peg in a round hole." Moreover, our internal puzzle changes in tune with the experiences we have every day. As we learn new ideas and master new skills, our comfort with the unfamiliar grows. Discomfort and fear lessen as we gain mastery over parts of our lives. Our occupation, school, parenting, being married, dating, and changes in family dynamics all become easier when we gain mastery through experience. In essence, the construct of the puzzle is never static but is changing constantly, from our very first breaths of life until our death.

The theory we espouse from the puzzle metaphor is when we see our most comfortable and safest people in our world (people like us: white if you're white, black if you're black, Hispanic if you're Hispanic, handicapped, blind, cancer survivor, diabetic, African, Indian, Russian, and so on) we assign a value or a polyomino that is easiest to fit into the construction of our mind's puzzle. Moreover, other human emotions and experiences along with our choices all are assigned a value and polyomino shape. As you can imagine the more complex the polyominos, the more difficult it would be to complete the internal brain puzzle. Piecing together complex polyominos into a symmetrical three-dimensional square is more difficult than connecting and stacking simple monominos and dominos. The crux of the challenge is that on a daily basis for us to feel complete, whole, at peace, and safe, we must complete our puzzle daily before we go to bed and process the accumulated or shared narrative we participated in. Our minds have a need to comprehend, process, and distinguish the familiar from the unfamiliar. Moreover, we assign a value to everything so we can organize it. Our world is co-created with every other human being, animal, plant, and living matter. When the unfamiliar becomes the familiar, we are able to simplify the polyomino structure and fit the interlocking pieces easily. But an inability to adapt and create order in the puzzle sequencing can leave us feeling incomplete and distressed. Seeing the unfamiliar and being around people who make us feel uncomfortable because they are different can create anxiety and fear.

Our need to feel safe requires simplicity, familiarity, understanding, acceptance, basic needs being met, and connection. These elements

when felt and experienced simplify our puzzle construction in the
mind by changing the complex polyominos into simple monominos
and dominos that are easy to construct into a puzzle that makes sense.

In order to simplify our own personal polyomino puzzle and piece our thoughts and experiences together to make sense, we assign a value judgment to everything we do, everyone we meet, and all personal experiences. Things that are familiar and people that we feel safe with allow our brain to create a simple monomino or domino to represent the known and the familiar. Someone who is 'like us' doesn't raise as many cautionary messages in the brain. As the values are being assigned throughout the day, our brains then lay these polyomino pieces onto a puzzle grid and attempt to complete the puzzle every day. This example is easy to picture if you imagine an expanded checkerboard, nine by nine with 81 squares. Placing single monominos and dominoes side by side is significantly easier to interlock and fill the gridded puzzle than more complex tetrominos and pentominos.

Completing this puzzle daily is relatively easy as long as we process the known and familiar. However, unexpected circumstances, unfamiliar people, and situations that may cause discomfort or fear cause our brain to complete a far more complex polyomino puzzle. These challenges become stumbling blocks and their assignment of value as a triomino, tetraomino, pentomino, sexomino, or a larger polyomino can potentially push into conflict in our brain. The result of this uncompleted puzzle could cause distress and unsettled feelings. The consequence may lead to fear, anxiety, worry, and becoming reactive rather than responsive, grounded, and centered.

The value system we assign to people who are unlike us and the complexity of the polyomino structure are parallel reflections with one another. Every experience and impression is assigned a value or polyomino pattern. So even the lessons we learn from parents, community, teachers, news, books, friends, and other people who influence our beliefs tilt our polyomino structures toward the simple or complex. Therefore, if you're a Caucasian male and you've grown up in a small mid-western town with people who are mostly white and blue-collar individuals, in all likelihood you're going to assign a complex polyomino structure to a black man from the south side of Chicago. If you grew up without exposure to many people of color, you become more likely to assign complexity to the interaction. Even though he may have been a hard-working college-educated man, his appearance, *being different* than the familiar creates difficulty for the brain to fit him into a simplified puzzle. Therefore, he seems unsafe. This becomes even more tenuous if growing up there are messages taught in a child's home to distrust people who are different than they are or to even hate based on color of skin, ethnicity, sexual orientation, class, tribe, and religion.

Once again, we come to understand bias. The ability to accept and embrace people who are different than we are is a learned behavior. Moreover, the earlier the impressions are formed, the stronger likelihood we will assign simple value or polyomino structure to a variety of people and life circumstances.

However, there are requirements that all people possess in order to experience their own personal understanding of security. If a child has incredibly diversified messages and images with inconsistent routines, forming cohesive bonds and security is difficult. Jean Piaget, one of the most influential researchers on childhood development, researched and discovered there are crucial developmental milestones all humans must pass through to have proper physical and mental health. Piaget determined children pass through four stages of development.

Stages of Cognitive Development

Piaget identified four stages in cognitive development.

Sensorimotor stage (infancy). In this period (which has six stages), intelligence is demonstrated through motor activity without the use of symbols. Knowledge of the world is limited (but developing) because it's based on physical interactions /experiences. Children acquire object permanence at about seven months of age (memory). Physical development (mobility) allows the child to begin developing new intellectual abilities. Some symbolic (language) abilities are developed at the end of this stage.

Pre-operational stage (toddler and early childhood). In this period (which has two sub-stages), intelligence is demonstrated through the use of symbols, language use matures, and memory and imagination are developed, but thinking is done in a non-logical, irreversible manner. Egocentric thinking predominates.

Concrete operational stage (elementary and early adolescence). In this stage (characterized by seven types of conservation: number, length, liquid, mass, weight, area, volume), intelligence is demonstrated through logical and systematic manipulation of symbols related to concrete objects. Operational thinking develops (mental actions that are reversible). Egocentric thought diminishes.

Formal operational stage (adolescence and adulthood). In this stage, intelligence is demonstrated through the logical use of symbols related to abstract concepts. Early in the period, there is a return to egocentric thought. Only 35% of high school graduates in industrialized countries obtain formal operations; many people do not think formally during adulthood.[38]

If each stage of development unfolds properly, children are able to adapt and assimilate with the unfamiliar more easily than if a breach in the development occurs. Giving routines and knowing the familiar can also allow children to venture into the unfamiliar and unknown. *Existing simultaneously, a child given routines he can count on, while also exposing him to outside experiences and people in opportunities to learn and trust the unknown, can be a positive equation for a well-balanced adult who will provide a strong leadership of compassion and justice in the world.*

Regardless of race, religion, sexual orientation, nationality, or social class, all people have the same basic needs and go through the same developmental stages of life. Therefore, a black woman growing up in the deep south of the United States may also struggle to assemble her own puzzle within her mind, accepting the friendship of a Hispanic neighbor or trusting a Caucasian immigrant from Russia. ***Bias is not specific to any race, religion, ethnicity, nationality, or social class. Discrimination is often specific to individuals or whole groups of people. The inability to organize constructive thought as we have been presented is the seed for its destructive existence.***

One of the troubling consequences that may result from the unsettled completion of interlocking polyomino puzzle sequences daily could also be violence. Violence against other people might be attempts to simplify complexity and perception that people are unsafe. Violent behavior could be a reaction our brains default to when there are no other ways we can make the pieces all fit together. In other words, if there is a need to create a secure meaning from our daily interactions with life, then the threat of not being able to assemble order to the events can create grave frictions within the brain. Moreover, if there has been cause through personal experience that made us feel unsafe, experience mistrust, or have a heightened sense of personal safety, the active fight or flight systems of the human body will also take hold in the brain, hijacking the rational construction of a symmetrical polyomino puzzle. Crimes of hate, superiority, dominance, and other modes of violence can be related to the unsettling our brains have with an unfinished construction of familiar, safe structures daily.

Puzzles of different types can also help us to have an image from which to build a conscious landscape, for peaceful coexistence with the unknown in men and women who are different than we are. The Rubik's Cube, invented by Hungarian inventor and sculptor Emo Rubik in 1974, became the most popular toy in the world following its introduction in 1977. With over 350 million Cubes produced worldwide and numerous people playing with it for recreation and competition, the Rubik's Cube is one of the more daunting puzzle challenges for many who attempt to solve its colored, squared mystery. Solving the puzzle is simple in theory but difficult in practice when attempting to move the articulated blocks each holding a colored square as a marker. To solve the puzzle, each of the nine colored squares on the six sides of the Cube should be an identical color. However, often people find this very difficult to do as the articulating mechanism of the puzzle has only a few correct sequences, which must be followed to be successful. Frustrating and too challenging for many, often the Cube is manipulated for a while and then abandoned with the various color combinations now mixed in varying degrees but held together by the connecting points of the toy on the inside of the Cube.[39]

Considering the Rubik's Cube and the metaphorical premise it may represent in bringing people together, it's apparent there is a natural symmetry in the puzzle that is undeniable. Connected in the middle at the core and able to move and articulate but different on the outside, each square could be compared to the differences we all see in one another's color, race, ethnicity, religion, sexual orientation, class, or tribe. There is a desperate need to separate and create unity bringing all the like-colored monomino pieces together on each side of the Cube to solve the puzzle. However, if we were able to personally examine each of the 350 million Rubik's Cubes that have been manufactured since its introduction in 1977, in all likelihood we would find far more uncompleted puzzles on tables, in drawers, or under beds. Yet, these unsolved puzzles remain connected, and the colored squares create a beautiful tapestry in their mixed union on each side of the Cube. Like continents on the world map, we should also consider how the Rubik's Cube can be looked upon as a symbol of unity we could also achieve. Even with a vast array of colors, ethnicity, beliefs, and differing views of life, we too can coexist and stay connected at our core.

But the paradox of the Rubik's Cube as a metaphor for the beautiful tapestry of our colored planet with people of varied nationalities, beliefs, and backgrounds is the difficulty we have in solving the puzzle. Like the Cube, we have struggled with the complexity of how to intertwine our lives and comprehend the need to be compassionate with others. We struggle with the complexity of poverty and what to do about the suffering that exists. Our hearts and minds have difficulty with the magnitude of the problems, and we often quit in frustration, throwing up our hands and tossing the problems under the bed, in a drawer, or on a table like the complex Rubik's Cube. The Rubik's Cube is a great metaphor, whether solved or unsolved. In its unsolved state, there is symmetry with all the colors blending together and forming a beautiful array. While the solved puzzle is uniform and demonstrates order. Either way, it is possible to see the unique opportunity a Rubik's Cube provides to understand humanity.

Aristotle's 'Golden Mean' Teaches Us Virtue

Seeking to enlighten his students and create order in the world, the great Greek philosopher Aristotle proposed geometry as a tool for understanding virtues and vice. It was Aristotle's belief that all humans harbor the nature for good and evil with good habits becoming virtues and bad habits, vices. Practicing virtuous habits produces happiness and bad habits, unhappiness. His observations along these lines led him to write, "Neither by nature, then, or contrary to nature do the virtues arise in us; rather we are adapted by nature to receive them, and are made perfect by habit." [40]

In the book *The Middle Way*, Lou Marinoff, PhD, seeks to enlighten with a parallel thread of conscious thought many great philosophers and teachers shared during their formative teaching. Finding a common thread of philosophy weaving itself within the writing and messages shared by great minds like Aristotle, Buddha, Confucius, and others, Marinoff proposes that satisfaction and happiness are achieved with conscious avoidance of extremes and seeking a path of middle ground being perhaps the most desirable road.

Marinoff writes of virtues and Aristotle's philosophy of the golden mean by stating: "Virtues cannot be imposed by legislated laws or political orders. Man-made laws can be bent or broken, can be unjust on their face or in the application, can become outmoded or superseded; and so man-made laws cannot be allowed to constitute the basis of moral behaviors. We legislate against vices that we do not wish to see practiced in civil society, yet each individual decides whether to obey or to flout the laws. The laws we follow should reflect, but cannot dictate, our morals...." [41] Aristotle knew, too, that moral order could not be imposed on a society, any more than it could be legislated. For the imposition of moral order can only take place in tandem with the suppression of individual development and the restriction of personal choice. Western morality rests squarely on each person's choice and depends upon a majority's preference for better over worse thoughts, words, and deeds. To impose morality is an affront to its very meaning. It can be done but only by political tyranny. And Aristotle knew that tyrants did not usually embark on campaigns of moral edification. Benevolent despots are few and far between." [42]

Marinoff sheds light on an incredibly important feature of humanity in examining the role all of society has on the continued suppression of people and the inability of the poorest on the planet to climb out of poverty. Our laws and efforts to become virtuous have followed a mostly legislative path, when the essence of any change we hope for must come from a truly holistic center.

Aristotle recognized the faulty thinking and ineffective result imposed laws and suppression of individual thought would ultimately have on society. So he turned to geometry to explain morality and help his students understand virtues. Virtues could be explained in the simplest of forms in the following way: Geometric shapes constitute a plethora of possibility, and some are purely symmetrical while others assume odd dimension and shape. Aristotle taught that virtues were like well-proportioned shapes while vices were ill-proportioned.

Known as the 'golden mean,' Aristotle recognized that if given an assignment to choose a rectangle, many people if provided with the examples in this diagram would opt for a proportionate rectangle similar to rectangle #5

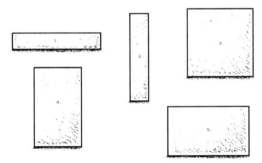

Most people select rectangle #5 because it is naturally more appealing to the eye and has a proportion that most people regard as the correct dimensions of a rectangle.

Aristotle reasoned many would consider rectangle number #1 to be too narrow and long while number #2 is too tall and narrow. Observers would recognize number #3 is a special rectangle, a square, where all four sides of the rectangle were equal. However, #4 and #5 would usually be selected as the customary classic rectangles of proportion. Like rectangles of proportion, Aristotle believed virtuous thought, moderate thinking, balance, and symmetry in life were reflected correspondingly to the balance of a well-proportioned rectangle. Furthermore, the proportions of rectangles #4 and #5 were frequently observed in nature. Known as the 'golden ratio,' Aristotle determined extremely common and clear proportions were found within this geometric proportion in nature. Rectangle #4 and #5 came to be known as the ratio of the Greek letter phi. The golden ratio is inimitable because phi = 1/(phi − 1). As a result, we can subdivide any golden rectangle into a square and another golden rectangle. This proportionate subdivision can continue indefinitely, but only with the golden ratio.

When Aristotle discovered this well-proportioned golden rectangle, he could not have known how distinctly and commonly this proportion resided in nature. It permeates architecture and art, from Classical Greece to the Italian Renaissance and far beyond into personal identification, business, and global markets. Leonardo Da Vinci, using the golden ratio in precise proportions, painted the Mona Lisa. Innumerous architects, sculptors, and painters have similarly utilized phi in their expression. Even credit cards, driver's licenses, and social security cards resemble the golden ratio originated by Aristotle.

Aristotle's golden ratio also gave rise to the famed Fibonacci series (0, 1, 1, 2, 3, 5, 8, 13, 21, 34, 55, 89, 144...) discovered by Leonardo Pisano Fibonacci (1170-1250). Each sum in the series is the result of adding the previous two numbers. As a result of this remarkable symmetry, the inclusion of these values within a golden ratio gives rise to nearly perfect aesthetics. The natural coincidence does not stop there but continues when observing a nautilus, a head of cauliflower, or even shrimp tails. Symmetrical measurements and natural phenomenon are evident throughout nature and could even help understand why certain people are considered more beautiful.[43]

Our recognition and familiarity with proportion create an internal sense of comfort and attraction when the geometric ratios are proportional. When geometric proportion or parameters outside our conscious understanding of our spatial world are breached, it becomes difficult to balance and harmonize emotions. However, it's not entirely impossible, and the astonishing fact is that human beings are actually capable of far greater levels of adapting and creating new norms than many would consider, like the theory we have proposed using polyomino puzzles and Rubik's Cubes, geometry, and the common ratios, we can all see and experience become a connecting point.

These points can then become the foundation for our care, compassion, and service to people inhabiting the world who suffer and hold little hope for survival or forward progression in their lives. Knowing all men are responding to universal truths, the observation of these virtues allows us to speak common languages. Math, observation of geometry, and puzzle solutions may hold a key to unlocking the difficulty our world has in relating to one another and feeling moved to aid the most vulnerable. Certainly, if we are to create any sustainable solutions to end suffering around the globe, we will need to find commonality in language and experience.

Lessons Humanity Can Learn from World War II and Auschwitz

The atrocities of World War II Nazi Germany have left permanent scars on humanity. Few words can describe the enormity of the loss and the senseless killing. However, in the midst of these turbulent years, the will to survive and adapt has been revealed through the accounts of brave survivors. As Jewish author Primo Levi recounts of his tortured years living in Auschwitz, survival under extreme duress can often require a certain psychological trickery along with enormous capacities for adaptation. Levi, an Italian Jew deported to Germany and then transported to Auschwitz for ten months, gives a powerful account of his execrable time in the death camp, and helps us to understand with more clarity the mammoth efforts people living in desperate poverty and near the edge of survival have to manage.

Like the most vulnerable living in the world's deepest holes of poverty, Levi discovered concepts such as 'just,' 'right,' 'moral,' and 'fair' lose any sense of meaning, and it is only through the adaptation and dismissal of any attachment to their meaning is survival possible. Surviving the brutal, reprehensible, loathsome treatment within Auschwitz required men to take on the brutish character of an animal and dismiss all attachments to civility. Moreover, ethics and moral behavior were frequently discarded if survival were even a faint possibility. Many opted for thievery when possible if the result meant the differences between life and death. Additionally, Levi came to recognize the insane were more apt to survive than the sane because they lacked the context for normalcy even in the face of brutal hardship. In a parallel way, we may also consider the ways the poor survive hardship, tossing out notions of 'just,' 'right,' and 'moral' when faced with difficult decisions to steal or embark on criminal acts.

As Levi himself, along with the few who made it through, eventually learned, the attachment to anything of significance and the anticipation of something changing for the good had little hope or possibility. Instead, setting short-term goals of survival like making it through the winter, or even just being able to get a few hours of sleep became goals worth living for. Adaptation was the way humans survived Auschwitz, and releasing attachment to morality were codes of conduct required to withstand and live.[44]

The parallels in thought and ideation many of us create in order to survive our daily lives are also connecting points of similar experience. Moreover, the under-resourced and most at-risk people living also share some of these same survival characteristics in order to stay alive. Like the survivors in Auschwitz, when our real or imagined hope for fairness or understanding of the dire circumstance is stripped, stolen from our grasp, we must be willing to diminish and narrow our possibilities. Limiting goals and taking a more immediate, in the moment view is the only way we can truly survive. What is particularly compelling about Levi's discovery of survival is the way it draws humanity to focus more on the present and the appreciation for the mundane, rather than the attachment of us to something far off while putting our happiness in the hope this distant desire occurs.

Whether rich, poor, a survivor in an Auschwitz death camp, or any other genre of humanity, the only thing we have to share with the world is the exact moment we are living at this time. We cannot live in the future or redo the past. The presence of now is the present of life. As well, the uncomfortable experiences we can feel when pushed against difficult experiences in life are reminders and opportunities to gain perspective. Even the most difficult and possibly life threatening situations can give a glimpse into the emotional strain many under-resourced people around the world experience continually. The more we learn to feel like others feel and are placed in the situations they feel, the stronger our compassion and drive to help solve the challenges of poverty around the world.

Further, our ability to create thought and ideation with universal language and truths can become launching points for us to act and deeply care about the desperate lives of many around the world. Whether living 'with' or 'without', all of us must learn adaptation and survival at some point in our lives in order to *survive*. But for most of us living with plenty, we can never know the true meaning of survival in the truest sense of no food, water contaminated with waterborne pathogens, deplorable sanitary conditions, and possibly even the exploitation of human trafficking. Any of these recognized associations that frequently exist in poverty would stretch most of us beyond our comfort zones, but eventually we could adapt. But in our adaptation we would change and become more humble, possibly with greater tolerance, and on some level connect with humanity's most impoverished and come to know how desperate their lives are. Then we would see it is not someone else's job to worry about the poor or to 'do something.' No, instead we would feel compelled on our own to take action to change the injustices and correct the imbalances that exist between the vast number of people who live below the poverty line and the minority who enjoy relative lives of ease and comfort.

In a social experiment video on YouTube, the acts of compassion a homeless man shows a freezing boy in New York City demonstrate how profound compassion affects the heart of even the most unlikely people to do something! Filming on a bustling street corner in five-degree Fahrenheit weather, the OCK TV production crew placed a young boy, about twelve, on a busy street corner dressed only in jeans and t-shirt. He is given a plastic garbage bag and is instructed to stand and wait. Obviously shivering and frightfully cold, the boy waits and waits while busy New York commuters pass him by. Some pause, only a few moments to notice, but don't stop to offer any help. Sadly, others seem to not even notice, walking past him as if he doesn't even exist. After a while, he becomes so cold he wraps the plastic bag around his body and lies on the ground, curled up like a dying animal in the bag on the frozen sidewalk. Still commuters pass, most not even noticing his dying body beginning to shut down from the cold. Two hours and no one has stopped to help! Then a miracle appears: a *homeless* man stops to help! Yes, a homeless man who knows what it feels like to be an outcast, to be out in the cold on a busy New York sidewalk and not have anyone care that you exist. He stops, he questions the boy, "Are you homeless? What happened to your parents?" The boy answers, "My parents abandoned me." The homeless man gives assurance to the boy, telling him he's going to help him and then he takes his *own* coat off and wraps it around the boy. He goes on to say, "I know what it feels like to be homeless; we need to stick together."

The OCK TV production program has struck an emotional nerve around the world with their films like this one. Taking a look at how we treat one another and act toward each other is causing some to wake up and see we all have the ability to *act*, *do*, and *change* something to improve the life of someone. At the end of this YouTube video, a call to action is given: "If you wait until you can do everything for everybody, instead of something for somebody, you'll end up doing nothing for nobody."

Compassion fueled with action and dedication can change the world. Our awareness that poverty and people we never meet are our brothers and sisters is the beginning. Then we will heed the words, "Do unto your neighbor as you would have him do unto you." [45]

Summary Questions for Discussion

1. In his book *The Hole in Our Gospel*, Richard Stern provides a simple formula to help end poverty. The people who have the means are supposed to be helping those who don't to end their own suffering. As we have theorized as well as Stern, there is not nearly enough active participation to end poverty around the world. What are your thoughts about poverty and the role you personally have in this world to help people?

2. As Stanley Milgram discovered in his experiments with connection, we are more connected to one another than we realize. Only six links were required to connect any person with another somewhere in the world. Now with more connectivity and a plethora of social media sites, the number of links may be further shortened. How do you see this unique opportunity of connectivity as an opportunity to help people working to climb out of poverty?

3. The polyomino puzzle theory we wrote about in this chapter is a simplified way we can understand the possible ways we struggle to connect with one another. As well, it is also a possible explanation for some of the reasons violence and hatred exist. What are your thoughts about this theory and how can you see this being used in the real world to help people acquire the ability to gain tolerance, appreciation, and celebration of the diversity of the world?

4. Aristotle's golden mean is a universally recognized mathematical model, which presents itself throughout nature. As Aristotle believed, virtues that are balanced and more appealing to our nature have comfort, whereas the less symmetrical is less appealing and less virtuous. How could Aristotle's golden mean be used to help people understand their similarities and need for balance and be a connecting point for humankind?

5. In the last example provided in this chapter, we write of a video experiment where a young boy was standing on a busy New York street corner on a sub-zero freezing day. The sign he held said he was homeless. Hours passed before anyone stopped to help this boy who was without a coat and dressed only in a flimsy t-shirt. What do you imagine you would have done if you had encountered this boy while you hurried to your next appointment and were anxious to get out of the cold yourself? Would you have stopped and helped? Would you have called for help?

CHAPTER 6

THE POWERFUL RELATIONSHIP BETWEEN POVERTY AND THE BEGGAR

What keeps some persons poor? And what has made
some others rich? The true answers to these queries
would often make the poor man more proud of his
poverty than the rich man is of his wealth, and the
rich man more justly ashamed of his wealth than
the poor man unjustly now is of his poverty.
– Charles Caleb Colton. *Lacon*

Poverty's Impact: Every day, 22,000 children die due to the horrific consequences of poverty.

Labels Paradoxically Separate and Connect Us

Impoverished, poor, down and out, beggar, destitute, rich, goodie-two-shoes, jock, fat, skinny, short, tall, robust, black, white, Hispanic, sexy, athletic, handicapped, Republican, Democrat, chatterbox, nosey, dumb, brown-nose, illegal, homosexual, Bible thumper, Barbie doll, welfare mother… and thousands upon thousands of other words are often used to label people! Some are intended to cut, inflicting emotional pain and racially slur. Others evoke personal inferiority if we find ourselves unable to measure up. Still some labels are used to prop up our emotional health and give us a sense of superiority over another class of people. Whatever the feeling or need for labeling others and ourselves, the sad reality is labeling is frequently the wall that stands between our hearts and most human connections. But the paradox we must also recognize is the labels we ascribe to ourselves and others also provide us with a sense of connection, helping us to know where we belong and fit. Even our first and last name can be, in a sense, a label, connecting us to one family or group of individuals. "He's a member of the Waxman family" or "She's one of three Jordans at this school" are examples of typical comments that exemplify the use of labels to ascribe a connection to a group of people. Moreover, the human need to label may even run deeper, aiding our survival by helping us to know whom we can trust and with whom we should exercise caution. In other words, if we stay close to people more like ourselves, our subconscious survival instincts recognize this strategy has a stronger likelihood of survival than placing us in unknown places or circumstances and with strangers.

Thus, our labels are paradoxically important in helping us understand 'who' and 'what' we have connection to and also the important relationships in our lives. In a sense, they give order, association, and importance to our lives. Disregarding them would not be healthy to the human psyche. Labels are like pieces of a puzzle that we use to fit people, events, and circumstances together in order to make sense of our world. They can operate like mechanical pieces we place into our neurology, as we discussed in the previous chapter when we introduced the concepts of polyominos, Rubik's Cubes, and Aristotle's golden mean. The challenge we must consider is, ***how can we still have our human need to label the world and not exclude people and experiences, which can help us grow and feel connected even more richly?***

Labels Alienate the Poor

In the book, *The War Against the Poor*, Herbert Gans describes labels as a continuum that begins with knowledge and understanding. He proposes that life is a never-ending flow of moral surveillance. We survey each other to see if actions live up to norms and expectations we carry in our brains from past experience. We shape a surveillance system, using it to help us judge rather than merely to observe or to study situations. We create a set of moral imprints based on our observations of people. With family, friends, and people we trust, their actions are assessed. With people we know less, and especially strangers and groups, we move from judging actions to judging character! Character judging moves to the forefront particularly when the actions we observe strike us as wrong.[1] This finding is further supported by recent research coming from the Rochester Baby Lab and may even indicate character judging is inherent from infancy in all human beings.

Affiliated with the University of Rochester, the Rochester Baby Lab is a research facility focusing on early human development. It is part of the Department of Brain and Cognitive Sciences, where researchers observe children while they watch movies or play. Studying their interactions and behaviors, they analyze eye-gaze patterns and brain activity to study how children think, learn, and make decisions. One of the most fascinating studies the lab has undertaken is to determine the role of familiarity and how it can influence our decisions. In particular, researchers wanted to understand why humans prefer to associate with people more like themselves, and often disregard or may even allow harmful actions to befall someone who is different than them. This idea is possibly one of the great paradoxes of humanity. Why do we prefer to only act in a kind way to our familiar friends or people who are like us in color, ethnicity, educational background social class, etc.? Moreover, why are we apt to hurt, speak unkindly, or justify a penurious attitude with those who don't look like us or don't like our choices? Perhaps understanding the seeds for labels and the mechanisms could help create a new paradigm of thought and possibly move us closer to one another.

To study the earliest seeds of morality and preference for people who are similar to us, researchers used a series of puppet shows. Using babies as young as three months old, each child was shown a puppet show with two identical characters wearing different colored shirts. In one of the tests, babies were provided with a bowl of Graham Crackers or Cheerios and allowed to select their favorite snack. Then a puppet show was shown to the baby with the two puppets also enjoying either Graham Crackers or Cheerios. Each puppet had a bowl of Graham Crackers or Cheerios to demonstrate a preference for one food or the other. To test the baby's bias, another puppet show was performed. But this time, the character that had selected the bowl of snacks different than the one the baby had selected was trying to perform a difficult task. The puppet was attempting to lift a lid on a plastic box that was stuck. Intervening in this experimental puppet show, two entirely new identical puppet characters wearing different shirts provided assistance or opposition. One offered to help lift the lid, giving the puppet that had selected the different snack than the baby some assistance. The other puppet jumped on the lid, slamming it shut as the different snack choice puppet attempted to lift the lid. The two puppets and different modes of action were observed by the three-month-old baby. Would the babies prefer the helpful puppet as earlier experiments had demonstrated they tend to do when given a choice to choose a morally more responsible puppet over an oppositional one? Or would the babies go with a puppet that wanted to be unhelpful and thwart the attempt by the other puppet, which seemingly was different only because of choice in snacks he preferred. To test the results, random researchers offered the babies a choice of either of the two puppets—helpful or discourteous. Then by monitoring eye gaze in the younger infants or their reaching for the preferred choice, each infant was assessed for preference of puppet. Shockingly, what researchers found was that over 80% of the infants surveyed in this way would select the puppet that was discourteous and had thwarted the attempts of the puppet that had a different snack preference than the infant. These findings seemed to indicate that labeling and preferring people that are more like us have some innate origins. In other words, we are born with a preference to prefer the self, and probably out of survival, we recognize preference, similarity, and people who make choices like ours will more likely help us survive than perish.

In addition, studies at the Baby Lab revealed that while labeling and choice for self were inherent, even if it meant harm to others who were not like us, babies also demonstrate the seeds for recognizing right from wrong.

Moreover, further research demonstrated that early preferences to select more favorable results for self could change as children grew in cognition and learning. Using a simple board game, researchers tested older children to determine if moral attributes could be learned to favor others over self. Surprisingly, what they found was in the early developmental years of childhood from ages three to about eight, most children preferred to favor themselves over being fair with another child or even offering more to another child. But as children grew older from ages nine to eleven, the maturity of their brains, coupled with taught behavior, started to reveal a new possibility of morality emerging. ***Children became willing to offer a complete stranger some of the reward they would receive. Moreover, in some instances, children even offered to give another child a reward, even if it meant they would receive none. It would seem they were demonstrating the moral message, 'to give is better than to receive.'*** [2]

Thus, labeling and preferring the self, while inherent in human beings according to the research, are adaptable and thankfully influenced by teaching fairness, compassion, and justice. So the seeds for melting the walls of ice that separate us by our need to label and prefer the self are found in the ways we teach our children in daily life. Furthermore, the teachings we learn from the Bible about caring and loving the poor are demonstrable within each of us if our mentors, parents, and leaders are also willing to change and heed the call to serve others over self. The labels we place on one another can be self-imposed and pass through generations if there are not programs created to change beliefs. Certainly in America, many minorities have experienced negative characterization while also burdening themselves with their own. Indeed, even the word 'minority' can be a label indicating a segment of our population that has a less meaningful voice. As Todd recognizes from his experience growing up black in America, the messages he learned from his parents and others in his community are strong. His grandfather and other relatives passed on a sense of identity that sticks with him. Moreover, others may also share his identification with these messages and labels within the African-American community. When passed from generation to generation, these labels and the fear created by them have dire consequence for some. As Todd explains in this conversation he had with his grandfather about being black in America, and the role this may play in the deadly consequences of recent racially charged incidents in America, there are deep rivers of belief which have imprinted themselves on our minds.

Passed-Down Mentality

As I have grown in my understanding of people who live in poverty and now having experienced the desperate living conditions of people in Africa, my thoughts are troubled. I wonder, how did our world and society become so difficult for so many people living in poverty? My thoughts of poverty are not only confined to material possessions like homes, cars, and money. I wonder about the dreams people have for a brighter future and also the mindset of poverty. I also think about my own family and the ways I felt as a kid growing up as a black youth in America. And I think about how I feel as a black professional, married with two children and working hard to earn a living for my family. I am drawn to my own desires for a better life while wondering, why it is so difficult for black Americans and other people living impoverished lives in America to succeed?

As I shared some of the exciting details of my work in Africa and aiding many of the children in sports and education, my grandfather and I engaged in some healthy conversations that helped piece together answers to some of my questions. He believes black Americans have a built-in poverty mentality, possibly dating back as far as the early slave trade. However, he advises we move past our sorrowful history and allow a prosperous future to take ahold of our lives. My grandfather believes that, until we look to the future with new focus and not hold on to the negativity of the past, we will remain in a poverty mindset. Though my grandfather has eight decades of wisdom, his notions are confined to his own experience and don't help to explain the depth of beliefs held by people from centuries of beleaguered opportunity to move outside the stiff confines of poverty's steel gates.

My grandfather's wisdom on this subject also leads me to question when we should let go of the negatives in the past and allow new thought patterns to take ahold. We continue to blame when we should be concerned with how to make our lives and our surroundings better. A beggar's mentality is complex and can last many generations. What a powerful prison we live in through our experiences, in our minds, and still in our labels, which separate us.

Questions of epigenetics, our DNA, and the imprints of poverty shaping our behaviors sadden me. Complexities exist with the rich becoming wealthier while the poor are slipping and falling precariously fast into a black hole from which there is little hope of return. Swirling about is the role our political landscape, power, agriculture, ample jobs, education, morality, compassion, justice, and fairness all play in the poverty question. As I began to recognize, with the help of my grandfather's insights, my personal labels were even holding me back. Moreover, I began to discover some paradoxes in my own thoughts surrounding race, ethnicity, social class, and other matters that came into question as they relate to the origins of poverty and its continuance.

Children growing up in rough, urban neighborhoods with ties to gangs, poor living conditions, and few opportunities seem to make breaking the cycle of poverty and achieving healthier outcomes slim. It isn't just the drugs, gangs, violence, and educational disparity that trouble me. The mental state of kids growing up this way seems to be the crux of the problem from my grandfather's viewpoint and what I am learning about poverty. The stress that children feel with all the worry and anxiety they have about guns, violence, and not being good enough are real issues for many kids. This same kind of gripping fear and stress is also in other areas of the world, like East Africa and other impoverished areas, too. Entire nations of people seemed to have their lives laid out with little hope of any real economic or quality improvement in the near future.

As I also reminisced about my own childhood and my friends, I thought about the ways we were perceived. I had a close group of friends. We called ourselves 'Showcase,' and there were seven of us who hung out regularly. No, we were not a gang, fighting, selling drugs, causing trouble for the law, but we were perceived in that way, getting hassled by law enforcement and authority figures. There was something ominous about seeing a throng of black male youths hanging out together. Furthermore, if we crossed paths with another group of black young men, there were also possibilities for conflict. There was a code we lived by, and it reminded me of the experiences Geoffrey Canada wrote of in Fist, Stick, Knife, Gun *concerning urban violence in America. Canada, while growing up in the South Bronx in the 1960s, recalled the role fear played in his childhood and the notion that to show fear was unacceptable, even if it meant possible harm or death to oneself. I also experienced fear within the community, and I knew the need for self-preservation seemed to harbor violence as a safeguard to protection and survival. Even the lack of protection from policing bodies or other institutions seemed to add to the dilemma we faced. As a result, we came to mistrust one another as black males and were always looking over our backs to see who might be following us or looking to pick a fight. This was the tempest I grew up with and recognized I still hold on to today. So in a way I was confronted with a paradox in my heart and thoughts when I began to dissect the actions and consequences of two extremely racially charged court cases that took place recently.*

Treyvon Martin and Jordan Davis, two young black youths not all that dissimilar from myself when I was growing up in California, were the victims of bullets coming from the guns of adult assailants. Their deaths and the media frenzy gave me cause to reflect on how I would have reacted to the possible threat the two assailants may have perceived was possible.

While the media sensationalized the cases as racially driven, I saw a deeper complexity here. Instead of looking at the color issue, I saw the stereotype issue. I must admit that initially I viewed the case as everyone else did, as just a race issue. But then I put myself in those different circumstances of those young boys and the men that murdered them. Because of the stereotypes of young black males, I can understand why jurors might sympathize with the assailants being scared of young black men. I am not saying that what those men did was right. They should be punished. However, I am saying that because of the circumstances of our worldview on young black men, there leaves doubt in the mind of people. Our country is scared of young black men, and as a result clouded judgment on the part of juries sometimes prevails. Yes, we could say that these men who shot the victims were prejudiced and meant to do harm. However, this is not the root or the source of the problems we face in America. The issues come down to misunderstanding, fear, and the inability of our culture to accept diversity. But young black men must also work to change stereotypes. Only young black men will be able to change the perceptions that they are unsafe. When young black men become community leaders, doctors, and teachers, the stereotype will change. Unfortunately, it won't happen overnight. I must admit that even my own demons to judge and stereotype creep out as I write this. Even though there are many black leaders, including our president, I still have a mindset that there are not enough. I also admit, as a black man, I still fear the labels. And if I were in the circumstances as the two men who murdered these two black youths, I can't lie, I would have had fear myself because of the perception of black males in America.

I view stereotypes as a disease, and diseases can live through generations. I can take it a step further and look within my own family history and friends' families, which had the mindset I could only succeed if I was in sports. Where my father and stepmother did a great job of raising a good young black man, because of social reasons and stereotypes, my upbringing was centered on sports. Of course, financial reasons made it hard for our family to afford college, so that was a big motivator in my parents' minds; but a lot of black families that I knew put their hopes in their child becoming a sports star or R&B/rap star. Education wasn't a big push. There wasn't enough emphasis on becoming teachers or policemen or politicians. Unfortunately, some stereotypes keep us in an impoverished kind of mindset.

Todd's grandfather's thoughts about the self-imposed labels, along with the paradox even Todd felt as a young black man when judging the safety of a situation involving possible violence, seem to indicate a need to be more definitive about facts versus possible fiction in assessing people. But the challenge, as Herbert Gans points out in *The War Against the Poor*, is as the increased social distances between strangers' judgments are based less on actual knowledge and more on indirect knowledge including information gained from the media. Sometimes the information can even be based on imagined knowledge coming from stories and preconceived ideas filtered through personal values of the people in various positions in society. The result of this continuum is that imagined knowledge becomes a label, according to Gans.[3]

Labeling is the method we create to designate people outside our moral and character comfort zone. In some cases, this becomes negative and pejorative with demeaning consequence as the result.

Poor people are customary recipients of labeling. Words like vagrant, destitute, delinquent, criminal, under-class, vagabond, skid row, white trash, spics, bums, shiftless, hobos, drifters, loiterers, homeless, tramps, street urchins, class failures, dregs, lower-lower class, and *beggars* are derogatory terms cast upon the poor. The labels are hurtful and demeaning. Moreover, labels ascribed to a class of people that are cast without care of how it feels to be on the receiving end are at the root of many social issues existing today. As well, the unwillingness to consider the other person's perspective and life experience are also responsible for the thick walls that still reside around the hearts of many people. Without an opening to visit, learn, take time, and share with people living in the margins of society, we lose an opportunity to be transformative as a generation. As we've said previously, we are all living at this point in history for a reason and to not recognize we are being given an opportunity to connect with one another with all the methods of communication and travel existing is tragic.

Understanding separation to protect the self and yet also knowing we must learn a way to connect and trust certainly seems like a paradox. Moreover, we question the role the labels can play in favor of the seemingly oppressed and how the *beggar* and the *waver* in everyone, whether real or metaphorical, has a role in connecting us. There is a purpose inherent in all human interactions. Exchange of thought and connection is always present even in a *beggar-and-waver* interaction.

What value is the *beggar* providing in return for a payment he receives? Is it acceptable for a man to simply stand on the side of the road and shake a cup with jingling change and beg for money? "Do you have any spare change?" "Can you help a brother out?" "Hey, I need something to eat, can you give me some money?" The pleas may sound different, but the end result is they all add up to begging. So is there a benefit or a payoff for a true *beggar* to continue begging if the opportunity to end the need for begging presents and now he can become a *waver* again? Perhaps at some deeper level there may even be a deeper philosophical meaning the role of begging plays in society at large.

Examining the relationship a *beggar* has with poverty is not unlike the relationship a fish has with water or an athlete has with sport. *Beggars* are symptoms of poverty, and in many ways they depend on the poverty to serve their needs. Poverty has created an economic reality and a paradigm the *beggar* may accept as his destiny. It changes his mind, his perceptions, and expectations. Poverty also draws volunteers, charities, and governments to rescue beggars and provide resources. While it may seem an enigma to consider *wavers* and *beggars* both being served by poverty, the tragic reality of the most under-resourced communities is that *wavers* and *beggars* serve together in a symbiotic relationship. There are *wavers* along the sides of the roads and the *waver* inside each of us who may have the necessary resources for our survival without much worry. While we each may feel a connection to the *waver* inside every man or woman along the side of the road, we also can feel connection to the feelings of the *beggar.*

But, unlike the *beggars* along the side of the road who may not be able to change their circumstances and their threat to survival is imminent, we can harbor those begging feelings inside our minds and hearts without the outward need to become a physical *beggar* ourselves. So in a sense, while we can feel alongside the most desperate, we cannot truly know what it is like to be in their shoes unless we have had to live as a *beggar* alongside the road.

Begging Occurs in Nature

Though begging may seem cast as a negative act, it cannot be viewed in this way. The act of begging and the metaphor of the *beggar* are parts of normal behavior for men just as they are found in nature. In the wild, begging behavior is found when dependent young mammals beg a mother to feed them. As well, it is seen as an act of submission to demonstrate to a stronger or more dominant animal, the willingness to surrender. Birds are completely dependent on their mothers to find and forage for food: begging is the method they use to get Mom's attention to feed them. Like human begging, it is a way to satisfy a survival instinct and is necessary when a tiny bird has no other way to find food. As well, when people beg alongside the road, they may have no other way to receive food. Begging is the only recourse.

Infants display begging behavior when they are hungry, too. But, as they mature and can open a refrigerator themselves or a cabinet, they can feed themselves. Though some mothers would tell you that their children stop begging and begin whining! The natural order for young mammals is dependence. But in healthy maturity, most mammalian animals will eventually be able to care for themselves. ***So the act of begging is a kind of metamorphosis or stunting that occurs to the poor. It's as if they are confined or relegated to be needy and dependent like babies or other young mammals.***

Paradoxically, begging also displays an immense amount of courage on the part of the *beggar*. The judging stares and shame cast in the direction of a man or woman begging for food can't feel empowering. Still, the will to live, to survive, and do what it takes even if it means begging shows a unique power that is present in almost every person. It means, "I'm not going to quit!" "I'm not going to die!" "I want to live!" "I want my children to live!" There is a power in begging that anyone who has cast judgment should reconsider his or her dispersive thoughts. Many of us would be too embarrassed to take up begging and hold out our hands to plead for money.

Beggars have a story to teach humanity and their courageous will, ironically enough, gives an opportunity for charity. Moreover, their faith may be stronger in God's promise to supply what they need for life because there is no other choice. Either believe that prayers will be answered today to supply food and water, or die! The *beggar* teaches each of us to trust Jesus's words in Matthew: "I tell you not to worry about your life. Don't worry about having something to eat, drink, or wear. Isn't life more than food or clothing? Look at the birds in the sky! They don't plant or harvest. They don't even store grain in barns. Yet your Father in heaven takes care of them. Aren't you worth much more than birds?" [4]

If each of us examined our own lives with deeper conviction to the archetype of the *beggar*, and the role it plays inside our own heart, we would recognize there are not large miles that separate us. I recognize there is a spirit of begging within my own story, and even discover daily in my prayers to God that I beg and plead with Him. Many of my begging prayers sound like this, "God, please fix this broken car!" "God, please heal me!" " God, please give me a new job!" "God, please be with them through this trial!" My prayers make God seem like the Wizard of Oz is passing by as a tourist in Africa, and I have my hand out begging like the *beggars* in Kenya I encountered. But what am I giving in return to deserve any notice from God? Yes, the Bible says God loves us regardless of what we have done, whether good or evil, deed or no deed, but I have discovered the notion of myself as a *beggar* before God something I want to cease. Instead, I want to *wave* to God and let him know I am ready to be seen and used for His purpose.

Recognizing that both *waver* and *beggar* are served by poverty is the beginning to end the strife. For the *beggar*, his need for survival means receiving food, clothing, and economic opportunity to claim autonomy. For the *waver*, assisting the *beggar* gives him a sense of fulfillment, a feeling of empowerment, and a deep sense of purpose. Teaming up to find viable ways to help people living in poverty escape this life are paramount. But theories for eradicating poverty and dependency are often easier to conceptualize than put into practice. In particular, aid to the poor in the United States has an ongoing dialogue between social experts. But the hurdles to climb and the definitive solutions are unclear to many. As an example, in the United States some believe the low minimum wage we have is the reason for furrows of deep poverty; they believe raising the minimum wage would transform poverty. However, as you will see from our discussion, issues like minimum wage and other economic policy changes are not linear solutions to eradicate poverty. It's possible the implementation of new wage increases could cause more hardships for the poor. But we cannot let *analysis* lead to *paralysis* in matters like minimum wage or any other social program created to help shift our economic inequality.

Conditions Can Lead to Begging

One of the possible factors holding many to the shackles of poverty in the United States is the low minimum wage paid to entry-level workers. The accumulated wages a someone raising a family in America could earn from a minimum wage would seem wholly inadequate to amply provide for all the needs a family or even a single person requires living without some type of means-tested system such as food stamps, Medicaid, or similar program. Working a forty-hour workweek and earning a minimum wage in 2013 of $7.25 provides $14,500 annually to a single man or woman. Per the 2013 poverty level for the United States, this puts a working wage slightly above the United States poverty line of $12,119.[5] Thus is the argument that raising the minimum wage seems necessary to provide a required boost to low-income workers, enabling them to move above the US poverty line. But minimum-wage changes are not always simple to implement. If wages are raised too high, employers claim they will be forced to hire fewer people, lay people off, and raise prices that will cause spiraling inflation. On the other side of the argument, a higher minimum wage is thought to reduce dependency on federal assistance and drain on taxed monies. Both sides of this discussion seem to have merit.

The United States minimum wage might also have further rippling effects through other economies as well. If workers are paid more for unskilled entry-level jobs in America, there could be a further illegal immigrant influx into our economy to take advantage of the uptick in wages. This possibility could cause a drop in available labor in neighboring countries and inflationary consequences. The uptick in prices could also influence the trade balance between our nation and others as our products become more expensive to purchase by our exporting partners and slow economic growth in our nation and new job creation. In addition, the pressure placed upon rivaling nations by their populace to follow the lead of the United States could also lead to more political unrest and labor dissatisfaction. Our national policies around setting a wage structure have direct and distant effects on global markets and must be carefully administered to seek the most advantageous outcome.

The Heritage Foundation, a nonprofit research and educational institution founded in 1973, has published controversial arguments speaking against aggressive minimum-wage policy in the United States. Their arguments certainly are warranted and bear weight in the overall picture. As the Foundation points out in their research briefs, more than half of the labor force securing a minimum wage is teens and young adults who are not the heads of households. Most are unskilled laborers who are working their way to another position and higher earning potential. The Foundation also goes on to point out that the vast majority of the workers who start work at minimum wage move on to higher wages within several years and many even receive a higher wage within the first year of employment through employer-directed wage increases for strong work ethics and job talents. The concern the Foundation raises about aggressive forced increases in minimum wages is that employers will seek to employ fewer unskilled workers, leaving many without jobs. Moreover, according to the Foundation, it's possible that employers will find ways to operate their business with fewer laborers and lay off or fire those presently employed. [6]

Countering the argument that raising minimum wage aggressively would detract from aiding the most under-resourced in America, consider the possible role a moderate capture of profit over aggressive profitability as a new target of business. Corporate social responsibility is the term used to describe this approach along with care for environmental impact, community relations, and consumer care. The focus in a more corporate socially responsible model places a holistic concern more on the role a business plays in society than only a focus on profitability. While corporate social responsible behavior holds promise to balance wages paid against profit, some would argue there isn't nearly enough importance placed on the broad role a company can play in making sure all employees are paid adequately. Some would argue there is no need to mandate minimum wages and should let corporate social responsible behavior create the balance. The sad reality is there are not nearly enough companies willing at this time to take a bite out of the top income earners in the companies and allow the profits to flow throughout the company. Knowing there are no easy solutions, many would agree there is cause for reflection and a need for change in the systems of imbalance between the highest income earners in a large multinational company and the lowest paid. Whether in America or abroad, the economically disadvantaged are falling further behind with each successive generation, and mandated minimum wages may hold some measure of accountability for companies who may not be able to exercise corporate socially responsible action toward fair-wage practices. As well, the graduated income opportunities following entry-level minimum-wage jobs must be strengthened to give room for advancement. The middle-income jobs available are dwindling in part because many of the jobs have become automated or are provided by foreign labor now. Indeed, this discussion garners strong debate from varying viewpoints. But like other discussions, it cannot stop there. Action and commitment to change to help the most vulnerable have to occur.

Poverty Conditions Us for Generations

Unfortunately, one of the tragic consequences of begging is the learned comportment it manifests in people. Without other opportunities to cease the need to beg, many beg for years and learn the act of submission as a beneficiary way to get what they need. There are always types of begging that warrant a helping hand in the form of money, clothing, or food; but then there are others, which are contrived. Many have discovered methods to position themselves in perceived locales of need and take on the role of a needy individual acting and playing the role of *beggar*. In American cities, there are customary patterns and people who seem to always be working a street corner with a cup held out, jingling change and asking for money to buy a sandwich. Near train stations, bus stops, sports venues, and other high-pedestrian traffic areas, begging is prolific. Sadly most people walk by without even a passing glance, find the display frightening, or place a judgment on the begging individual. When the perception is that a person never takes a step to make his or her life better and works a street corner year after year, it becomes annoying to many. Often, tourists in locations of severe poverty are frightened by the enormity of the begging and the pleas associated with them. For the people desiring to help and having a compassionate heart to give, knowing the truly needy and the ones who have taken up the look and act of a *beggar* but are not really destitute can be confusing. Certainly in many locations around the world where the needs outstrip the ability to secure the necessary resources for survival, acts of begging are rising, both real and feigned.

Feigned begging takes advantage of the impoverished circumstances and preys upon the compassionate heart of passersby. For some, it is as if they punch a time clock and have their assigned corner. It would almost seem working to secure a real job would make more sense if the regularity and precision needed to beg have the look of a job anyway. A man may even gain a respectable income from his begging and therefore sees no reason to stop, and may even begin to believe begging is a worthy occupation. The unfortunate paradox in most circumstances of begging is there is a complexity of matters that have led to this choice. As mentioned earlier, low minimum wages and limited access to decent-paying jobs contribute. Educational equality and mental health weigh in as possible agents to the ongoing choice some make to beg over working regular jobs. Whatever the impetus that leads people to cup their hands upward and beg instead of waving and providing value and exchange with the world, it's clear this is not how God intends for his creation to manifest the purpose he has instilled in us.

Summary Questions for Discussion

1. Labels are often hurtful and spiteful, though some labels are esteemed; still other labels help us identify with a group of people and feel connected to them. The paradox is we seem to require labels for ourselves to create identity but we also can use them as divisive tools of separation. What are your thoughts about how you use labels to connect yourself to others and also separate yourself from others?

2. As Todd shared in this chapter, labeling, feeling the effects of poverty, and low self-esteem caused by oppression can be passed on through generations. When you look at your family and some of the values you have today, what effect do you believe your family has had on your morality, your self-esteem, and your character?

3. Begging occurs in nature in the wild and is a natural action to help mammals get their needs met. All of us as babies had to beg our parents to feed us. Is it possible the need to beg pulls people back to a more immature developmental state that hinders their maturity and ability to lift themselves beyond poverty? What are your thoughts?

4. There are vigorous debates about minimum-wage standards in the United States and other countries. What are your thoughts about this controversial issue and how do you believe a wage restriction upward or downward would influence poverty around the world and domestically?

5. What are your thoughts about the relationship between poverty and the *beggar*?

We were helping families in a remote village 1½ hours from our Kimana, Kenya campus. Pictured: Todd, my son, Austin, and me.

The children love the tablet computers we provided with our Dreamweaver education programs. They all piled up on me in this little school because they wanted to see the screen and get a turn to play.

I call this photo *The Healer's Blessing* because the healer (me) and my patient are being healed together. Sometimes, the healer is healed more than the patient. This photo was taken in Amboseli National Park in Kenya.

Two little guys, probably friends forever, posed for this great picture in Kenya. I thought the way they supported each other was adorable.

Todd was overwhelmed as children crawled into his lap to get a look at the pictures and video on his phone. Most of the children had never seen a smart phone with pictures and video.

My daughter, Montana, was very popular with the girls in the Kenyan schools because she could dance and had awesome African rhythm songs on her Ipod.

Ken and Sandy Taylor, devoted 25 years to serving the poor in Kenya through their missionary work. We took this picture together during one of our trips in Kenya. Sandy is now deceased but her vision for Africa lives on through Dreamweaver.

The children followed my daughter, Montana, around like she was the Pied Piper on this visit to Kimana, Kenya during their annual games competition

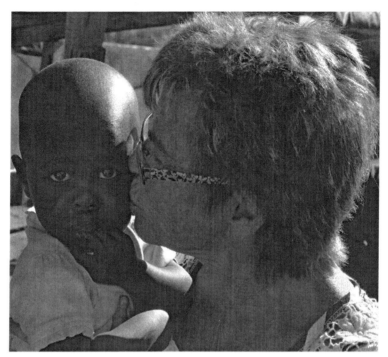

My mom loved the children and little Mercy was one of her favorites.

The Kimana School of Leadership and Professional Studies provides college studies to young people in one of the most under served areas of Kenya. This picture was taken when Todd and my son, Austin, were visiting Kenya on one of our work trips. Students, teachers, Sandy and Ken Taylor are pictured.

Mr. Joseph Nkaapa is one of the most dedicated leaders in Kenya and works with all the operations of our projects in Kenya. Joseph is like a brother to Todd and me.

Todd had this magical moment with this little girl on one of our days traveling to a remote boma to provide chiropractic/medical care and sports training. You can see the joy in both their eyes.

Anxious students in a remote schoolyard in Kenya awaiting our arrival to teach them about tablet computers. They had never seen a regular computer or a tablet before our visit.

This 85-year old Maasai woman fell and sustained a hip fracture. She was taken to the nearby hospital, one hour away, by motorcycle. Then she wanted to return to her home because people in the hospital were dying around her and she feared she would be next. We were able to create a brace for her out of PVC pipe so she could stand and get out in the fresh air.

The town of Kimana is located four hours from Nairobi and is near our Kimana School of Leadership and Professional Studies campus.

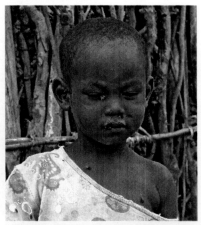

All of the children have a dream and love their homeland.

The flies are so abundant it is impossible to keep them off the children.

Sport brings hope for children around the world. Gear for Goals (G4G) has been able to help bring hope. Just moments before I gave these boys this basketball, they were kicking around a nearly flat soccer ball.

These young Dominican players participated in a parent-child baseball event. Every child's parent or coach was provided with a bat, a ball, and a mitt to give to the player. Baseball is one of the ways children in the DR can lift themselves out of poverty.

It's a huge undertaking collecting, transporting, and providing sports gear to children. But the effort is worth it!! In Kenya, we began Mt. Kilimanjaro Little League with a vision to see children in Kenya come and play in the Little League World Series in Williamsport, PA.

The smiles say it all. Taken at our parent-child baseball event in the Dominican Republic.

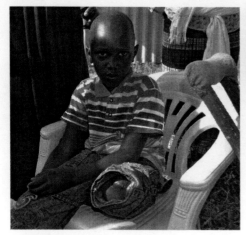

Malua lost his left leg in a motorcycle accident when he stuck his foot in the spokes

Malua lives in an extremely poor family that could not afford a prosthetic for him. Dreamweaver was asked to help. I was able to examine and provide chiropractic care to help heal the trauma he sustained in the accident.

I told Malau we would help him receive a prosthetic limb but he had to promise two things. 1.Stay in school & get his education. 2.Do something amazing as a leader because his life was spared by God to help lift his brothers and sisters of Africa from poverty.

From the first picture of shock and pain to this picture only 15 minutes later, you can see the power of chiropractic healing, sports, and compassion to heal the soul.

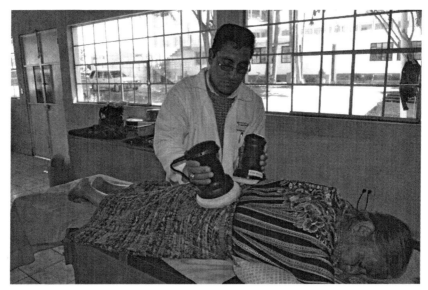

Dr. David works in a Guatemalan medical clinic. We provided instruction using percussion massagers and chiropractic, to help his community have a better way to address pain and suffering. The percussion massager is a unique healing tool we intend to teach the world how to use to help alleviate pain and suffering.

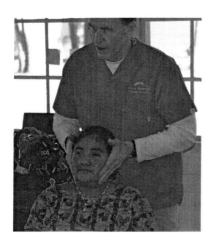 

Helping people and giving them reliable healing tools is a good strategy for improving health outcomes and alleviating poverty.

CHAPTER 7

WHAT DOES SCRIPTURE HAVE TO SAY ABOUT WAVING AND BEGGING?

"And if you give yourself to the hungry, and satisfy
the desire of the afflicted, then your light will rise in
darkness, and your gloom will become like midday.
And the LORD will continually guide you, and satisfy
your desire in scorched places, and give strength to
your bones; and you will be like a watered garden,
and like a spring of water whose waters do not fail."
– Isaiah 58:10.[1]

Poverty's Impact: 1.4 million children die annually because they don't have clean drinking water or adequate sanitation.

Understanding why there are enormous struggles and hardships for so many people is difficult. It doesn't seem fair! In the United States, we are blessed with abundance and though people live in poverty, the challenges faced here are less formidable. We have social safety nets like Medicaid, unemployment compensation, welfare, and Medicare. But, most of the countries around the world where millions live on less than $1.25 a day in deplorable poverty don't have systems to help people. Circumstances are unspeakable and would probably leave most of you in horrified disbelief. Philosophically, there are few historical documents and places to turn for insight to know the ways we should act in the face of poverty. However, the Bible is replete with wisdom on matters of the poor and provides sound direction to understand how to help. The parable of the Good Samaritan exemplifies the honor God wants bestowed upon the weak, sick, beaten, and the poor. Jesus teaches through this parable in the book of Luke how we are supposed to regard 'our neighbor.' An expert on Biblical law questions Jesus about the ways he must live to inherit eternal life. In answering, Jesus replies, "What is written in the law? How do you read it?" The man answers Jesus's question. "Love the Lord your God with all your heart and with all your soul and with all your strength and with all your mind… and Love your neighbor as yourself." Jesus, satisfied with the man's correct response, says, "You have answered correctly. Do this and you will live." However, not fully satisfied with Jesus's response and wanting to further justify himself, the man asks Jesus, "And who is my neighbor?" Then Jesus answers him in this way.

"A man was going down from Jerusalem to Jericho, when he was attacked by robbers. They stripped him of his clothes, beat him and went away, leaving him half dead. A priest happened to be going down the same road, and when he saw the man, he passed by on the other side. So too, a Levite, when he came to the place and saw him, passed by on the other side. But a Samaritan, as he traveled, came where the man was; and when he saw him, he took pity on him. He went to him and bandaged his wounds, pouring on oil and wine. Then he put the man on his own donkey, brought him to an inn and took care of him. The next day he took out two denarii[c] and gave them to the innkeeper. 'Look after him,' he said, 'and when I return, I will reimburse you for any extra expense you may have.' Which of these three do you think was a neighbor to the man who fell into the hands of robbers?"

Seemingly obvious, the expert in Biblical law answers Jesus, "The one who had mercy on him." Jesus then provides a four-word exhortation to the scholar of law: "Go and do likewise."[2]

Go and do likewise! Jesus doesn't suggest it would be a good idea to help the beaten man out or give it some thought and see how your heart leads you. He doesn't say pass him by until your retirement when you feel you're really ready to help out and have some time now. He doesn't include the notion of waiting until you win the lottery and then you can give some thought to helping out with a few denarii. No, Jesus says very clearly 'go and do likewise'! Notice the Samaritan not only provides assistance in the moment but also took the next step to take the beaten man to an inn, dressed his wounds, and then provided the money for his continued care until he could return. His care was thorough, complete, and left no question of his intention to see the beaten man returned to health again.

Practicing Jesus's edict in this parable, we wonder if the problems and suffering around the world would finally end. If each person picked up a beaten man, a man rolled over by life, born into desperate circumstances, and placed him on his donkey, in his car, or over his shoulders and took him back to a warm bed, a hot meal, and dressed his wounds with care, would we begin to finally see many of the horrible injustices of poverty, starvation, human trafficking, etc. end?

Scripture cites numerous passages concerning help for the poor and disabled. In Deuteronomy, God is called the "defender of the fatherless and the widows." [3] In Psalms and Isaiah, he is referred to as the "rescuer of the poor." [4, 5] One of God's primary vehicles he provides to change circumstances and to offer help to his creation, man, is prayer. Often prayer is all people living in poverty have available. Sometimes the answers to desperate prayers are US! It can be our money, time, knowledge, skill, education, and ongoing mentoring. Maybe our friendship and relationship is an answer to a prayer for a lonely man or woman who has lost everything!

In the Gospel of Matthew, Jesus further declares, "But many who are first will be last; and the last, first.[6] Jesus tells his disciples they will be rewarded for taking the burden to walk with him in ministry to the weak, the afflicted, the sick, the poor, and the brokenhearted. The care of the poor appears throughout his messages and in frequent verses of the Old and New Testament. In 205 instances, the word poor is mentioned in the King James Bible.[7] Twenty-three books of the Bible give a voice to the poor and their requirements for care.[8] The admonition is clear: God does not want us to forget the poor, and he is revealing something wonderful to us about his plan. Jesus seems to affirm the special place God has in heaven for those who will have endured extreme trial while living in their earthly bodies. Still, does this mean God wants men to live in poverty, to live in squalor, to suffer, and wonder why they seem to have been forgotten? Does God prefer poverty to wealth?

Looking closer at this paradoxical Biblical passage in Matthew, which states those who were first will be last and the last first, helps us recognize God has given the riches of the earth for us to know His blessing. Being poor in money, clothes, food, water, and anything of material wealth does not have to interfere with the nature of God's opportunity for wealth and connection to him. ***Many who live in poor circumstances and under-resourced opportunities sing out with stronger prayer of intention for God's help and blessings for his providence, while the most materially wealthy may not even acknowledge God's role in their comfortable lives.***

The remarkable realization we learn from this simple Biblical passage is that our connection to God has nothing to do with anything material, including food or water. In Deuteronomy 8:3, God gives credibility to his desire for our lives with these words: "He humbled you, causing you to hunger and then feeding you with manna, which neither you nor your ancestors had known, to teach you that man does not live on bread alone but on every word that comes from the mouth of the Lord." [9] Jesus reiterates this message in the fourth chapter of Matthew when he has retired to the desert praying and fasting forty days. As Satan is tempting him by offering him the earthly needs one would consider man requires at his weakest moments, Jesus responds: "It is written man shall not live on bread alone, but on every word that proceeds out of the mouth God." [10]

Scripture continues to lay the foundation for active care of the poor and the understanding that our earthly comforts are only temporary. Moreover, the messages assure God's intentions are clear to comfort, care, and stay with the poor, no matter what. In Isaiah 41:17, we read, "The poor and needy sear for water, but there is none; tongues are parched with thirst, but I the Lord will answer them; I, God of Israel, will not forsake them." [11] Jesus echoes love for the poor in Luke's gospel: "Blessed are you who are poor, for yours is the kingdom of God. Blessed are you who hunger now, for you shall be satisfied. Blessed are you who weep now, for you shall laugh." [12] Again in Matthew, Jesus responds to the questions of the poor, declaring, "Blessed are the poor in spirit, for theirs is the Kingdom of Heaven." [13] Our understanding of the promise the Lord has for us should lead us to know he has a plan for all people regardless of material wealth and circumstance.

Tzedakah is the Jewish practice of giving to the poor, and although in Hebrew it means 'justice' or 'righteousness,' tzedakah has come to signify 'charity.' Though charity is often considered a spontaneous act of goodwill and optional, tzedakah is an obligation practiced by Jews. The customary requirement of Jews is giving 10% of all their monies to charity. This is similar to the practices of tithing in Christianity. Further, Judaism practices tzedakah as a religious obligation to do what is right and just, which is further emphasized as an integral part of living a spiritual life.[14] In Hebrew school, it is customary for youths who attend to bring money as a gift of tzedakah for a worthy charity the synagogue supports. This regular practice gives Jewish youth a sense of responsibility to share their blessings with others. Moreover, when Jewish children approach their thirteenth birthday, the practice of B'nai Mitzvah encourages an act of service to the community. Volunteering to work at a homeless shelter, raising money for educational supplies, or helping beleaguered youth sports programs are examples of serving that Jewish youths will do when called to the Torah as a young adult. Even the Bar Mitzvah ritual to be recognized as a young leader in the synagogue and being called to read from the Holy Scripture is a symbolic gesture giving the Jewish youth a newfound sense of responsibility.

The word poor is described in the Bible using five different Hebrew words in the Old Testament and two unique Greek words in the New Testament. Besides describing destitution, the words elaborate the oppression, humility, afflicted, in want, needy, weak, thin, low, dependent, being defenseless, and socially inferior. In Greek, the word 'penes' designates the working poor who own little or no property. They are the people who possess little in the way of material goods, but they earn what they have from their daily labor. Another form of this word, 'penechros,' describes a poor widow who may be receiving a small subsistence from a relative or social agency. In The

Beatitudes of Matthew, when Jesus speaks of the poor in spirit for theirs is the kingdom of heaven, the word he uses for poor is translated from the Greek word 'ptochos.' Ptochos literally means 'to crouch or cower as one helpless.' It signifies a *beggar*, a pauper, one in total destitute poverty, totally dependent on others for help and necessities of life. Later in Galatians 4:9, it is translated as 'beggarly.' [15]

At first, the word 'poor' signified someone lacking material possession or basic necessities like food and water. But as time passed, poor took on additional meanings in the Bible. Weakness, frailty, feebleness, fragility, dependence, subservience, defenseless, affliction, and distress are among the descriptors. Sometimes poor was also associated with people who had become outcasts because they were lepers. The poor had few opportunities, and the Bible cast their lot with spiritual overtones because the perception of their survival was placed solely on the refuge of God. Even the great King David, who had profound material wealth and power, found himself at times weak, afflicted, and in distress and thus impoverished in hope. The moments of desperation led King David in Psalms to write, "This poor man cried out, and the Lord saved him out of all his troubles." (Psalm 34:6)[16]

The revelation of God's unbending love for the poor in spirit and his desire to touch them is also found in the prophecy of Isaiah and lends support to the ministry of Jesus. These words are not spoken to comfort only the materially poor but also the lost souls who may have departed and are now far from God. "The Spirit of the Lord GOD is upon Me, because the LORD has anointed Me to preach good tidings to the poor; He has sent Me to heal the brokenhearted, to proclaim liberty to the captives, and the opening of the prison to those who are bound." [17]

A person can be poor regardless of how much money they possess. The human spirit can be broken even when living in grand houses, driving luxury cars, and wearing the finest clothes. One may be lost in addiction to alcohol or drugs to numb the pain of a failed marriage, loss of a loved one, or a deep hole of darkness in depression. Those of poverty can also feel these same feelings of loss and horrible failure leading to addiction. They may feel God has abandoned them. The possibility of disconnection and personal relationship with God resides for all men and women regardless of material possession or lack thereof.

Regardless of achievement and worldly status, each of us has to determine where we settle for less than a devoted a relationship to God. Human nature often creates apathy along with a disinterest in praise for God's generous provision. When our needs are satisfied, even overflowing in abundance, we tend to not think of God's loving gifts and we don't praise him nearly enough. When circumstances change and we lose something or tragedy comes, then prayers often come and our desperate pleas follow. Paradoxically, we may also blame or accuse God of not providing for our needs if we have fallen into difficult circumstances or have had to suffer our entire lives in destitute poverty. Our willingness to believe God loves us and is there for us may be strained and broken. We may abandon him when our need is greatest and become broken beyond our ability to repair our spirit. However, these times are when we can find God's greatest work is ready to unfold and demonstrate his unfathomable love.

A man I know shared how, after losing his job, he had begun to feel God had forgotten him. His self-esteem had crumbled and after being unemployed for nearly ten months; he wondered if he would ever find a job again. Searching but coming up with nothing in his hometown area around Chicago, he received good news when a firm in North Carolina hired him. But now he would need to leave his family and take work in another state. Nonetheless, he let God's will for his life dictate this move and discovered God's unfailing love as he began to piece his life back together and found an active and living church in the North Carolina area where he could minister to others. Eventually, he moved his family to North Carolina and started a new life with a deeper sense of faith. He shared with me how he had begun to doubt God was alive in his life. But he now recognized this low place he had come through was preparing him for something much greater in ministry. He and his wife had felt a calling to ministry in Chicago but had come upon numerous obstacles, coming to believe ministry was not for them. But the job loss, the faith he had to exercise to weather this difficult place, and the restoration had given him hope again. Now he had a clear picture how God had always been with his family and he could share the victory with others. My friend's story is a common one many of us have heard or maybe even experienced. It is often in our most desperate trials we learn how much God loves us.

Every Man, Woman, and Child Matters to God

It's easy for many who live lives of relative ease and comfort to disconnect from the needs of the afflicted around the world. We may even become haughty and feel entitled acting as if our station in life has resulted because we were blessed and have done something elegantly right with God to deserve the vast opportunity afforded to us. However, if we are seeking purity in our hearts and want to know the deepest meaning of how God feels about each and every creation he fashioned, we must consider the words of Jesus in Matthew chapter 10: "But the very hairs of your head are all numbered. Fear ye not therefore, ye are of more value than many sparrows." [18]

God has spoken through Jesus to teach us all that we are counted in his grace. However, an apathetic regard to helping many people we choose to not see, or simply don't acknowledge, takes away the incredible opportunity God is seeking to give us a profound gift. In Deuteronomy we learn that care of the poor is an expected duty.: "If there is a poor man among your brothers in any of the towns of the land that the LORD your God is giving you, do not be hardhearted or tightfisted toward your poor brother." [19] The image of being tightfisted is an unwilling desire to wave, to say hello, to give, to teach, or to even acknowledge. How can we be tightfisted? Often, a tightfisted response comes from the deep places of fear that if we don't hold on, we will fall or lose something of value, even our lives. However, God does not desire a tightfisted heart but instead a heart of open love and care with the willingness to embrace our brothers and sisters who may have fallen.

Perhaps there is a connection each of has with the *beggar* that is deeper than we realize if we examine our actions closely and our requests we place before God. Although some choose not to believe in God, the vast majority of the people in the world, when surveyed, believe in the existence of a god or as some choose, to speak of a deity as a higher power. Nonetheless, with a belief in God also comes a hope that He is listening to our requests and prayers, he knows our needs, weakness, and sickness and is present in our pitifully dark, lonely places. When we pray, we ask, "God please…" We request, "God if you are there and see me, can you provide me with…?" We beg God, "Please, God, please don't let him …" Our frequent refrain in our sacrament with God is begging and pleading instead of coming to God with the spirit of the *waver* and saying hello to God. God, I am here and see you and I want you to see me. I want to have a relationship with you in which I come into your presence as a willing soul who has a plan to produce, be fruitful, and provide resources for myself, my family, my community, and the planet of living creatures, both man and beast. I want to steward the resources for which I have been given providence though I may only know my small section of the earth during my lifetime. I know I am seen and I see you.

However, we might choose to turn a tightfisted hand toward a brother in need because we cannot acknowledge our own *beggar* inside ourselves. We may actually be in need as greatly or more than the *beggar* pleading along the side of the road for a scrap of food, money to drink, or clothing. ***Yes, recognizing there is a connection we all have with one another and knowing the child who pleads on the side of the road is no different really than any of us is the beginning of transformational change.*** If we recognize he is our son, brother, or friend, even if we have not known him before, we will act in a different way from the heart. ***If we are not willing to at least look at him and see his eyes and try to see his crying needs, then we are probably not willing to examine our own heart's fragile need for compassion, empathy, and love.***

I have a close friend who has developed a phenomenal healing technique taught internationally called the Lifeline Technique. Dr. Darren Weissman is a recognized speaker and is well known for his cutting-edge thoughts on healing and the role the mind and spirit can have in the process. One of the frequent messages Darren repeats over and over again in his sessions with clients when speaking about the beliefs, emotions, and negative associations we frequently make is that these are just that—belief patterns. When confronted with the choice, would we ever choose to feel sad, in despair, without love, weak, alone, frightened, overwhelmed, poor, needy, hungry, without hope, robbed, or as a *beggar*? And without fail, if we truly examine our highest ideal or motive, most of us would answer with the response: "No way!" But why do we allow ourselves to create these limiting beliefs?

For each individual there may be a separate and distinct reason, but we know when we've examined our limiting beliefs we have chosen to package them as a way to protect and rob us from fully knowing joy, happiness, and possibility in life. In some ways, limiting beliefs make it all right to stop and play it safe in the world, to just climb so far, and to just touch so many people's lives. In short, limiting beliefs allows us to stay safe in the world and, in truth, is another version of our tightfisted response to our brother. However, if we begin to don a new coat of belief not wrapped up in sorrow, weakness, pity, poverty, being without, or fear of rejection, we can open our hands first, then our arms, and then our heart to God first, then ourselves, and our brothers and sisters who are in need. If we can acknowledge we have been a *beggar* wanting to know how God cares, then we are coming to a closer connection with our brother and sister in Africa, India, China, Bangladesh, and right here in America.

Ask!

In Matthew chapter 7, Jesus teaches his disciples and followers to Ask! He continues saying, "Ask and it will be given to you; seek, and you will find; knock, and it will be opened to you. For everyone who asks, receives, and he who seeks finds, and to him who knocks it will be opened." [20] While begging is a form of asking, I would assert in this exchange that Jesus further qualifies his directive with two other action steps, and even the action of asking is a teaching cue to do something. Jesus is telling his followers that there is a God who cares for them, and asking God to deliver them from their needy place will be found with blessings and results if two other steps follow. Seeking and knocking are to follow the asking. Webster's defines 'seek' as the act of searching, trying to discover, or making an attempt.[21]

In this teaching, Jesus is instructing us to take the necessary steps once we have asked to now seek a way to discover how we can acquire the needs, wants, and desires for which we are asking. While some who beg on street corners have resorted to this as their action step, this is not the ultimate destiny God would have wanted for his child, to lead a life of effortless work. Seeking inspires the act of initiative and the pattern of solution and fact finding. How can I solve this problem and what can I do to get my present need or desire met? Then Jesus gives the final directive: knock. Knocking implies a physical action to tell someone you want to walk inside and be seen. You want to be noticed and welcomed into their home and have time with them. Knocking is an action requiring effort to be seen and be allowed to enter a home. In many ways, knocking demonstrates a willingness to participate in life as a *waver*.

God has a plan for every soul, or he would not have created them. However, his plan is higher than ours, and the ultimate understanding of 'why' many suffer while others live in relative comfort with plenty will not be revealed until we have passed. However, from the depths of the scriptural evidence and historical perspective, we can learn a great lesson, particularly as we experience how service to those in need changes our own hearts. God knows our bodies and our needs better than we do, and he wired us for compassion and service to one another. Acts of altruism bring about physiological changes, bringing joy, peace, and increased longevity.

At the University of California Berkeley, longevity among residents aged fifty-five and over was studied from 1990 to 1995 to discover if volunteerism had any effect on life expectancy. Studying 1,973 residents, researchers discovered the participants who volunteered for two or more organizations experienced a 63% lower likelihood of dying during the study period than did non-volunteers. Even after controlling for age, gender, number of chronic conditions, physical mobility, exercise, self-rated general health, health habits (smoking), social support (marital status, religious attendance), and psychological status (depressive symptoms), the effect on survival was only slightly reduced to 44%, representing a substantial positive result to longevity.

Further research has also demonstrated immediate physical gratification during acts of altruism and volunteering. In a February 1987 issue of Better Homes and Gardens, an article reporting on a survey of readers revealed remarkably how altruism and volunteering gave immediate benefits to respondents. Over two-thirds (68%) of the 246 surveyed, indicated experiencing a distinct physical sensation while they were helping. Half reported feeling a 'high,' 43% felt stronger and more energetic, 28% felt warm, 22% felt calmer and less depressed, 21% experienced greater self-worth, and 13% had fewer aches and pains. Indeed, Christ's teachings to help the poor and the practices of tzedakah demonstrate wisdom in health and happiness steeped in the acts of servanthood and giving. ***Jesus's message was clear and as you will discover in the next three chapters, there continues to be more evidence that the more we do to help improve the lives of others, the more benefit we personally receive in our happiness.***

As Todd discovered when he began to extend his hand to help the poor, he was rewarded in ways he never imagined.

Witness to God's Calling to Help

My relationship with God was, I thought, very good. While my presence in church wasn't what it should be, I felt I was grateful, I prayed every night and I was a positive influence in my kids' lives and in the community. But this was before I went to Kenya and saw people who felt God had forgotten them. In the bushes of Kenya, the lack of basic necessities made me feel God wasn't there until I saw the Kenyan people pray. The powerful way they held services and called to Jesus was astonishing. Before going to Africa, I used to always say I was poor. How could I help out anybody else when I was just trying to get by myself? But through the help of family, friends, and generous donors I was able to go to Africa and see for myself that God's work is also going on in the sub-Saharan deserts.

After the trip, my relationship with God improved because I felt he wanted me to help and see what my strengths are and how I can make the world a better place just from my small stature. My mission and joining together with others who cared deeply about the people of Kenya helped me to recognize I have a big purpose. Strong messages in the Bible state that God wants us to help those down and out. It does not say God wants rich people and people who just have resources to help. At first, when God sent Warren to call on me, I met his offer with resistance. I didn't know what I could do to help and really didn't believe there was anything I could do to help overseas. However, I was terribly wrong to have considered my help unneeded. The children and the college age students appreciated my coaching skills, teaching ability, and love. I learned sometimes that relationships are the most important bonds we can form with people, especially people living in difficult places like Kenya. No matter what your circumstances, you can make a difference—that's what I learned!

Summary Questions for Discussion

1. How would you define the word poor? What descriptions would you use if you needed to describe 'poor' to someone only using descriptions and no pictures?
2. As you consider your own spiritual walk with God, how is He calling you to act in more direct ways to serve the poor and connect with His desires for your life?
3. Consider people you admire that help others and the way you describe their work. What is it about their care of others you admire and what can you incorporate into your own life to be a better servant to the needs of others?

CHAPTER 8

WHAT WORKS AND WHAT DOESN'T TO END POVERTY

*"Do you think, because I am poor, obscure, plain and
little, I am soulless and heartless? You think wrong! – I
have as much soul as you – and full as much heart!
And if God had gifted me with some beauty and
much wealth, I should have made it as hard for you
to leave me, as it is now for me to leave you!"*
– Charlotte Brontë. *Jane Eyre*

Poverty's Impact: There is no health care available for 270 million children
worldwide.

Reflecting on history once it has been revealed, world events are usually
easier to analyze, seeing facts and outcomes with more clarity. Every
nation has a story and often they are woven together. High-speed
telecommunications and rapid travel have connected the world. In a matter
of hours, we can travel the same distances men spent months traversing
before via ship, rail, and horse. Instantaneous telecommunications allows
people a way to call a loved one ten thousand miles away and see them
through a computer or a phone. These marvels are the imaginative genius
of science fiction novels written only a century ago. Yet, they are now
reality and people in the modern world have access to these wondrous
advances. But there are still many who have not participated in these global
revolutions. Not much, if anything, has changed for them.

The living conditions and opportunity for billions suffer from a time warp of isolation and stagnation. In Africa, Asia, India, and within every major developed nation, poverty still resides as a neighbor to opulence and excess. The American Dream signifying an improved economic future, modern conveniences, leisure, and a 'better life' has only been achieved by a small percentage of the world's people. But these are not experiences only Americans hope to have. On every continent people have a strong desire to for a better life, and while some have attained the dream, the vast majority languishes far behind. Yet, there is hope, and some remedies are stronger curatives than others.

In this chapter, we examine charitable endeavors that have helped us gain perspective in assembling an approach for aid to help the poor. Moreover, we look at the physical realities of our world and the great teachings of masters like Aristotle and Newton, so we recognize what connects us and draws us closer, as opposed to the separation many feel on both sides of the lines of poverty and wealth. The basis for all change in our world centers on two basic premises which we cannot escape and must come to freely embrace or our hope for changing the divide will continue. We are created by God regardless of our wealth or circumstance. *Therefore, both those of poverty and wealth are not living separate lives. Instead, if we can experience the feeling, the way it makes us feel to help the poor change their lives and gain new footing and move into economic sustainability, we can literally change our brains and our biology. Our cellular systems will resonate with new connections that bring us closer and give us a stronger desire to help and inspire others.*

When our empathy grows, our aspirations to change the circumstances that have allowed deplorable poverty are amplified. Jesus understood the enormity of this opportunity and taught an ongoing regard for the poor. As he instructed in Matthew, "Love the Lord your God with all your heart, and with all your soul and with all your mind," and "Love your neighbor as yourself." His words should remind us that every decision men make about the futures of others that can cause suffering, or are an inclination to discount some in favor of greed and selfish elevation are wrong. Instead, his teachings have the ability if practiced to replace the cold, frigid love toward others with a warm embrace and glow some have probably touched but few have truly known.

Admiration of our great servants to the poor has always received the highest recognition. Mother Teresa and Francis Assisi are among the most well known. They totally invested themselves in the care of the poorest. Their love and devotion to the poor demonstrated a selfless regard few have attained and likely few will touch again. Though we are each capable of doing more and we know this, what stands in the way of serving with more fervor, giving to the poor, and changing the world with our focused action? Our perception and caring desire is often affected by the messages and the ideas we plant in our own minds about the importance of the giving and the impact it will have on people's lives. If we feel a recipient is worthy and the needs are justified, we often rise to standards of giving even we didn't know were possible. In times of tragedy, like the fall of the twin towers on September 11th, our care for one another stands out. At these moments, our ability to access the most compassionate loving parts of our humanity seem to transport to the surface with tremendous ease. There are few objections that can stop the rally of men, women, and children who will organize and work to bring aid to the afflicted. In part, the images we see and the experience of tragedy come so close to our own lives, making the reality unmistakable. Indeed, humans require the experience and the connection to feel compelled to act. This brief anecdotal story called The Blind Beggar Child, illustrates the importance of how we report the needs along with the images that will move people to action.

A Blind Beggar Child

On a roadside, a blind child was begging. He had a sign resting by him, "I'm blind, help me with money." As he sat on the busy road, many people passed but few responded and shared money or time to acknowledge the boy. However, one man passing by noticed the boy and offered some coins in his cup but he also went one step further and erased the writing on the boy's sign which read, "I'm blind, help me with money" and wrote something else.

After the man left, the boy noticed other people passing by seemed more interested in donating to him and he was amazed. As the day wore on, the success the boy experienced after the stranger had changed his sign was remarkable.

Toward the end of the day, the man who had changed the sign came back down the sidewalk and noticed there were significantly more coins in the boy's cup. As the stranger approached, the boy recognized his footsteps and stopped him to ask him what he had written on his sign after changing the message. To which the stranger replied, "Nothing much, son. It gives the same meaning though I used different words. I wrote, 'Today is such a beautiful day but I can't see it, I'm blind.'"

Anonymous

To see with our own eyes and interact personally with the recipient of our aid is often the catalyst for deeper levels of giving and serving. But our ultimate goal should be giving without the need for reward or for seeing the recipient who will benefit. Moreover, the gifts we provide have the strongest benefit if our desire is forming a partnership and eliminating reliance. As the great Rabbi Moses Maimondes wrote in the 13th century, giving is graduated and as we grow the giving spirit within our hearts, our levels of gift will also grow. Rabbi Maimondes catalogs a progression of giving in the Mishneh Torah, which serves as a blueprint for the personal giving levels we might strive to achieve.

1. Giving an interest-free loan to a person in need; forming a partnership with a person in need; giving a grant to a person in need; finding a job for a person in need—so long as that loan, grant, partnership, or job results in the person no longer living by relying upon others.
2. Giving tzedakah anonymously to an unknown recipient via a person (or public fund), who is trustworthy, wise, and can perform acts of tzedakah with your money in a most impeccable fashion.

3. Giving tzedakah anonymously to a known recipient.
4. Giving tzedakah publicly to an unknown recipient.
5. Giving tzedakah before being asked.
6. Giving adequately after being asked.
7. Giving willingly, but inadequately.
8. Giving 'in sadness' (giving out of pity): It is thought that Maimonides was referring to giving because of the sad feelings one might have in seeing people in need (as opposed to giving because it is a religious obligation). Other translations say "giving unwillingly." [1]

Aristotle on Moderation and a Happy Life for Everyone

In the book *The Middle Way* by Lou Marinoff, PhD, the value of moderation, seeking an agenda, which is neither too perfect nor imperfect is one of the most congruent and realistic measures to achieve lasting peace and happiness. Aristotle believed, 'the good' in people was a byproduct of practicing virtuous actions, virtues being the golden mean between the two extremes of excess and deprivation. Good and evil therefore cannot become locked as cosmic forces in perpetual struggle but instead become interwoven in the midst of virtues favoring egalitarian life and value for the role we each hold in the global society.

As Aristotle further espoused there are two extremes in life; virtue and vice. Vices are the extreme that can marginalize our expression of good away from a virtuous center we would normally seek. On the other hand, relative indifference to the dangers and evil tendencies, which exist because of human emotion, further contrives an extreme absolute causing profound sadness and despair. If our expectations of life assume everything is always all right and no matter what, nothing bad can happen to us, then our unrealistic belief system is poised for a hard fall. Thus, the golden mean is Aristotle's attempt to create a way of viewing the world that limits the highs and the lows that may cause mental strain for people. [2]

Moderation and thoughtful use of how much we require for our happiness and how little others may have can create a symmetrical congruence and lasting peace. However, present modern societal efforts stray divergently from moderation and careful planning of resources. Instead, as Thom Hartmann writes in *The Last Hours of Ancient Sunlight,* our modern societal norms are invested in competition, accumulation, and subjugating large segments of the world's population to extreme poverty so that we can have, to obsession, extra measures beyond our actual needs. As Hartmann identifies, our modern political landscape based on a city-state structure where the few govern the many has always led to collapse and the obliteration of the national system of governance. Ancient Rome, Greece, and the powerful Khan Dynasty all ended with nothing more than ancient ruins and artifacts—the lasting impressions from their domineering nature of governance and conquest.[3]

On the other hand, tribal societies, which dotted our various continents, provided a lasting tribute to the value of a more temperate and moderate approach to societal discovery. North American Indians, The San of South Africa, and the great Inca populations all survived for thousands of years in relative peace and without destructive demise, until the arrival of settlers seeking to exert their dominance and destruction on ancient tribal ways of life. Demonstrating similar disposition, many of the ancient tribal cultures bestowed virtues of political independence, egalitarianism, utilization of renewable resources, a unique sense of identity, and respect for other tribes.

Whereas city-state governance tended to espouse ideation of political dominance, established hierarchy, acquiring resources through trade and conquest, absorbing cultures into their own identity, and genocidal warfare against others, the tribal systems were sustainable and highly egalitarian. City-state governance demanded resources from the populace and, as a result, slavery, high taxation, and submission were necessary to stimulate the explosive growth and widespread expansion of the commonwealth. Though only a few would hold the power of governance and many people were subjects of this power, the ability of the large populace under governance to counter the fear-based polity was unattainable. Millions over centuries lived and died without ever knowing the meaning of equality or actively having a sincere voice of reason and need heard by their governors.

When the city-state system of governance eventually landed on the many tribal societies of the world, there was little tribes could do to stop the demise of their ways of life. Time and again, as explorers wielding military strength and the desire to dominate charged into them, tribal communities would soon discover there was no compromise—only submission or death.

Christopher Columbus's conquest is a classic example of the city-state's voracious appetite for resources and power. As we covered in chapter three, when Columbus left Spain in search of new lands and the opportunity to secure the massive wealth other explorers had spoken of, his ships eventually landed on the island of Hispaniola, known today as Haiti and the Dominican Republic. Living in relative peace for centuries, he found the Taino tribe actively engaged in a communal-based lifestyle. The word 'taino' means good or noble. Though peaceful and trusting, the Taino were savagely exploited by Columbus as he stole their precious metal resources of gold and silver. Forced to work as slaves for Columbus and other early settlers from the Europe, the exposure to new infectious agents brought by the Europeans led to prolific disease among the Taino. Believed to have numbered in the hundreds of thousands, or possibly over a million, when Columbus arrived in the late 15th century, the Taino people began to rapidly die. Eventually, Columbus's disregard for their livelihood and ways of life through forced slavery and extreme work hardship would lead to the demise of an entire populace of people, obliterated in the name of progress and discovery.

The experience of the Taino people and millions more is a testament to the wretched ways many city-state governance bodies treated indigenous tribal populations. While the moderate and peaceful ways of tribes were considered savage, uncivilized, and without merit, the savagery and domineering methods of the conquering bodies were considered progress. We now look back on these brutal and tragic losses of so many innocent people with disdain, but today our societal norms still subjugate many to similar and tragic circumstances, only in more subversive ways. When our policies and use of resources favors less than a quarter of the world's population, and perhaps even less, in trade for billions living without even adequate water, food, or the ability to recreate purposeful existence, there is a deeply troubling firestorm advancing.[4]

As Hartmann eloquently testifies in his accurate and sober analysis, the planet cannot sustain life in the imbalanced system we currently know. Our most vital and necessary resources are declining at a rate that will not sustain a return and support for the nearly seven billion people alive today. Deforestation, carbon-based fuel depletion from the earth's deeper recesses, the catastrophic pollution of natural aquifers, and the explosive elevation of greenhouse gasses are thrusting us toward an eventual cataclysmic ending that will likely destroy humanity as we know it. Though it is likely man will survive this eventuality, the history of the world leads to a day of reckoning not too far off in the future.[5]

However, if we act now and consider alternatives and ways we can submit ourselves to moderation and the achievement of responsible action with every thought, response, and choice we make, there is a chance for reprieve from this likely scenario. Some steps we can take to begin are simple and will require little effort or inconvenience, while others are going to be significantly harder. The sustained effort and action steps necessary will have to begin with a conscious desire to change and cannot come from legal recourse and the criminalization for not joining in concert.

From Aristotle, we learn once again our indulgences have become our vices and the forced abstention will never sustain a long-term favorable change in cultural norms. Instead, criminalization often serves as fodder for organized crime and select individuals seeking the achievement of false power. But our desires moving toward sustainability like the ancient tribal practices of self-governed societies interested in respect and appreciation for resources can lead us back to a way of sustainability desperately required today.

When Helping Hurts

Some organizations and individuals take the issues of poverty seriously and make attempts to change the culture and strain placed upon the poorest around the world. However, frequently these efforts are met with resistance and limited success. Moreover, as Steve Corbett writes in *When Helping Hurts*, more harm can be done to the poor when efforts to help are detached from the real root of poverty and the emotional well of despair and shame enveloping the unfortunate.

Corbett discovered when aid was provided that there was frequently a disconnection from the desired outcome and the actual result. Writing of the experience of Creekside Community Church, a predominantly Caucasian congregation of urban professionals, Corbett illustrates the ultimate demise of aid when the process ignores all the possible variables that might hinder or even halt the hopeful aid. Members of the Church had decided during the Christmas holidays to reach out and visit African-American residents in a nearby housing project that was fraught with high rates of unemployment, crime, and teenage pregnancy. Though some congregants had reservations about serving these people, and even showed some disdain for them, Pastor Johnson insisted they were in need of God's love and Christmas was the perfect time to show God's compassion.

Since most middle-class and upper-class Americans believe poverty is a lack of material resources, members of Creekside decided to address poverty in this community by purchasing Christmas presents for the families. Then, church members visited children in the housing project, singing carols and delivering wrapped toys to each apartment. At first, the sharing was awkward, but the warm smiles of the children and appreciative mothers moved the congregation to expand the ministry to include delivery of candy during Easter and turkeys during Thanksgiving.

However, after several years, Pastor Johnson found that it became more of a struggle to get enough volunteers to deliver gifts to the housing project. Being somewhat perplexed by the lack of enthusiasm for the housing project ministry, Pastor Johnson decided to ask congregants why they had cooled to the serving opportunity in the housing project. At first, it was difficult to get a clear answer from the congregants at the congregational meeting. Then one congregant stood up and shared, "Pastor, we are tired of trying to help these people out. We have been bringing them things for years now, but their situation never seems to improve. They just sit there in the same situation year in and year out. Have you ever noticed that there are no men in the apartments when we deliver the toys? The residents are all unwed mothers who just keep having babies in order to collect bigger and bigger welfare checks. They don't deserve our help."

As Corbett reveals, there was a reason few men were around when the Creekside church members delivered the toys. Often when fathers heard the carolers outside their homes toting presents for their children, they were embarrassed and hid in the bedroom or left abruptly to avoid shame and the sadness of personal failure. For various reasons, many African-American males find it difficult to find jobs and retain work. As a result, there are rivers of deep shame and inadequacy that prevail in the community. When church members thought they were providing a valuable and needed resource that might contribute to a reduction in poverty, in reality they were likely increasing the poverty and shame many men felt. As a consequence, now feeling more inadequacy and shame, these men were less likely to gain the confidence and motivation to find and hold work. Moreover, the congregants of Creekside also suffered an unfortunate consequence in denying any further opportunity to serve the poor of this housing project because of their disdain for them. As Corbett explains, they had developed an undesired side effect of their service, which he refers to as 'compassion fatigue.'

Corbett raises a number of important points to consider in the role poverty plays from both sides of the equation. Whether one lives in poverty or lives a moderately or even supremely easy economic life, the relationship we all have to poverty is shared. We cannot separate ourselves from the people who are forced to live in the absolute poorest economic conditions nor can they separate themselves from us. As Corbett later details, part of the solution congregants at Creekside eventually came to discover was that engaging the recipients in the giving was a more thoughtful strategy for success. Providing low-cost pricing for the donated toys allowed the recipients to purchase them on their own and feel the pride of giving the gifts themselves. Ultimately, this solution eliminated one of the significant elements in the disease of poverty–shame. When a mother and father felt they were earning the money and then providing the means for their children to have Christmas presents, the parents' pride and confidence swelled.[6]

Moreover, these positive feelings were translated into other areas needing a renewed sense of self and possibility for the recipients of the program. Waking every morning with a purpose and seeking opportunity for gainful employment, becoming willing stewards of loving care for their children, and feeling on equal footing with other parents who provide for their children were all unintended results. By allowing the recipients of the aid to purchase the gifts, they were given an opportunity to feel needed, valued, and appreciated. They were transformed from the need*y* to the need*ed*! As a result, they became more like *wavers* than *beggars*. This is an important feature of poverty that cannot be overlooked if we are to have any sustainable change in the future of billions around the world. ***Everyone wants to feel valued, needed, and appreciated.*** When parents can provide for their family, they feel needed and valued. However, when the provision for service to the community is nonexistent, the begging spirit can take hold like a cancer unresponsive to treatment.

Corbett further details a number of vital ingredients that anyone interested in serving the poor should consider. "Never do anything for someone that they can do for themselves." Strong words in a master plan for success in aiding the poor. However, all too often there is a disconnect in many efforts to assist. As aid in dollars and time has grown, a predilection toward short-term missions has become commonplace. Between 1989 and 2006, the number of missionaries providing short-term mission trips (less than two weeks typically) exploded. In 1989, approximately 120,000 individuals participated in this way to reach out and extend helping hands to the needy. But by 2006, over 2,200,000 had begun to engage in service, spending over $1.6 billion. While these numbers are gratifying to know that more Americans desire to help, the ramifications are important to measure. Some care programs can leave more scarring than healing if there are no efforts to create a sustainable program that facilitates the ongoing transference of service or resource from within the community. As Corbett explained and bears repeating: "Never do anything for someone that they can do for themselves." However, the wisdom to recognize the actions and processes which the under-resourced can do for themselves and the motivation to also respond and do them are difficult sometimes. Human nature leans more toward inaction and relying on others. People can become accustomed to having things given to them and not being held accountable to work for them anymore. If people are not given an opportunity to earn their livelihood, there can be a gradual regressive dependency on others. This familiar scenario probably contributes to the burgeoning weight of social programs that seem to have spiraling costs and no way to slow the declining hope for a change toward personal responsibility over passivity.[7]

Animals are imbued with the reward action gene, and numerous studies have documented that when you provide a reward for a specific action, the action is trained to occur repeatedly. By nature, mammals are driven by a reward-based system. If cheese is found by a mouse down a specific tube in a maze, the mouse continues to deploy a strategy of visiting that tube over and over, even if the cheese ceases to be in that location. *In the same way, people will continue to beg for a reward even when begging provides little reward in comparison to the healthier reward that is possible to achieve through work.*

While there are extreme circumstances of poverty that give begging men almost no opportunity for value-based exchange, the lack of creative institutional programming to afford transformation in this area cannot be overlooked. Living below the poverty line is a common position of life for most of the world's people. They don't know anything better, so their life is their life. To say it another way, their fish bowl becomes their paradigm from which all of their life's expression comes. To know something other than their life is impossible. However, while living in this impoverished milieu, they teeter dangerously close to death on a daily basis without adequate access to basic necessities such as water, food, proper shelter, or clothing. If given an opportunity, a gift of proper drinking water devoid of disease, food packed with nutrition, shelter, clothing, and most importantly knowledge in education, then there is the possibility of transformation and change

There is no doubt about the role of education in the transformation of poverty into opportunity. Countless examples exist, including the forming of the great European, American, Japanese, and South Korean empires over the last two centuries. Education and implementation of structure, which provides a way for men to sustain their own lives, results in success and change. What doesn't work in systems of poverty is simply using money to buy food, water, or goods and services. As the saying says: 'Give a man a fish and he eats for a day, but teach a man how to fish and he eats for a lifetime.' Today, we have to provide the man with a fishing pole, bait, hooks, string, and a lake with live fish in order to properly execute this old proverb. So it isn't as simple as teaching him to fish if the other resources are not available. This is where it might be necessary to utilize money and delivery to bring the fishing pole and other necessary ingredients to the man so he can fish. However, we must also teach him, once we have brought the resource to him originally, how to secure the resources again when he runs out or his pole breaks. Frequently, the collapse of institutional involvement falls in this deep crack when time, money, and resources have been given to developing nations. While it would be easy to blame the recipient for his failure to properly execute on the delivery of compassion and resources, that would be an incorrect assumption. The blame rests on the delivery of the service and the plan for follow-up and execution of a comprehensive plan to follow through with adequate training and help in securing resources locally to properly implement any sustainable change. The problem with this strategy is that it is not always possible to provide this link and connection.

Many times, a developing nation simply does not have the infrastructure, manufacturing, or the resources to sustain a program that has been implemented by an outside agency. So what is the solution when this happens? The first solution is to recognize that there isn't an answer to the truncated plan to implement sustainable change. Then, the next step is to execute a strategy to determine a solution that does not presently exist. If the interference that plays out has political chaos as its driving force, there may be a significant obstacle toward sustainable change. However, the opposing force is susceptible to active counter-forces; with time, economic and political leaders do fall and pass on to younger and more progressive thinkers. The world is constantly evolving and great empires rise and fall every few centuries. This is simply history.

Charities: What Doesn't Work About Them?

In his book *With Charity for All*, Ken Stern details some of the serious deficiencies that befall many charities in America. With good intentions, and sometimes ulterior motives, many charities lack effective execution to significantly affect any measurable positive change. According to Stern, there are 1.1 million charities in the United States, with the number of charities growing fifty thousand every year. Sixty-one million Americans volunteer for charities, adding over eight billion charitable hours of effort annually. This tallies to over five million full-time employees. Stern further elaborates that charities receive a staggering $1.5 trillion each year in revenue and have $3 trillion in assets. A full 10% of all economic activity in the United States is attributed to charitable work. When calculating the financial support provided by the United States government of roughly $500 billion annually, it's evident that charitable endeavor is big business.[8]

However, as Stern points out, numerous shortcomings exist in the results of the charitable sector. Often, elaborate sums of money pour into the coffers of organizations like the American Red Cross, only to see the care of the recipients in most need still wanting for services and resources. Going unchecked, and often without any accountability, the non-profit sector can be hampered by red tape and abundant waste.

In 2005, an example of this inefficiency played out in the handling and response to one of the most devastating disasters ever to occur on American soil. Hurricane Katrina was bearing down on the Louisiana Coast, and the American Red Cross, along with countless other agencies, sprang to action, sending immense manpower and resources to the stricken zone. While the precision that the Red Cross displayed in mobilizing and bringing aid was remarkable, the systems of quality control ended up in shambles and terribly mismanaged. Goods poured into warehouses and the systems to monitor the needs for resources that arrived were inappropriate. Stale Danish pastries, Uno cards, buns marked 'perishable,' and radios without batteries ended up shipped to the field, regardless of usefulness. Goods coming into the warehouses were not registered or recorded, and pilfering and theft were common. Commenting on the effectiveness of the American Red Cross, Mike Goodhand, who heads logistics for the British Red Cross, said of their efforts that they were 'amateurish.' He notes in his descriptors to Stern that at one point a Red Cross vehicle manager admitted to him that he had no idea where a large portion of his entire fleet was working in the field. More than a hundred cars and trucks were unaccounted for.[9]

Goodhand went on to detail further how across the entire storm-damaged region inefficiencies and waste prevailed. Shelters were undersupplied or incorrectly stocked. Perishable supplies rotted in warehouses, shipments went to the wrong places, cash disappeared, and supplies walked away. Too many key leadership points were managed by volunteers ill-equipped to handle the enormous challenges. High-cost items like rental cars, generators, and computers disappeared without record. In the end, it appears evident the Red Cross supply-chain and inventory-control systems cracked. While these failures are glaring, Stern points out they are not dissimilar to the same mishandling of the 9/11 disaster.[10]

The damage and tragedy waged by Katrina and 9/11 stood as opportunities for hundreds of organizations to benefit from the gold rush of funding and outpouring of compassion so many felt. In both cases, many organizations rushed to help and some were even granted fast-track status to a non-profit organization. But ultimately, confusion and lack of real expertise were the demises of real tangible help for so many who had been devastated by these tragedies. Saying these events were unique and perhaps out of the ordinary would not be accurate when reviewing the unfortunate inefficiencies across the globe so many charitable endeavors share. Massive action with poor execution and planning seems to be a repeated theme playing out all over the world.

In her book *Beyond Good Intentions*, Tori Hogan learned firsthand how aid provided for some of the most needy recipients is often not only mismanaged but it's gobbled up by wasteful employees and volunteers. Hogan, as a young and perhaps somewhat naïve volunteer, made a decision to devote her life to service and, as a result, traveled to one of the harshest and most poverty-stricken places on the planet, Somalia. During the summer of 2002, Hogan decided to work as an intern with Save the Children in a refugee camp near the Kenya and Somali border. As she details in her book, she would soon learn there were many recipients of aid in the camp who were not experiencing any real tangible change or opportunity to improve their barely above-surviving existence. Wanting to learn how she might help and what could be done to provide tangible aid, she took on the role of interviewer of students in classes meeting in the camp.

At first, she was disappointed to learn many students' remarks were familiar refrains of thanks and appreciation for all the wonderful aid agencies were providing. However, deep down, Hogan knew this couldn't be true in light of what she could see with her own eyes in the camp. She referred to this set canned script as a riveting play called, 'What to Tell the Aid Workers.' Fed up with the canned responses, she pushed a little harder to see if anyone was willing to speak up and actually say what was on their mind. It was the words of a tall Somali boy who ended up cutting to the truth in a few parsed words.

"A lot of aid workers come and go, but nothing changes. If the aid projects were effective, we wouldn't still be living like this after all these years. Do you really think you have the answer to our problems?"

Hogan recalls hearing the truth this young Somali boy spoke and thinking he was finally saying what she had hoped to hear from all the others she had interviewed. Who do I think I am? Who do we think we are? Her reflection of this truth led her to question if anyone who was there had the solution to the problems existing, and to further complicate matters, maybe they were part of the problem. As the one boy became willing to speak the truth, the floodgates of other truthful responses came in waves. Broken promises, waste, corruption, distrust were witnessed on a daily basis. Horrors of sexual exploitation by aid workers of children and failures of international aid agencies who neglected to protect the very people they were here to help.

As Hogan lay that evening in her bed, the words of the boy echoed in her mind as reverberant messages impossible to ignore. While she felt she could justify her efforts by stating, 'at least I'm doing something!' she found it impossible to convince herself that their work in this camp was effective; rather, could potentially be harmful. At that moment, her naïve dream of saving Africa was shattered and her reality was cemented.

Hogan's sobering realizations and the truthful honesty of the Somali boy in class are cause for us to examine our intentions when we want to help. Moreover, the accumulated experience of others we have mentioned and the vast resources we attempt to share must be carefully considered as 'seeds' and the process for growth of seeds should always follow basic principles. All seeds must be planted in good soil, fertilizer needs to be applied, water given daily, sunshine abundantly provided, and cultivation executed. The process is then repeated yearly. Hopefully, the growing of food will provide the necessary sustenance for a community. Further strengthening the yield, when we actively engage in educated crop-yielding technologies, more food results. In the same way, all resources provided to any community, including chiropractic care, medical care, physical therapy, education, water, food, shelter, business development, recycling, sports, arts, and leadership development must take an approach of cultivation and harvest. Never doing for someone what they can do for themselves and teaching them the skills to execute this strategy is the most sustainable model.[11]

What Can We Learn from Isaac Newton?

In the Nova PBS documentary 'Newton's Dark Secrets,' some important and remarkably revealing answers to mysteries of the universe are revealed. Sir Isaac Newton, from an early age was enthralled with the nature of the universe and science. His need to understand how our universe functioned and explain the observations many saw but could not explain was paramount to him. At a very young age, Newton poured over books and was drawn to a particular to a book called *The Mysteries of Nature and Art*, a manual for building mechanical contraptions and investigating the natural world. Newton seemed to be preoccupied with things that physicists pined to understand: time and motion. He made windmills, tiny boats, and flew kites with burning candles, which were mistaken by some townspeople for comets in the sky.

As a child and young adult, Newton endured hardship and loss. His father died when he was only three and his mother remarried, only to move away and leave him to be raised by grandparents. These painful losses would shape Newton's need to understand the nature of why the universe operates in this manner and how the unseen was constantly present even if concealed from human vision. His rage and anger for his parents' abandonment haunted him. He would admit later in his life that he had secretly thought of violent retribution against them. His hardships were elevated further by the turbulent times in England. A violent and bloody civil war and a beheading of a king were a backdrop to his life. Enrolling at Cambridge in the mid-1600s, Newton immersed himself in solitude and pensive study often choosing an insular life over social pursuits. His focus and solitude became his truth; he would say, "Truth is the offspring of silence and unbroken meditation."

It was during his time at Cambridge, and afterward, that many of his astonishing discoveries and laws of physics would come to light. Drawing on the popular theory of the day concerning the nature of the earth and the solar system, which traveled around the sun, so thought, Newton would dispel the theory proposed by French philosopher Rene Descartes. Descartes believed the universe was like a giant machine or clock and the individual parts moved like gears in the framework of an intricate machine.

Leaving Cambridge to avoid the plague, Newton returned to the countryside of his youth.

It was here, his famous 'taking a nap in the afternoon under the apple tree' observations would take shape. He explained that while he was sitting under the apple tree pondering the nature of the earth and the moon relative to the distance and attraction of the two spheres, an apple dropped to the ground. As he observed the apple dropping, it dawned on him that the very same energy governing the pull of the apple to the earth was simultaneously working on a much grander scale between the moon and the earth. He recognized there was a force drawing the moon and the earth together, just as the apple had been drawn to the ground after breaking free from the small branch, which had held it securely.

His discovery and the parallel connection of all things in the universe that are pulled by gravity would become the foundation of virtually everything we know in the physical sciences today. Moreover, Newton's experiments with gravity led him to discover an entirely new branch of mathematics called calculus. It was his desire to know the exact speed at any given point in the flight of the apple that enlightened his discovery of calculus. Now it was possible to know, with absolute certainty, quantities of constantly changing matter, like the speed of a falling apple or how a planet or a moon's position changes over time. Calculus became a science that could help man understand the way things change, including populations. How fast is a population changing over time?

Newton then went on to study light and the spectral quality of sunlight. He learned through active investigation using prisms that he could engage a rainbow hue of all the colors when passing sunlight through a prism. His discovery led him to conclude that sunlight is not a pure form of light but instead is a mixture of many colors. Moreover, when a single color of light was passed through a second prism, the color remained pure to the original. Revolutionary for the time, his newfound understanding of light would help him change the way telescopes gathered light and showed images. Fifty years prior, Galileo had built telescopes using lenses as magnifiers to increase the size of observable planets and stars. However, the refractive quality of the lens caused observers to always see a hue of light surrounding any object viewed in the telescope viewfinder. Newton determined if he were to use a mirror to bounce the light in a series of steps within his tubed telescope he could accurately depict any objects appearance without light hue and therefore portray all images accurately. His finding would forever impact the way telescopes are made, even today. From the smallest children's telescope to the largest NASA scopes, all have working reflective material almost identical to Newton's original.[12]

Newton's discoveries in physics, calculus, and astronomy have shaped our understanding of our universe. His observations could also lend support to help us better understand ways to address many of the social challenges existing today. Using calculus to understand the rates of change populations are undergoing helps us appreciate the effectiveness of economic, health-care, and education programs that are implemented to help the most under-resourced. As well, bringing people together from different nations and beliefs is spurred by the recognition of the common threads all humans share. Gravity, sunlight, oxygen, water, planetary movement, our moon, and other physical laws are common to all of us. By appreciating how we are connected, rather than separated in experience, we also move closer to Jesus's message regarding the second greatest command: to love our neighbor as ourselves.

Newton's three laws of motion are relevant in the observation of waving and begging. His first law—every object in a state of uniform motion tends to remain in that state unless an external force is applied to it—gives a basis to examining the act of waving and begging. A man who can wave instead of beg by nature has more energy, even in his motion of his hands. Newton observed motion was something that once started and actively maintained continued to stay in motion unless met by an opposing force sufficient to stop or divert it. An object in motion tends to stay in motion. A *waver* waving his hands and staying engaged in active exchange with his community through work and serving would be more likely to continue as a *waver*. A *beggar* holding a cupped hand and looking for spare change would likely continue as a *beggar* unless a sufficient healing force occurred in his life to change the course of his direction. Therefore, it is imperative to retain the spirit of the *waver* in mankind and not allow degrading forces of life to change the course toward the *beggar* over the *waver*.[13]

Newton's third law—for every action there is an equal and opposite reaction—helps us understand the critical role a foundation plays in poverty alleviation strategy. A solid foundation of family, community, and spiritual strength is a strong pushing point for those living in poverty to begin to hold them up and climb. A concrete walkway is a solid foundation to walk on and the opposing forces it pushes up against our feet gives us the ability to walk on it. However, if the ground is soft and the foundation is weak, we would tend to sink and require more effort to walk. Walking in sand is an example. Therefore, it is Newton's third law that tells us that in order to alleviate poverty, we have to have solid foundations for people to push off of with their steps. Weak, soft, and unsteady programs will not be enough to give people the proper footing. The value of Newton's laws of motion when thinking about execution strategies is they can help us look at the bigger picture and know if we are on the right track or if we are wasting time with the program likely to fail.[14]

The reflections of light Newton discovered in his telescope are similarly a metaphorical example of how we must reflect one another's light to bring into focus and clarity objects that seem too distant to grasp or see. Our ability to touch and locate the solutions to our challenges in the world may be the reflections we cast on one another when we wave in friendly greeting. How simple the beginning to 'love your neighbor as yourself' is in the simple gesture of a wave and the reflection we see of one another in the mirror. Like Newton's telescope and the improvements he made upon earlier designs, we too can improve upon the vision and efforts of previous leaders who have labored to alleviate poverty. We have the intellect, the heart, and the desire to change when we cultivate this inner hero in ourselves. But the links that connect us begin with our earnest desire to favor diversity and the opportunity it inspires in strengthening people not weakening them. Using the wisdom of the masters alongside the collective knowledge gained through the centuries holds the foundation to asking different questions and, as a result, learning new answers.

A Collective Effort will be Required to Solve Poverty

Many programs attempting to alleviate poverty have solutions weighted heavily in economic revival. More money, opportunity, clean water, ample food, and education are thought to be the solutions to lift the masses glued in poverty and unable to climb out. Political activists, social service organization, governmental entities, and charitable sectors are all attempting to make an impact. Concerned individuals and organizations are taking positive steps to empower people and communities. However, as Duncan Watts writes in *Six Degrees*, academicians and the actions they pursue in the alleviation of poverty are often incongruent.

Academics are a fractious bunch, rarely inclined to step across the boundaries of their disciplines for more than a polite hello. But in the world of networks, sociologists, economists, mathematicians, computer scientists, biologists, engineers, and physicists all have something to offer each other and much to learn. No one discipline, no single approach, has a stranglehold on a comprehensive science of networks. Nor is that likely to happen. Rather, any deep understanding of the structure of real networks can come only through a genuine marriage of ideas and data that have lain dispersed across the intellectual spectrum—each a piece of the puzzle with its own fascinating history and insights, but none the key to the puzzle itself. As with jigsaw puzzles, the key is the way in which all the parts interlock to form a single unified picture.

Watts describes the unification of ideas coming from diverse organizations of people who have the power to create a cohesive embodied transformation. But the reality is that many people in nations around the globe never speak, learn, or seek to know one another. Many academic organizations do not work to know one another and gain perspective and strength from each other. Instead, fear of loss and the struggle for who will receive credit for a new idea that will change the outcomes for billions of lives becomes the conflict. Thus, many political systems, well-intentioned organizations, and individuals with grand visions come up dramatically short of their desired impact to improve the suffering lives around the world.[15]

The thoughts we have shared in this book have purposely come from unlikely places to offer new insights and possibly tangible hope for lasting change. One of my grave concerns about poverty alleviation strategies and many of the social challenges facing humanity is the lack of healers who participate in the discussions. Rarely are chiropractors, physical therapists, occupational therapists, medical doctors, dentists, nurses, and other healing professionals sitting at policy tables making decisions about the welfare of people. Moreover, there is often little input from local healers within communities who may not carry a degree but are regarded by the community as a healer. The reason this is troubling is because the problems we are considering require healing. Like a patient who has become sick, the myriads of social issues weighing on the planet are symptoms. When healers examine people, they consider not how to alleviate symptoms but how to get the patient well. If a procedure is likely to have a terrible side effect, hopefully it is avoided. When decision making is steeped in the traditional ways with leaders of politics, law, economists, and educators making decisions, new ways of looking at a problem go unseen. As well, we need to consider the value of other types of thinkers coming to the policy tables of the world.

Scarcity: Why Having Too Little Means So Much

In order to help people living in poverty, it's important to understand the physiological effects it has on their minds. Though the needs of the impoverished in the poorest areas of sub-Saharan Africa, rural India, and urban Detroit may require different resources, a similar psychological phenomenon emerges inside all poor people anywhere in the world. When someone is forced to live in scarcity, it changes them psychologically. But this change is not only confined to people who live in financial scarcity, it also appears in someone living in scarcity of time and of love or connection. In other words, human nature dictates a set of possible responses that are predictable and may explain why the poor, or anyone who internalizes deep feelings of scarcity, may continue to spawn neglect, poor judgment, or ineptitude.

In the book, *Scarcity: Why Having Too Little Means So Much*, a new way to examine poverty emerges. Sendhil Mullainathan and Eldar Shafir take a significantly important look at the ways scarcity preys upon the human brain and why conventional thinking about impoverished people may be wrong. Moreover, their findings and research provide compelling motivation for facilities and programs that aid the poor to take a forward approach in their creation of new curricula.

In studies designed to measure the cognition and effectiveness of people operating under the strain of scarcity, it's been discovered that the brain, if confronted with scarcity, often creates modes of thought that hinder financial and tangible progress toward economic revival. Moreover, the limited resources available, coupled with the automated thought patterns scarcity creates, makes any significant progress forward nearly impossible. Known as 'bandwidth tax,' when poor people are strained by the daily worries associated with paying rent, having enough food to eat, or the heat being turned off, their attention toward executive function or higher-order thinking is significantly altered. Moreover, an extremely focused mode of thought takes shape called 'tunneling.' often leading the poor to neglect vital tasks.[16]

When confronted with pressing and worrisome matters on an almost continual basis, survival instincts are accessed in often-detrimental ways to long-term survival and personal growth. By tunneling focus on the immediacy of some tasks which are pressing, other matters that may positively affect the future are often neglected, sometimes with drastic consequence. The heavy burden of debt many poor accumulate is one example.

As Mullainathan and Shafir point out, a common practice among poor is taking on loans with unfavorable terms and exorbitant interest. The rationale for the bad loans is usually because there are few or no other options available for the poor. If a father comes up short and doesn't have enough to pay rent because his car needed an unexpected repair, he may have no other option. Or an Indian woman takes daily loans to purchase products to sell in the market with an extreme interest rate. While she is successful in selling all her products she purchased with her daily loan, the extreme interest paid on the principle leaves little profit to make any significant stride forward in lifestyle or security. The father unable to pay rent takes out loans in America called 'payday loans,' loans secured only until payday and then repaid. The assumption is the loan is only for a very short time, maybe a week or two at the most and then paid off in full so no long-term interest or penalty will ensue. But when the father receives his paycheck, he is once again confronted with another unexpected expense or simply does not pay the loan in full because terms are made available that lead him to continue to hold the payday loan or, worse, take more money. The endless day-to-day existence has no end and the poverty cycle continues.

Why does this happen? On the surface it seems the loans are taken because an immediate need exists and the loans are helping to fill a gap in financial resources. However, as Mullainathan and Shafir point out, poor people afflicted by symptoms of scarcity in their lives seem to be unable to practice saving because their vision is tunneled on the immediacy of their present need, without having insight into how they may plan for the future. In both examples, the American father needing to pay rent or the Indian mother requiring capital for merchandise purchase, a higher order of thought unhindered by the scarcity thoughts streaming through the brain would be necessary for appropriate executive action. A plan and a simple approach toward a reasonable savings program could significantly increase the likelihood of success of both parents in vastly different parts of the world.

But higher-order thinking or 'executive' thinking is nearly impossible in the presence of tunneling. Moreover, with the constant barrage of worries, unsettled matters, and inadequate resources, the bandwidth tax becomes narrowed to a point where few other opportunities for advancement and climbing out of the hole of poverty are entertained or acted upon.

Bandwidth tax is demonstrated in virtually every category of scarcity, not only in areas of financial poverty. People living in scarcity of human contact and feeling lonely experience this mentally stretched state, which hinders the brain from focusing on things outside a very narrow scope. Like a narrow radio band on a dial, people living with scarcity of time, emotional connection, and money, all have a tight band of concentration available for creative and fulfilling desires in life. Instead, this narrow bandwidth is self-created by a tragic override in the brain caused by the shards of scarcity, either real or sometimes self-imposed. Further consequences of bandwidth tax are human error, irrational decision making, and emotionally agitated feelings.[17]

Frequently, there is difficulty finding a job, keeping it, and performing well at it. The poor are plagued by a sort of malaise created by tunneling and bandwidth tax, according to Mullainathan and Shafir. As they point out, often the outside world has little understanding or empathy for what the truly poor really feel and how difficult it can be to function within the realm of poverty. Although the authors don't suggest there shouldn't be attempts to aid these side effects of scarcity, they regard many of the present approaches unsatisfactory because they simply are not looking at the true problem. ***Scarcity changes the brain and the way it functions! Therefore, our programs must take this fact into consideration.*** One of the unfortunate side effects poverty has on the brain is the tendency to create human error, forgetfulness, and poor decision making. When these tendencies are demonstrated in an environment without scarcity, there may be cause for alarm if they seem excessive. However, among populations living in extreme scarcity they are more prevalent because of the tendency to tunnel and have bandwidth tax. Therefore, programs must be designed with these unfortunate realities. It can't be assumed the same outcomes are likely in an educational program if methods are used to teach scarcity-driven populations the same way as populations unaffected by scarcity.[18]

Mullainathan and Shafir further elaborate on a conceptual model they refer to as 'the suitcase' of the poor. If you were to consider your own life and the purchase decisions you make daily, some purchases would require more careful thinking than others depending on your financial wealth. If you have a well-paying job and money saved in the bank, a nominal purchase of a new pair of hundred-dollar shoes may not require much thought. But a woman living in extreme scarcity and poverty would have to consider first if the purchase is even possible and second, what would she have to give up or not have, like food, rent money, or other basic necessities. In other words, she would have to consider giving something up to make this purchase. You, in contrast, may not have to give anything up to make the purchase of the new pair of hundred-dollar shoes. As Mullainathan and Shafir demonstrate, we all have various sizes of suitcases that hold our daily requirements of financial, personal, and emotional material. If we are financially secure, our room in our suitcase tends to be significantly larger and more 'slack' exists. However, a woman living under the duress of poverty and struggling to survive has a decidedly smaller suitcase and therefore almost no slack. If she were to purchase the shoes, she would have to decide what is she going to take out of the case while another individual would simply add the shoes to his/her roomy suitcase filled with large quantities of slack.[19]

This problem becomes the self-fulfilling prophecy of the poor and the ongoing distress leading to more strain on bandwidth and further tunneling. As well, when the poor are afforded a lift or a break in the form of aid to create more slack, the patterns of thought already created by scarcity for sustained periods will usually land them back in the same predicament as before. This plays out when the poor win lotteries and don't have a strong concept of how to manage large amounts of financial resource, or when young athletes are given generous monetary contracts and they end up squandering the money and declaring bankruptcy. Time and again when given a resource and the immediate ability to have more 'things' put into their suitcase, the poor end up mismanaging the opportunity and in more debt than before. While this has often been considered as an educational gap the poor have in managing resources, what Mullainathan and Shafir discovered sheds new light on this phenomenon.

While tunneling and bandwidth tax may be responsible for much of the poor decision making and misuse of resources, the poor have very strong notions and consciousness about value. As an illustration, Mullainathan and Shafir posed a question concerning saving money on a purchase to two groups of people. If you were going to purchase an item and you could save fifty dollars on the purchase, would you be willing to drive forty-five minutes to do so? The same question was posed for different value items: a one hundred-, a five hundred-, and a thousand-dollar purchase. When two groups of people in different financial positions were asked this question, the results were surprising. Financially secure individuals tended to say they would drive forty-five minutes to save fifty dollars if the item was a hundred-dollar purchase but tended to be less enthusiastic about driving if the cost of the item was five hundred or a thousand dollars.

Why would they be less inclined to save the same amount of money regardless of the value of the item? Individuals who had less slack in their suitcase and, of course, much tighter budgetary constraint said they would be willing to drive forty-five minutes to save fifty dollars regardless of the cost of the item. Of course, the savings relative to the cost of the item became a smaller percentage as cost increased. Therefore, those with more slack in their suitcase tended to find the drive less appealing and unnecessary. However, if we examine this from a purely economical standpoint, saving fifty dollars regardless of the actual cost of an item is irrelevant—the poor demonstrated more economic clarity in their decision making. This exercise in saving money illustrates an important and salient concept about human nature and the capacity poor people have to make good decisions about money.[20]

But the strain of scarcity still looms and the effect of tunneling and bandwidth tax are probably stronger reasons that end up derailing the best intentions of many poor and the well-meaning people and programs attempting to help them. However, programs to aid the poor should not be considered hopeless because of these tendencies of human nature. Instead, creating programs that understand and prepare for the eventual failure the poor will demonstrate because of bandwidth tax and tunneling are likely to be met with greater success. Shafir and Mullainathan further explain the success of any program to aid the poor must consider the likelihood they will make mistakes frequently, show up late for important meetings, and demonstrate difficulty with focus. However, the capacity of people living under-resourced lives with scarcity also creates incredible resourcefulness. Because the suitcase of life is so small for so many, they must consider carefully their decisions and consider creative ways to make more fit in their suitcase of life. Stretching food, money, or any resources further become second nature. Even begging and the approach taken to create more value from the time and opportunity during begging will often develop. The plea, the posture, the location where the greatest reward will take place are considered carefully.

Shafir and Mullainathan share a story of how scarcity of time and energy in the form of fatigue could create devastating results but a simple cure changed the outcome once it was recognized. During World War II, flying B17 and B52 bombers, pilots were having trouble with the landing of the planes, frequently turning them upside down at the critical moment of landing. Many thought the cause was pilot fatigue or lack of proper training on landing procedures. However, addressing these two issues alone did little to stop the problem. Perplexed by the regularity of this occurrence, the design of the cockpit and the position of the controls were considered. Looking at the landing gear and the mechanism for the wheel elevation, it was soon discovered the controls were placed too close to one another and at a very critical moment, when split-second decision making had to occur to successfully land one of these big planes, pilots were simply reaching for the wrong lever.

Once this was discovered, a large knob resembling a wheel was placed on the lever for the wheel lowering system and the problem was solved. The size and the easily recognized knob left little room for error, and the landing problems no longer occurred. The answer was not in further training or adjusting the schedule for the pilots, it was in designing a user-friendlier cockpit that took into account the tendency to pilot error in a very critical period of scarcity. In the same way, the efforts toward lifting the vast numbers of under-resourced people around the planet must also look at each situation as a 'cockpit' and consider carefully the design of the programs serving their needs. Taking into account the role scarcity will play on the brain and adjusting systems to thwart failure will render successful execution and more rapid advancement.[21]

The Role of Mental Health on Poverty

In 1995, the World Health Organization (WHO) published a paper entitled *Bridging the Gap*. In this article, WHO states, "The world's most ruthless killer and greatest cause of suffering on earth is extreme poverty." Adding to WHO's commentary, Vijaya Murali and Femi Oyebode expanded on the role of poverty in mental health in an article entitled *Poverty, Social Inequality and Mental health*. Murali and Oyebode write that "poverty is a multidimensional phenomenon, encompassing inability to satisfy basic needs, lack of control over resources, lack of education and poor health. Poverty can be intrinsically alienating and distressing, and of particular concern are the direct and indirect effects of poverty on the development and maintenance of emotional, behavioral and psychiatric problems." They further elaborate how the effects of poverty can be responsible for the development of mental health disorders because of the expanded stressors people experience when living in extreme scarcity and under-resourced environments. On the other hand, the mental health disorders of many are the seeds leading to their fall into poverty. Unable to secure employment, retain a job, or gain any economic footing, many suffering from mental health disease become homeless, become lost in society, even commit suicide.[22]

In some instances, the psychosis of individuals may lead the descent into poverty, while at other times it is poverty's elaborate system of strain that erodes the mental capacity of people. Drug abuse, alcoholism, personality disorders, high rates of suicide, and mood disorders are common among the poor. As well, the vast majority of mental-health disorders begin to develop during adolescence, when poverty and other familial stressors tax brain development. As WHO points out, much of the world's population is under the age of twenty-five, and nearly one million die from suicide every year; a life taken every forty seconds. Likewise, rates of teen suicide are increasing so rapidly they are now the highest-risk group in one-third of the developing and developed nations of the world. Suicide is now the third-leading cause of death among people fifteen to forty-four years of age.[23]

In an effort to repair the tragic loss of life ensuing, the World Health Organization has provided several remedies. Though comprehensive and likely to require substantial collective efforts of many organized bodies, the implementation of these recommendations would no doubt save lives and right many of the troubling trends.

1. **Help people help themselves**. Self-care: Give people knowledge and skills to recognize, discuss, and manage stress and emotional problems as they arise. Also, provide the knowledge to know when to seek help.

2. **Community education**. Using media, community leaders, role models, and well-known, respected figures in the community to raise awareness of mental-health problems arising in youth and to de-stigmatize the issue.

3. **Intervention in schools**. Work with teachers and administrations to provide skills to recognize mental-health problems in students, and then offer students and families support or appropriate referral services where required.

4. **Set up life-skills programs to enhance self-esteem, coping skills, and health decision making**. *This has been demonstrated to reduce the risk of suicide among the youth*. Promoting social and physical environments conducive to good mental health, e.g., strategies to reduce bullying, promote social inclusion, promote sports and leisure activities to develop good social relationships and networks.

In addition to the mental-health needs that must be addressed in saving lives of people, other vulnerable populations must also have programs to help them. Among the most at risk are:

1. Orphans of parents who died of AIDS
2. Displaced populations
3. Child soldiers
4. AIDS infected
5. Political or economic migrant populations
6. Marginalized groups

"The difficulties faced by the youth of vulnerable populations in integrating into society and accessing educational and economic opportunities jeopardizes not only their own future, but the future of entire nations." World Health Organization [24]

Poverty Challenges Created by Mental-Health Conditions

Reduced economic development

- Poverty of individuals and families affected by mental health
- Inequality
- Less social capital and economic development

Increased vulnerability

- Stigma, discrimination
- Violence against the mentally ill
- Abuse of the mentally ill
- Civil rights restrictions
- Exclusion from society's opportunities
- Less access to health care & emergency services
- Less educational opportunity
- Increased disability & early mortality

Elevated mental-health disease scenario

- Despair, sadness, fatigue developing
- Hopelessness and helplessness take hold
- Fear about the future
- Societal withdrawal & sleep problems
- Concentration and problem-solving challenges

Education is the Foundation of Poverty Alleviation

Education is one of the most pivotal instruments communities utilize to raise living standards and increase economic prosperity. The introduction of public education for all children in the United States is an example of the enduring power that knowledge holds for the betterment of all people. The early period of American education, like many developing nations today, had struggles and limited access. Only the elite and those who had the financial means could afford to send their children to private schools in the 18th century. As a result, taking a snapshot of the American culture of the 18th century, the lives of people and the literacy rates of the United States were not unlike many of the under-resourced countries around the world today. Scores of children never learned to read, write, or perform basic mathematical computation. Poverty was prevalent and only the wealthy, through private institutions, were able to provide education to their children. Educational equality was non-existent. However, Thomas Jefferson and other reformers felt this was inequitable. Certainly driving their determination was a deeply held belief that equality was the foundation of the new nation. Moreover, they knew hidden throughout society were great minds and potential leaders, and if they were never to receive a proper education, America would be robbed of their brilliant initiative.

As America emerged from the Revolutionary War, unified as a nation, many competing needs vied for attention, and Jefferson and his colleagues had limited success passing any legislation favoring public education. However, in 1826 Horace Mann, a political reformer and legislator, with tireless

197

determination changed the history of education in America. Promoting, speaking, and traveling throughout his home state of Massachusetts, Mann successfully lobbied for the first laws requiring public education. Other states would follow, and eventually laws requiring mandatory student attendance in school were enacted.[25]

The emergence of public education in America also paralleled a stratospheric rise of ingenuity, skilled labor, and entrepreneurial pursuits previously never found in the world. Advanced communications, transportation, energy exploration, health care, and other socially required sectors for an industrious and fertile society to develop were created and fueled through education made available to the majority of the American people. America became the prosperous society other countries around the world sought to emulate. Legions of people flocked to America in the latter half of the 19th century and early 20th century seeking refuge and hope in the opportunities born from the foundations of a strong educational system. America's reputation and economic brilliance continued to escalate throughout the 20th century, while other nations duplicated the successful inclusion of public education to achieve economic prosperity also.

Still, billions around the world never participated in the emergence of global economic prosperity and still struggle because of inequitable education. Stifled resources, coupled with economic and political instability, have been harbors of stunted possibility for the past century, and continue today. While reforms and technology have engaged children in education in many regions of the world, millions still are illiterate. Without radical efforts aimed at changing this sad commentary, many of these young minds will also end up wasted. Yet, there are some hopeful signs in the work of service organizations to reverse this trend. World Teach and Teach For America are nonprofit organizations enlisting the support of recent college graduates to teach within poor communities where educational disparity is rampant. Focused on education and excellence, Teach For America, places value on the leadership and mentoring the college graduates gain through their service. Simultaneously accessing the youthful energy and fresh knowledge many young college graduates have to share with children desperately needing an education, Teach For

America's motto is "One day, all children in this nation will have the opportunity to attain an excellent education." [26] While Teach For America places the emphasis on educational excellence within the United States, where huge gaps still exist despite the economic resources available within the richest country of the world, World Teach addresses the needs of the international community.

Teach for America and World Teach mirror a common purpose by eliminating the educational disparities around the world. They focus on literacy, job skill training, language development, and broad-based educational reform. In combating one of the unfortunate parallel components to poverty, educational disparity, they also address the enormous economic gaps that exist between highly literate well-educated and the uneducated societies.

The promising results of strategically implemented educational reform around the world are evident. In the emerging economy of East Asia, primary school enrollment was virtually universal (99%) by 1997, up from 86% in 1980. Though South Asia lagged behind with only 77% of the children enrolled in 1997, this represented a huge improvement from data collected in 1980 when enrollment was only 64%. While both of these increases were marked by economic benefits to the people of these nations, sub-Sahara Africa still faltered appallingly far behind. Enrollment peaked at 54% in 1996 and then abruptly turned backward to 50% only a few short years later. Even more heartbreaking, disabled children in Africa suffered even more from the disparity, with only 5% attending a school when 70% would have been able to if facilities and access had been available. [27] But frequently parents regarded begging a more fruitful reward than sending them to school.

Standing in the way of many poor children around the world, corruption is also an ever-present nemesis. Not uncommon, some government officials may shun spending on schools in favor of high-cost expenditures like defense, roads, and building projects, where kickbacks and deception can reward the leadership with unjust financial gain. In some cases, this problem is further complicated by foreign donors who regard investment in large capital projects as more worthy than recurring expenses like salaries and textbooks.

Another stumbling block standing in the way of education globally is the accountability and standards placed on educational institutions and teachers. In many regions where standard public education has become reality, the inclusion of large numbers of students into classrooms has not always led to strong advancements in knowledge. In fact, in Malawi and Uganda where free public education began in the mid-1990s, user payments (school fees) were found to be more effective in improving educational outcomes. Working like private schools in America where parents pay tuition for a child's education, user fees have been remarkably successful.

Malawi and Uganda: Moving beyond user payments

The history of payment systems for education is salient to examine because they provide evidence for how structured programming needs to occur for success in many under-resourced regions. In the mid-1990s, Malawi replaced a system of user payments with free primary education. Though parents were still required to pay for school uniforms, examinations, and to aid in the maintenance of schools, the bulk of the costs were borne by the government. Although government spending on primary education rose sharply, quality declined as school enrollment surged 60% (one million new students), leading to overcrowding and a shortage of teachers. Anticipating additional funding from outside sources, Malawi's educational system was unprepared for the massive influx of new students. But the trouble extended even further than the overcrowding as teachers, who were now held less accountable by parents who had paid fees for their children's education, became indolent. With low morale among teachers and high student-to-teacher ratios in the classrooms, the results were disappointing. As a result, dropout rates soared and primary-grade level completion rates barely eclipsed 50%. Moreover, strong gender biased rates still favored males going to school and completing the primary grades over females.[28]

Uganda moved most of the way toward free universal primary education in 1997, when it waived tuition for up to four children per household. Families remained responsible for school supplies and contributions to construction, as in Malawi, and had to purchase uniforms and pay final examination fees. Uganda did better than Malawi, however, in preparing for the influx of new students. The government doubled the share of recurrent government spending targeted to primary education and used external aid to train new teachers, build classrooms, and purchase teaching materials. Even so, educational quality still declined with a free universal primary educational system in place in large part because of the high pupil–teacher and pupil–classroom ratios. As a result, net enrollment slipped from 85% in 1997 to 77% by 2000 with gender-biased enrollment still evident.[29]

Though funded public education is a model for improving the outcomes and providing economic lift, which many nations gripped by poverty seek, alone it is not the solution. Various competing forces, including inadequately educated teachers, inadequate supplies, honest governmental accounting, and cultural histories, play a significant part in success. Each country and its own economic, cultural, and historical values placed on education must be recognized. Countries with developed infrastructure are able to shift resources more rapidly while severely economically challenged ones are apt to move slower and have more challenges. But the resources a country has are not always indicative of the direction in which the education is heading. Certainly in the United States, as Richard Kahlenberg noted in his article *To Raise Graduation Rates, Focus on Poor and Working Class Kids*, America is struggling to keep up with other nations. As he notes, emphasis has shifted away from academics in favor of stronger social experience in many public schools. Proms, sports, and clubs have taken the spotlight over mathematics, writing, and sciences. While these are valuable to the development of well-rounded leaders, the shift has led some to not concern themselves enough with higher learning. More troubling is the disparity in the ability of the poor to access a college degree relative to middle-class and upper-class income earners. In the past thirty years, Bachelor's degree attainment has skyrocketed 45% among the top income quartile, while only 2% among the bottom. Moreover, by age twenty-four, the bottom-income students only have a 12% chance of graduating with a Bachelor's degree compared to a 58.8% chance among wealthier income-earning families.[30]

At the same time, graduation rates are falling in the United States and rising in more economically challenged nations. Even among developed nations, America is continuing to see a steady decline. In 2009, our graduation rates ranked twenty-first among twenty-six nations in the Organization for Economic Co-operation and Development. Though the rates of graduation have been consistently hovering around 76% for several years, other nations have continued to diligently pursue advancement and are now surpassing the advantages in education we always had. Moreover, 85% of foreign exchange students when surveyed have noted they find the classes in the United States easier than their comparable educational curriculum in their native country.[31]

In large part, the rationale offered for the decline in the United States along with the challenges in many underdeveloped countries parallels a similar vein. The wide disparity in the economic classes is frequently a core issue. The students who have the means are able to access quality education and attain higher levels of economic lift. While most of the bottom-income earners have little opportunity and find the climb upward nearly impossible. In America as well, the funding available for lower-income individuals and the cost of higher education has become unattainable. Tuitions, books, living, and other fees associated with attaining a higher degree are simply out of reach for many. Even those students who would rather not pursue a Bachelor's degree or Master's degree may be discouraged during high school if their interest lies in a trade over academics. Some drop out and end up never using a special aptitude for mechanics, artistry, or civil services. If a system were in place, as exists in many countries, to navigate a student toward mastery in a skilled trade if they desired this, we might be able to keep some in school and eventually graduate. The result would be a higher likelihood of social and economic advancement for our nation and improvement in the social wellbeing of our nation.[32]

Educational requirements are unique to each student, community, and nation. As discovered in Malawi and Uganda, achievement of a universally public-educated population is not simply a matter of instituting policy and hoping reform follows. Nor is public education without accountability possible. As well, the widening disparity in public institutions in America has caused a disintegration of many urban schools caused by underfunding and poor teacher quality. Every school, whether in America or a remote village anywhere in the world, faces challenges. But the achievements of education must also be celebrated and considered one of the greatest paths out of poverty and into abundance. Therefore, every nation must move with swift action to safeguard the minds and talents of its children. Illiteracy is not acceptable and high academic achievement must be the goal and the mark. If collectively our emphasis moves in this direction with compassion, service, and more egalitarian social order, the outcomes will be remarkable.

Summary Questions for Discussion

1. Maimondes' progression of tzedakah seems to favor the invitation and support to help people achieve independence through financial support. As you read the progression of giving that Maimondes suggested in the 13th century, what thoughts do you have about humanity and how similar or dissimilar we may have been to people living eight centuries ago?
2. The experience of Creekside Church provided by Stephen Corbett in *When Helping Hurts* demonstrates how important Maimondes' ideas of giving were, even back in the 13th century. Have you participated in programs similar to Creeekside Church and thought there was a better way to administer aid and help people? What experiences have you had? What would you do differently based on what you know now?
3. Tori Hogan's realization in *Beyond Good Intentions* that many of the children were telling her what they thought she wanted to hear helped her realize that often it's necessary to dig deeper to try and understand how aid is helping, hurting, or doing nothing at all to change circumstances. What are your thoughts about aid to foreign countries? What would you change to improve our programs of aid?

4. Mullainathan and Shafir discovered in *Scarcity: Why Having Too Little Means So Much* that, regardless of circumstances, anyone is prone to the habit-changing detractors created in the brain by scarcity. Tunneling and short-circuiting rational cognition can be responsible for some of the miscues humans make when facing deadlines and scarcity of money, time, or love. What thoughts are triggered for you around this idea of scarcity and how has it affected you personally? Can you remember examples of times you made mistakes you normally would not make when facing scarcity of money, time, or love? What could you have done differently to create a different environment to avoid the consequence you had?

5. Education is often heralded as a solution to end poverty. While the overwhelming data and experience of many programs around the world indicate this assumption is true, the administration of programs can affect results dramatically. Giving participants personal responsibility and ownership for the results is often crucial to success. What are your thoughts about education provided in America and other places in the world?

CHAPTER 9

A WORLD FULL OF WAVERS!

"Isn't it amazing that we are all made in God's image,
and yet there is so much diversity among his people?
– Desmond Tutu

Poverty's Impact: Four hundred million children worldwide don't have
any safe drinking water.

Imagine a world where everyone had enough and we had no poverty, no
lack, and there were people caring for one another. We have all experienced
the joy of giving and how wonderful that makes us feel. We have also
felt the sadness and pain of someone suffering. Our ability to access the
emotional connection with each other is paramount to our survival. For
Todd and I, we focus on the world as we hope to see it and not on how it
is! Though we are realistic that change comes slowly and at times it seems
like nothing will ever change to improve the station in life people hold, we
are hopeful. We believe it is possible for the citizens of our world to wave
joyfully at one another and for everyone to have enough. The blessings and
abundance our planet's resources provide for us are enough for all to have
a share—even more than enough. Like the manna God provided from
heaven in the Bible, our resources are provided and our responsibility is
stewarding their care. Our hoarding and incongruent selfishness are not
capable of sustaining man. But the way we will finally come to a readiness
to share and be connected will have to arise from inside of us. Our hearts

and our minds will have to change. Fortunately, we also have the capability to accomplish this change.

In this chapter, we look at the ways our brain is wired for empathy and connection. Sign language and the universality of the wave are also examined. Programming to end poverty and access the real possibility for a world full of *wavers* is further discussed. Finally, we delve into the concept of the shared narrative of life and the way this connects us, setting the stage for what we believe God has in store for us as His ultimate hope for man.

Motor Neurons Help Us Feel with One Another

The innate empathy humans and other mammals are capable of is remarkable and clearer because of research conducted in the early 1990s. While studying primates in Parma, Italy, a research team led by Giacomo Rizzolatti found that when primate test subjects reached for a peanut, they would activate specific sites within their prefrontal cortex known as F5. With characteristic consistency, reaching for the peanuts and the grasp would fire off a plethora of neurons in the exact locations of the brain in distinct and repetitive ways. Unexpectedly, Rizzolatti and his team stumbled upon another peculiar finding. When another primate did the same exact thing, reached for a peanut, it caused an uninvolved primate to signal in his F5 areas also. Surprised by the discovery, the team observed the exact brain sites that had fired when the primate volitionally grasped the peanut and opened it himself now fired without actually reaching for the peanut and opening the shell. Simply the observation of something the primate had done before was now causing his brain to fire. It was as if his brain believed he was reaching for the peanut and eating it. But instead, he was only watching another primate doing what he had done before. What seemed strange to Rizzolatti and his team was the replication of brain activity that could occur so readily even with no actual physical involvement.[1]

As a result of these findings, similar tests went on to discover humans also have the same capacities. If a test subject performed a task and also observed another doing the same task, the results in the brain activity were nearly identical. Rizzolatti referred to this new area discovered in the brain as mirror neurons.[2] Mirror neurons were also discovered to connect people in emotional ways. Now it was possible to explain why observing daredevil acts could make us feel tense and give an exhilarating rush, how seeing someone in distress and crying emotes feelings of sadness in others who were observing. Even seeing people do something that is painful can make us cringe and imagine what that pain feels like.

Wired in the brain of every human being, and perhaps all mammals, exists a remarkable system for compassion and empathy, which may hold the key to unlocking many of the social challenges that lie ahead for our planet. Working to understand the intricate nature of the brain's circuitry and how empathy is felt, Dr. Christian Keysers of the University of Groningen in the Netherlands, and others, have discovered a region of the brain that may be the central targeting site of compassionate feeling. The circuitry that makes us feel happy, sad, pain, and connection with others acts like a two-way system of reflection. Like seeing our own image in a mirror or a quiet, still lake, the emotional charges we feel in any moment, whether enjoyable or painful, have the unique ability to be felt through our own direct stimulation from the perpetrating cause or through observation of another receiving the same act.[3]

The theater in the brain for this astonishing neurological occurrence is the most advanced region, the prefrontal cortex. Known to be the site of higher learning and advanced knowledge, the cortex is the distinguishing feature of the human brain that sets us apart from other life forms, although the social engineering of empathy and compassion seems to exist in other living creatures as well. Keysers discovered acts of love or rejection could also be stimulated either by direct association or peripherally. Mirror neurons seemed to create learned responses we acquired as "a way to be social and honor our highest need—the need for connection with one another." People who exhibit the highest level of compassion and empathy have the largest network of mirror neurons firing. So, acts of service, being kind to a stranger, and observing individuals who demonstrate compassion and love help others also feel those feelings. We don't have to actually be a part of the experience to feel alongside someone else. Seeing people who are happy, sad, angry, or afraid evokes places inside us that make us feel those feelings too. We even use mirror neurons to recognize facial cues and body language. If we see a smiling face, we feel happy. If we see a sad face, we feel sad. If someone comes running frantically towards us, our brain signals us to be on the alert for danger. All of this is part of the mirror neuron system.[4]

Waving is the Universal Sign for Greeting and Saying Hello

The discovery of motor neurons and their importance in understanding empathy and connection for humans is possibly the reason waving has become a universal language of greeting around the world. Waving in American Sign Language and international sign language has the same or similar gestures. As a result, a wave virtually anywhere in the world means hello or goodbye. Without thinking, we all wave at one another, particularly when we want to connect and be friendly. I have noticed people in rural areas like to wave, especially if they don't have too many visitors drive by their home. This happens frequently in Kenya, where my original observations of the *wavers* and *beggars* took place. It also happens around the world, anywhere people want to connect with strangers passing by. The wave demonstrates a desire to connect. Our desire to connect comes from inner confidence and security, but also recognizes the important value of relationships. If we are friendly, the likelihood of friendly reciprocation is heightened. As we gather friends, our chances of survival are increased. Particularly, waving to strangers evokes a sense of connection that begins the recruitment and lowering of the natural guarding and shielding that separate us. ***Waving, unlike begging, as we have discussed, is a mirrored response esteemed around the world.***

Figure: Waving is a universal sign recognized around the world.

Human communication is elaborate and involves a myriad of nuances to convey a message. Though spoken language is the most common method for interacting with other people, body language and gestures are also interpreted and used to understand what someone is 'saying.' A simple 'huff' or a disappointed nod with a stern look of disgust can indicate displeasure. While a gleeful 'oh yeah!' with the hands elevated high in the air and a leap means something entirely different. Language is more than spoken words alone. Waving and begging are also part of a much deeper understanding of humanity's communication and can help us connect in more meaningful ways. Recognizing the feelings these two gestures emote in the giver and receiver can connect us. The mirror neurons that fire off when we see someone waving or begging inside our own brain can become a reflector. We see one another! We see the heart and can feel the feelings of a stranger if we are aware of our own *waver* and *beggar* spirit inside ourselves.

Sign Language Helps Us Understand
the Meaning of Waving and Begging

For the deaf, body language, hand gestures, facial cues, and reading lips are the ways they stay connected and communicate. As well, the complex system of language developed within the signing community is a testament to the enormous value gestures provide to understand what someone means to say.

Until the early 1800s, no known method of communication among the deaf existed in the United States, but was only found in Europe, predominantly in France. Many who were either born deaf or lost their hearing were regarded with disdain and considered deaf and dumb. If you couldn't hear, you were stupid. Now it seems ludicrous that people would have believed just because a child could not hear, he/she was dumb and incapable of learning. However, like other areas of study and progress, people slowly began to realize that if you could teach a deaf child like other children, they could learn a trade, work, and provide value in the world. In the United States, prior to the development of sign language schools, there were few options available for the deaf and most the time the children became a burden to their family, languishing without any real purpose. They often begged and lost any opportunity to be a *waver* to life. This fate changed for millions, though, in 1814. Thomas Gallaudet, a minister from Hartford, Connecticut, had a neighbor with a deaf nine-year-old daughter. His neighbor, Mason Fitch Cogswell, believed his daughter Alice was not stupid but actually extremely intelligent. She just needed a method to communicate her ability to speak and share her knowledge. Cogswell approached Gallaudet and asked if he would teach Alice. However, Gallaudet made little progress with any methods at his disposal. Recognizing his need to learn alternative methods to educate Alice, he gained the financial support of the local community and traveled to Europe to study methods of deaf education already existing overseas. Like many people living around the world today who require our assistance to educate them or teach local leaders more advanced education methods, Gallaudet recognized his limitations. Moreover, he was willing, as so many are, to help his community. His community also got behind him and sponsored his passage and training to bring the art of sign language back to the thousands who needed it desperately in the United States.

In Europe, Gallaudet met Abbe Sicard, Jean Massieu, and Laurent Cierc. Abbe Sicard was an accomplished educator at the National Institute for Deaf-Mutes in France. Cierc and Massieu were Sicard's students and later became accomplished educators. Gallaudet studied vigorously to learn their system and bring it back to the United States for Alice and others. Knowing the enormous stakes that were resting on his ability to learn this new way of communication, Gallaudet was committed and dedicated. Moreover, he recognized, probably because of his dedication to faith, that all children deserve a chance and the fate of being born deaf or losing one's hearing did not have to end God's plan for anyone. I am quite certain, as we mentioned earlier in this chapter, that his compassion was fully engaged. His mirror neurons were attuned to the plight he saw in Alice and others, and he was going to do anything he could to help the deaf have a chance at a prosperous and meaningful life of connection with the hearing world.

Once Gallaudet had learned enough to return and teach Alice, he asked Cierc if he would accompany him back to the United States. Cierc, who had been one of the premier educators at the National Institute of Deaf-Mutes, would be a tremendous resource to help start a deaf school in the States. Cierc agreed and joined Gallaudet, and together they returned to start the American School for the Deaf, established in Hartford, Connecticut in 1817. The school became the first free public deaf school in the US and represented a significant milestone in the history of the American deaf. The school grew rapidly and deaf students from all regions of the United States came to study. Students brought signs from their hometowns and many were incorporated into the language of the school as American Sign Language evolved. Eventually, Gallaudet retired in 1830 and Cierc continued teaching until the 1850s. By 1863, twenty-two deaf schools had been established throughout the US, and most of them had been founded by Cierc's students.

While the emergence of deaf education had grown substantially in this five-decade period, collegiate education still needed to be established.

Galluadet's son, Edward, would continue his work and answer that need in 1857 with the first all-deaf college, the Columbia Institution for the Instruction of the Deaf and Dumb and Blind in Washington, D.C. Progress in deaf education would continue in 1864 when Edward secured accreditation for the Columbia Institution to issue degrees. Eventually, the Institution would change its name to Gallaudet University in honor of Thomas Hopkins Gallaudet.[5]

Like billions of people living in the hopelessness of poverty, the deaf were often regarded as incapable and worthy only of begging. Many had no voice and no power to change their circumstance. Gallaudet, Sicard, and others who provided the institution for them to learn changed the destiny of millions in generations to follow. Similarly, education in under-resourced regions is also changing the future for generations of people. For some, simply learning to speak English provides a way to secure meaningful employment in tourism or international affairs. Gaining knowledge in math, science, and the arts also furthers economic opportunities.

Knowledge, experience, connection, and opportunity are all requirements for change and progress. The under-resourced must have a platform for their voice and dreams. The hope snuffed out in the *beggars* and the poor must not occur! Knowing they have enough food, clean drinking water, and a safe home are simple requests and not too much to ask of life. The international success that took place to provide the deaf with a way to communicate and provide purposeful value is a model for how we should approach poverty. Education and consistent attention to help the poor discover value in their lives is crucial. As we have discussed throughout this book, the poor and under-resourced are often the victims of societal challenges. ***Their willingness is evident, but the way is not clear!***

Ending Poverty to Help Everyone Stay a *Waver*

Internationally strong emphasis on alleviating poverty is ongoing. As we come together, not as individual nations but as global partners, we are capable of creating our vision of a world full of *wavers*. Though every large-scale change of consciousness followed by committed action requires us to change our own lives first, recognizing the status quo doesn't have to exist. Everything changes, and one day we too will look back at poverty and ask the question, "Was there ever a time when people didn't work together, share, and help one another?"

The Millennium Project End Poverty Campaign 2015 is one of the most promising programs now underway to alleviate global poverty. It also represents a real connection the people living with abundance and plenty are doing something to change the circumstances of the poor. The Millennium Project to End Poverty Campaign 2015 is a demonstrable program that shows a willingness and desire for the *wavers* of the world to help many who have to beg. It is a step toward a world full of *wavers*. At the time of our book being published, we are near the deadlines for the goals set by the Campaign; it appears there has been enormous progress. However, not all goals are met. Nonetheless, we applaud the world community in its effort to extend a hand and care to the people needing it the most. The goal is to reduce the number of people living on less than a dollar a day per day by half. Secondly, guaranteed stable employment and reduced numbers of people living with hunger are also goals. Remarkable progress has already occurred with over six hundred million people worldwide now earning more and overall poverty rates dropping. From 1990 to 2008, the Campaign reports poverty dropped from 47% of the world's population to 24%.[6] These initiatives have further been supported since September 2000, when 189 countries of the United Nations unanimously agreed to "spare no effort to free our fellow men, women, and children from the abject and dehumanizing condition of extreme poverty, specifically hunger and the major diseases that afflict humanity."[7]

In March of 2002, twenty-two of the world's wealthiest countries agreed to make concrete efforts toward poverty alleviation. Meeting at the Monterrey Conference, world leaders, including US president George Bush, French president Jacques Chirac, and British prime minister Tony Blair, agreed to give 0.7% of their national income as aid to the poorest countries, enabling them to raise the required $195 billion per year they felt was necessary to help the poorest nations.[8] Despite these efforts and grand visions of helping the impoverished, only five countries have satisfied the goal of reaching 0.7%: Luxemburg, Sweden, Norway, Denmark, and the Netherlands. Countries nearing the agreement in 2012 included the United Kingdom, Finland, and Ireland, while the United States, Japan, and Spain were woefully low and nowhere near reaching the 0.7% goal. In 2012, the United States was providing only .19 cents of every hundred dollars in actual GDP and Japan was even lower at .17 cents. The United States and Japan only led Spain, Greece, and Italy, three countries that had catastrophic debt crisis within their economy.[9]

While the resolution to raise aid in real dollars is only part of the solution, the dreadfully low contribution many of the wealthiest nations around the world provide is a strong message showing the disconnect with the necessity to act on behalf of the impoverished. However, the lack of adequate resolve may be something more psychological and genetically engineered within humans than merely a willful act of uncaring. When heroism is called upon in a crisis, Americans are among the most energized and quick responders. Hurricanes, earthquakes, and terrorism have given a glimpse of what is possible for Americans to come to the aid of the distressed. Among the most recent examples since 2000 are the terrorist attacks of 9/11, Hurricane Katrina, and the Haiti earthquake. In every one of these tragedies, Americans, and other people who had the means and the passion to help, stepped up and helped the victims. Sometimes, it was going to the site of the tragedy and helping; other times, it was helping on the periphery. And millions donated money to help rebuild communities. Though money and resources were often mismanaged, the real takeaway from these efforts is that people care about helping one another. So, why don't we do it all the time?

In his book *The Life You Can Save*, Peter Singer has identified a characteristic within humans that may explain the inability to act globally and provide economic assistance when combating global poverty. Singer found in his research that people were moved more by the plight of a single victim than by a large number. In his research, a group of volunteers was provided an opportunity to donate money for a job they had done for a charity.

Volunteers were asked to help a local charity, were paid a small fee for their time, and then given an opportunity to donate a portion to a worthy cause.

One group was provided information about food shortages in Malawi affecting millions of victims, while a second group was given information about only one young Malawian girl, Rokia, who was a victim of this crisis. A third group was provided information about Rokia and the immense crisis in Malawi. Singer discovered that when volunteers were provided insight into a single victim over the large group, charitable donations were far greater if only the single girl's story was told. Even hearing the single girl's story *and* the plight of the all the victims did not garner more support than only hearing the single story about Rokia.[10]

As a result, Singer realized that when we feel as though we can affect positive change with one person and identify with a single victim, our empathy is decidedly stronger. A possible explanation may be the way in which an individual need triggers our own mirror neurons. It's possible when confronted with a single need our mirror neurons are able to feel alongside the person with more empathy. We feel their pain and the desperate situation with more depth. On the other hand, when confronted with the magnitude of a condition for which we feel powerless, our tendency is to shut down and provide nothing rather than considering our actions can be the inspiration for others and with our one vote and contribution we are making a difference.

If we know about someone in trouble and in need, do we take action to help? Sometimes, the internal dialogue we each have may regard the matter as something we cannot help. It just seems too large. The notion of a world full of *wavers* is impossible. Really, we could end poverty? Come on, you're saying to yourself. There will always be poor people, corruption, and greed! But hasn't man evolved from the medieval world where savage killing was expected and life expectancy was brief? Sure, we evolve as men and women and adapt and change depending on the input and resolve we place upon change. Even in the United States, we provide more attention to children with special needs than only seventy-five years ago. There was a time when a child born with a severe or sometimes a moderate handicap was deemed

215

dumb and unable to learn. They were thought of as purposeless! We didn't bother to educate them or work with these special children. Why would you waste valuable resources on a child who has a handicap? But we evolve and have realized all children deserve a chance, and thus many schools and institutions provide special programming to reach these children, too. As well, we provide special parking and access so people with disabilities can also enjoy public facilities. These are acts of kindness and demonstrate our facility for compassion. But someone had to forge an idea and be willing to push, and most likely push some more, to make sure everyone got a chance. Pushing was an act, a resolve to see that we became a world full of *wavers* and the handicapped did not end up *beggars*. But we each have to ask hard questions sometimes about how far and how hard to push.

How far do we push when we know something is wrong and needs to be changed? Should I say something? Should I make that call? What if they reject my request or demand? Am I correct on this observation and does something need to change? This dilemma comes up again and again in matters of service and acceptable decorum surrounding the delivery of a service or items in exchange for payment. One of the problems we have to consider when caring for the poor is how we deem what is good enough. Most charity involves giving to an organization or individual to help them. Like expecting good service and food at a nice restaurant, we should expect the money and time we invest in change initiatives is providing the excellent service and delivery of our investment to the intended needs. But if the situation doesn't change, how far do we individually push to change the circumstances, and is our individual voice worthy and powerful enough to change the circumstances? Or, another way to view this dilemma is when do we say something if nothing is being said about a social problem or little is being done to improve the circumstances? How do we decide when to challenge the status quo and say enough is enough?

I can recall countless opportunities in my life to determine how far to push and how much to ask for in regards to the lack of service or delivery of a product. In a recent visit to Florida where I had arranged a family reunion bringing my family together, I had the occasion to ask myself the difficult question again. How far do I push for what I know is right? Though this example is not related directly to the care of the poor or challenging the status quo of poverty, some parallel questions arise about personal resolve to take action and be heard. In many ways, there are parallels to the ways we need to act with a myriad of global issues. There is no way to change the circumstances of poverty without questioning the way we are doing things. We have to take an approach that says 'enough is enough!'

My mother was recovering in Florida following bilateral hip replacement surgery and my stepfather had come home from Kenya to attend to health issues as well. This time provided a unique window for our family to come together and share some long overdue time with one another. My parents have been missionaries in Kenya for twenty-five years and their visits home to American soil are rare. Therefore, we wanted to make this time a unique time of love and togetherness. Desiring an unforgettable family experience, I arranged for a rental home on the Florida coast large enough for our entire family. Researching online home rentals can often be like searching out a small diamond in the middle of a large haystack. Making decisions often requires trusting the quality of the home and care provided by the company and owners. Unfortunately, it isn't always possible to make a wise decision from misleading pictures posted on websites or overly exaggerated descriptions and the amenities it includes. On this trip, my family got a full dose of both of these examples and more.

When we arrived at the property, we were greeted by a poorly maintained home in disrepair and fraught with safety concerns and violations. Where to start and what to do, if anything, to make this matter right? Do I call the management company or live with the problems and say nothing? Do I complain a little or extensively? How do I table my arguments for concession and remedy? So many questions to ask and do I want to appear too pushy? Since it is my nature to take action and not sit on the sidelines, I made the phone calls to the management company to begin the process to bring this property to the proper state for guests. Top of my list was the installment of smoke detectors in the unit since none were installed. Hard to believe in 2013 there could be a rental home without adequate smoke detectors installed.

Surprisingly and as is often the case, when blatant deficiencies exist and they are called to light, some leaders act to make the situations right. This was the case in this instance. Although the property was in disrepair and without hope to properly fix all the deficiencies, any positive change toward improvement would represent a victory. These small victories are not dissimilar from the small victories realized in the work of aid for villages and communities needing care. ***Small victories and incremental change are relevant.***

Among the remedies made while staying were the installation of five smoke detectors and a carbon monoxide detector, cleaning the soiled carpets, cleaning the heavily darkened dirty windows, fixing a broken gate on the deck, disposing of scattered trash around the grounds of the home, filling in large holes in the yard to reduce the likelihood of trip-fall injury, and estimates of repairs to fix deteriorated decks and outdoor recreation areas. In total, my desire to make things right took portions of four days of my vacation. But my efforts made a progressive leap to make this property safer and hold the owner and the rental company responsible for their negligence. While my stay with my guests was somewhat blighted by these matters, the satisfaction in knowing I had created some small change of improvement was gratifying.

This story is parallel to the need we have to ask for more care when we recognize the extreme deficiencies that exist in social justice. Throughout the world, billions of people living in poverty struggle to eat, find clean water, and get an education. Who is in their corner? Who is telling the management company this is unacceptable and needs to be fixed? Who are the champions of the poor? My experience with the rental is not unlike the broken lives many are forced to lead with inadequate resources. When there are few that have so much and many that have so little, the imbalance needs to be measured and recalibrated so the spirits of the many under-resourced will not crumble under the weight of poverty and despair becomes the result.

The Shared Narrative of Life

TED is a remarkable collection of fascinating presentations offered free of charge on virtually any mobile device or computer. One of the truly remarkable feats of this digital information portal is the wealth of information and knowledge one can gain in only five minutes. Created to allow viewers to watch a topic that will inspire, make them laugh, or deeply connect, the TED presentations are often provided by experts, scientists, educators, and leaders of social change. Among the many relevant topics discussed on TED, one of the presentations by Renny Gleeson, provided a humorous look at the various ways we seek to hide our addictions to mobile devices and shamelessly ignore people who are in our midst.

In his presentation, he shows the typical postures we all see in ourselves and others while we glance, tap, and engage with the small-screened smartphone devices like iPhones and Android phones. As Gleeson points out, our behavior is telling those whom we are with that no matter what is going on right now, whatever is being said or seen, this small piece of informational matter I am holding in my hand is more important than you and I am not with you.[11] While this may seem harsh, this is the reality of our digital age—being hooked to cellular data over actual life. While this is compelling and has enormous ramifications, the real takeaway from Gleeson's presentation is the incredibly strong urge we have to create a digitally synthesized shared narrative. Gleeson recognizes and presents in his elegant presentation a need we as humans all share to create a shared narrative of our lives. While we are empowered by our ability to create an individual narrative and enjoy, relish, and seek to have unique and powerful individual experience, it is our need to share our experiences with others and bring them in and for us to enter their experiences that draws us so magnetically to this virtual relationship with other people.

The shared narrative is the collective conscience of our world coming together. These new digital possibilities have never been imaginable before and perhaps are the forerunner of something that could be frighteningly potent. Technology allows us to see and speak to people thousands of miles away in other continents. We have the ability to assess facial cues and watch them as if they were in the room with us having a conversation at the dinner table. Visually seeing someone speak as if he/she were actually in the room with you allows new human connection. Even though the travel to a distant place may not be possible because of the high travel costs and time to transport people to meet, the evolutionary technology emerging today is allowing a virtual world of human connection. By connecting often and learning more about our brothers and sisters in distant lands, we co-create a new world thought. We begin to feel as though they are part of our lives and we *can* and *need* to care for one another. Working together, caring for one another, and establishing plans together creates a social narrative that focuses on *us* and not *them*. In essence, our biology can become more intertwined when we communicate and see one another because of the role our mirror neurons can have in connecting us. I believe the shared narrative of existence has enormous ramifications when we consider how shared narratives are used. An effective example is the shared narrative used in entertainment, such as in comedy.

In particular in improvisational comedy, there is a premise of agreement. In improv., I am co-creating a scene of life using a real world suggestion from the audience and seeking to entertain, develop characters, and raise the stakes of the relationship in a manner that makes our theater compelling and worth watching. Great improvisation requires a simple action to make it fantastic. An example: I must agree with my scene partner and say "Yes!" to all he provides for me to play with on the stage. My objective is to agree with his thoughts and actions and play along, offering only the words, "Yes and…" as I take his suggestion and build upon his narrative, creating a shared narrative of life and drama on the stage. Our shared narrative may have conflict, may have love, may have competition, but the true spirit of the shared narrative is a basic agreement.

In the world of opening possibilities and transforming economies and the emergence of billions of *wavers* the world over, we must clearly be ready to use a shared narrative of agreement. When all narratives start from the place of 'I agree with what you give me and will build upon it,' we are creating a possible narrative that moves a scene of compassion and justice along. We cease to have stops, still moments of no movement, and instead create a world where the desire to render movement is paramount to our survival. Never have we been in an age as this when so much can move so fast and this resolve to use the shared narrative of "Yes and…" will change the consciousness of the planet.

Of course, you are probably thinking to yourself that if we agreed with everything the bad guys around the world are doing, we would have chaos and destruction. We have to fight evil! On some level this is true, and we may need to recognize evil is afoot because we can culturally find ourselves in disagreement about 'what this life is supposed to mean.' Some believe life is only about seeing what they can get for themselves. It is survival of the fittest: the weak will perish. Others believe their god is the only god, and anyone who doesn't see it that way needs to die. Still some see their poverty as a medal and are willing to stay there even if opportunity comes knocking. We are not saying any of these are right or wrong; instead, we're making an effort to be in agreement, first because everyone is made in the image of God and each has something magnificent to give the world. Moreover, every life has a purpose, even the people who create evil and harm others. No, their actions are not justified or esteemed by God! But, by taking a position of agreement and trying to understand the unjust, we set the table for transformation. Many who have beset evil on others have changed and, as any believer in Christ knows, God knows the hearts of men and has the ability to change anyone.

The Garden of Eden: What the Story Teaches Us about the Hope God Has to Create a World Full of *Wavers*

For centuries, biblical scholars have debated the veracity of the Garden of Eden. The presumed author, Moses, writes of a garden with all the necessary water, food, and security for man's needs provided by God. God is generous and clear in His directions to the man and woman. They may have anything the garden provides and eat of all the fruit, except for a single tree in the garden. The forbidden fruit of the Tree of Good and Evil is disallowed by God as his instruction to the couple. However, Satan, disguised as a serpent entices, Eve to consume the lovely fruit of the tree, and then Adam also eats the fruit. Together, Adam and Eve become aware now of their nakedness. Their shame leads them to find clothing made of fig leaves and they attempt to hide from God as he comes to visit them in the garden.

God, recognizing they are clothed and observing a change in their behavior, questions the couple to find out why they are ashamed of their naked bodies. Not being able to lie, they confess the serpent enticed their weakness and their fleshly desires to eat the fruit of the Tree of Good and Evil. God, angered by what he hears, banishes the couple and lays the extreme pains of labor upon woman for her egregious actions. Adam draws hard labor, forced to grow and find food from the soil choked by thorns and thistles. Unable to enjoy the abundant resources of the Garden, they discover outside a life with extreme toil, marred by sadness within their family, including the death of a child.

While the story of the Garden of Eden is frequently told as the origin of man, present technology and ancient manuscripts tell a different story. Moreover, archeological findings and aerospace photo imagery may point in the direction of an earlier civilization than the people of the Garden. Dr. Juris Zarins, an archeological researcher, believes he has found the mysterious location of the Garden of Eden and theorizes the common story shared in Genesis may have been a borrowed tale of man's origins from a more distant civilization.

Using detailed imagery from satellite cameras and archeological discovery, Zarins theorizes Eden may have been found in the head of the Persian Gulf around 5000 to 6000 BC. In the details written to describe the Garden in Genesis, four rivers turning into one are described. Frequently postulated to have been located in Africa or even in Asia, the more likely location seems to reside within the region Zarins believes. Though four rivers no longer come together into one in this region today, Zarins postulates the Tigris and Euphrates reached further south into a land valley now covered by the Persian Gulf. He concludes there were two other rivers that would have emerged from this area but are now dry at some points along the riverbed and covered completely by the Gulf at the meeting point with the Tigris and Euphrates.

Zarins' findings are intriguing because they further elucidate possible explanations for the nature of the Biblical writing in Genesis and who may have been responsible for the original text and story. Moreover, the possible explanations for writing about the Garden and man's expulsion may also have come to light. The probable site of Eden was the ancient civilization of Mesopotamia. Zarins pieced together earlier archeological findings, which seemed to indicate an origin to the Garden story that may have existed within the Sumerian culture several thousand years before the Hebrew mention of a garden. Recognized as the earliest written language, Sumerian tablets tell a story of a people forced to leave this region and refer to a gardenlike existence.

Zarins believes the Sumerians were probably the culture that first resided in the region believed now to be the original Garden of Eden. However, they were forced to leave when climatic weather changes shifted the earth's waters and drowned the fertile valley. Zarins and others believe the stories of the garden-like region and the people's forced evacuation would eventually be described by man's sin against God and their forceful need to leave the fertile lands. Though no one knows for sure if a garden existed or the true nature of Adam and Eve, the historical relevance of the physical garden and the possible mythical implications present meaning in lives bereft by poverty, famine, and unattainable basic resources.[12]

If we examine the Garden of Eden from a mythical and metaphorical perspective, we can understand a deeper meaning to God's possible plan and ultimate wish for his greatest creation, man. God chose to make man in his own image and to breathe life into him from his own breath because he wanted man to know the greatness we can only imagine God understands. God is believed to have made all the astonishing creations on earth and in the cosmos. He is all knowing. Looking closer at the story of Adam and Eve, I believe there is a more powerful meaning perhaps unexamined and unmentioned in any previous study.

I believe there is a parallel wish and meaning to God's parental punishment of his children, Adam and Eve. Existing within almost all parental relationships, a hierarchy of respect begins in virtually all parent–child relationships. Children admire and seek to be like their mom and dad. This is called the 'respect phase' of a parent–child relationship. As children mature and they discover the independent nature of their mind and the individual aspirations, a 'rejection phase' often follows. Children say words to parents like, "I'm not sure I agree with your ideas, Dad." "Mom, I'm my own person and you can't make me do that." Children learn to individualize and find their own meaning. Though the rejection phase varies, in order for children to know themselves as individuals, they have to reject some of the thoughts and ideas of their parents or they cannot discover individuality.

The culmination in this lifecycle children take with parents is the 'return phase. In this culminating cyclical conclusion, children learn after having experienced some of life's trials and disappointments that their parents may have had some significant lessons of value to share with them. Not uncommon, many children as matured parents themselves and survivors of trials, return to their parents with words of love, admiration, and respect for all the valuable lessons they received in growing up. The return phase of life is a celebration parents often hope for and get to experience, but not always. When adult matured children return to their parents and acknowledge them, a glowing pride emanates from both. They respect one another again.

If we consider the Garden of Eden as a metaphor and God is our father, then we as humanity are involved in the cycle of return at this time. Though we appear to be far from the return to God's wishes, we are evolving, and have been for more than five thousand years. ***When man was banished from the Garden of Eden, the color or race of man was not mentioned in the biblical text***. He doesn't concern himself with the color of our skin or our ethnicity. However, when we fell from his grace, he showed us our nakedness and our cruelty. He allowed us to fall and know the pain a fall from his grace can have on our hearts.

The rejection phase of the respect–reject–return cycle continues today and will likely continue for many more years. Why? I believe God is calling us to change the way we hold our love for one another. He doesn't want us to fight and hurt one another. He doesn't want us to judge our brothers and sisters by color, religion, disability, or sex. He only seeks to have us celebrate with him the immense diversity he provided us in our lifetimes. His wish was, and still is, that each of us would be part of a greater whole. No one is singularly more valued by him or is more important than another. The weakest, sickest, and poorest child is just as important to God as the wealthiest and most powerful man in the world. God does not see the circumstances as relevant but sees the heart and soul as the true measure of character.

When we have learned a method to transform our minds to celebrate our diversity and seek it as an opportunity, then we will know the powerful possibility of a return to the Garden of Eden. The Garden is waiting. We have the tools, resources, and opportunity. Now God wants us to seize it!

Working Together to Personally Own Responsibility for Others

Near my home in a Chicago suburb, there's a program called Working Together. It was started in 2007 when a group of Hispanic mothers began coming together to talk and have their children play soccer with one another. The mothers were concerned there was a lack of opportunity for their children in the community and the damaging effect this was having on their spirit. Their homes were located among the wealthiest suburbs in North America and they discovered while many after-school programs existed for children in the area, costs of fees and travel, etc. made most of them cost prohibitive for their children. As a result, many under-resourced children were unable to gain the self-esteem and value others in the area acquired because of their inability to pay for sports, dance, and musical programs that enrich a child's learning experience.

It was evident to these mothers if they were to avoid passing on the disease of poverty, which can afflict children growing up in scarcity, they would have to take steps to make a change. The solution they created was a series of after-school and Saturday programs that would be offered to low-income students in dance, taekwondo, guitar, sewing, and jewelry design. They also developed a folk dance program, which celebrated the Hispanic culture, creating pride in their heritage and their roots. As director Margoth Moreno shared, the program gave her a way to help every student who attended the same high school she did in the 1970s and a way to avoid the discrimination and pain she felt. As she was growing up in this affluent community, she always felt like she was different and was shunned by other students. Although she had these intense feelings, she did not allow them to stop her from going on to achieving success in her life; but the pain of discrimination, racial slurring, and attack lingered in her heart for many years. In many ways, her resolve, like so many that are stepped on, was a testament to her faith and familial support. What was lacking when Margoth attended the same school where she now provides programs for students was a place where she could feel safe and feel she belonged. There were no activities for her to participate in because the costs were restrictive and language barriers existed. Moreno recognized this same problem was leading students today to make decisions to join gangs, quit on their dreams, and eventually develop the *beggar's* disease of poverty, a self-fulfilling downward spiral into despair and destitution.

Since developing the program, Moreno and her co-program coordinator Mrs. Alicia De La Cruz have experienced remarkable results with their students. No longer is the despair and hopelessness rampant among these students and their families. Their students now have some of the same classes wealthier students receive in the community, at less cost but with equal value. Though there is a long way to go and many more programs Working Together wishes to provide, the assistance they have developed for low-income families demonstrates the need to educate and care for children before the disease of poverty afflicts their mind and souls. Another benefit of the program is the opportunity it affords children who are blessed with financial resources in the community to volunteer and help the young children in the program. High school dancers volunteer to help the young children learn dance. Musicians in the high school volunteer to give lessons and the community rallies to support children who could be left behind but are receiving a chance to shine like others in the community. Working Together is an example and says it clearly in their name: we are supposed to work together to frame a better world. Creating a world full of *wavers* is a monumental task, and takes effort and strong will. As well, partnerships and focus on the impact we want to have in the world and not who is always getting the credit is the most effective way to challenge the status quo and change the circumstances of billions.

Waving on Camera Says Something about the Gesture

Is the desire to wave on camera natural? Does this common reaction say something more about our society and even our inherent need to be seen and noticed? Anyone who has watched a news broadcast or seen a live public event on television can recall seeing anxious people waving at the camera as they get their brief moment of fame. One of the most common places you will see this occurrence is outside the NBC studios in New York. Crowds of viewers watch the NBC Today Show through fully transparent glass into the studio. As a backdrop for the live television show, the host and guests talk about the daily topics and move about in the studio. As a viewer on television, we are afforded the opportunity to watch the show and catch a glimpse of excited fans seeking if only a brief moment to be on camera, that magic moment of fame. "Hey, Mom! Look at me! I'm on TV!" The refrain goes something like that inside the head of the anxious *wavers* hoping to be noticed. There are no *beggars* in view, only *wavers* with smiles and hope for a moment to be on camera. The same images are captured around the world on international sporting events like the World Cup and the Olympics. A camera focused on people and their opportunity to be noticed by someone and acknowledged inspires them to wave and smile.

The psychology of the *waver* and his desire to connect is evident. He wants to be seen! He wants to be noticed! He is happy! It's as if a *waver* on television is saying 'I want the world to see my happiness at this moment.'

He wants someone to respond, "Hey, I saw you on TV!" Being seen on television, if even for a brief moment, gives a *waver* a feeling of pride and fame. This simple and ongoing observation reveals how deep the desire is for our connection to one another. Moreover, it demonstrates how the more natural way we were born to communicate with one another is through waving and not begging. Waving opens us up and reveals our joy and desire to be seen for communication. Begging shuts us down and lowers our self-esteem. It would be completely unnatural to see a large group of people in the backdrop of the New York studio, begging instead of waving.

Schindler's List: A Movement of Thankful *Wavers* Came from One Man's Compassionate Act

In 1993, the hit movie *Schindler's List* was released, detailing the horrific killing machine of the Nazi regime during World War II in Poland. Living in peace and relative prosperity, many Polish Jews had lived in the region for hundreds of years among their neighbors, raising their families together and enjoying the fruits of labor and life. As we now know historically and through vivid imagery in the movie, the lives of millions of Jews were nefariously cut short by the evil psychotic dictatorship of Adolf Hitler and his master plan to eradicate the entire Jewish population. However, and thankfully, his strategy was extirpated by the eventual strength of the allied forces of the United States, Russia, England, and France, among others, who were able to amass their military efforts collectively and eventually topple the evil Nazi military machine. But the wake of Hitler's devastation and the magnitude would become a haunting artifact, leaving an indelible scar on humanity forever.

Nonetheless, the heroic efforts of many who survived and some who helped in the effort came to light as the stories and what had transpired during those darkened years from 1939 to 1945 would unfold and be told. One of those remarkable stories and the thousands of lives he impacted was the efforts of Oskar Schindler, a German businessman living in Poland, who recognized the opportunity the war presented for him to profit from the devastating circumstances and the needs of a massive military effort.

Schindler gained the attention and favor of the local Nazi leadership and devised a plan to use Jewish financial backing from compromised businessmen who had been forced to live in ghettos and give up all of their business assets and financial status. Seizing their misfortune and offering them asylum along with other Jews now harboring no hope living in the ghetto, he provided a factory for Jews to work in daily and exit the ghetto safely away from the disease, famine, and anguish felt by thousands clustered in the tight, unforgiving quarters they lived in.

Amassing a fortune over only a couple of years, he was one of the sole providers of cookware and artillery shells to the Nazi armies. His workforce was the cheap labor provided by compromised Jews unclear of their future and fearing death. All around them, every Polish Jew's life was crumbling under the harsh conditions and brutal, bloody Nazi regime's power. Rights to property, freedom, and access to the outside world were exterminated with each new policy. Polish Jews throughout Europe were the victims of a tyrannical leader who had visions of mass genocide and was working toward what would eventually be known to the world as Hitler's 'Final Solution.' In the wake of this backdrop, Schindler too felt little care for Jews but simply looked upon their unfortunate moment in time as his opportunity to seize his own money and power while giving them some comfort, but only for few hours while they worked in his factory. His heart, though not as harsh as many Germans and other Poles toward the Jews, was certainly not full of compassion and fully open to the implausible stripping of freedom and dire struggles Jews now bore.

However, as Schindler witnessed, and others alongside him also began to discover, the evil and heinous Nazi Party was brutal in the most inhumane ways and killing was almost like theater to them. Daily and without cause, it was not uncommon for a Nazi soldier to simply pull out his gun and shoot a Jewish mother, just because he was annoyed her baby was crying while he was enjoying the peaceful chirp of a nearby songbird nestled in a tree. Then he would also take the child's life in cold blood. These moments and countless others like them began to unravel and sicken Schindler in some deep place in his heart. Schindler began to see how the opportunity he had seized could now become a possible method to save lives as the rumors of the extermination camps began to surface and thousands were being shipped off to their eventual death in crowded trains and trucks.

Negotiating under the auspices of his need to have a skilled workforce that could exercise maximum production to feed the needs of the war machine, Schindler was able to navigate through countless setbacks the local Nazi leadership handed him. Eventually, as it became more certain that his laborers would be lost to him and be sent to their deaths if he did not act on their behalf, he came to a crossroads. As the scene is depicted in the movie, Schindler is negotiating with the childish, brutish Nazi commander named Amon Goth for the release of his Jewish workers. The discussions turn to how much a man's life is worth. As the banter goes back and forth between the two, Schindler poses the question to the commander but receives no answer. Instead, a rhetorically identical question is offered back by the commander. Wanting a bribe and willing to offer the release of men, women, and children for the right price, the Nazi commander asks Schindler, "How much is a man's life worth to you?"

Moving forward, the audience sees Schindler and his Jewish friend and key business operations manager pining over a list of names and determining the ultimate fate of each name. As they discuss the names and check the list again and again, Schindler continues and urges his Jewish manager to add one more, and then another and so on, each time asking how many is that now? It's as if Schindler is doing an accounting in his head, knowing how much money he has to pay for each soul and waging within his heart the grim reality that he will not be able to save everyone. We can only imagine this reality and how foreboding this may have been on his heart and his assistant's, knowing their decisions were determining the fate of men, women, and children was like playing God in a way. As they eventually completed the list at just over 1,200 names, both men could not have known how profound their tally would be in the annals of history.

Completing the transaction with Goth and now in possession of an agreement to deliver his Jewish workers to his factory by train, Schindler is relieved to receive the men but is terrified to learn the women who were sent in a separate train have been sent to a death camp instead of to him. Still undeterred, he visits Nazi leaders and once again demands and negotiates the delivery of his workers and the fulfillment of the agreement he had arranged with Goth to provide the workers for his factories. Though reluctant to comply, the Nazis eventually allow all workers to be delivered safely and continue working with Schindler till the end of the war.

The eventual liberation of Poland and the rest of Europe occur as the Allied Forces take hold of the war and defeat Nazi Germany. With the arrival of the Russian military, it is now official. Schindler realizes he has saved his Jewish friends, but he also faces a painful realization that he will likely be tried as a war criminal since he was a member of the Nazi party. But his Jewish workers come to his aid and write a lengthy letter of praise, with each member signing his name in thankfulness for what did for them. The movie ends with one of the most memorable scenes as Schindler is leaving the factory heading to his car to now leave Poland and move back to Germany with the likelihood of his fate sealed. But standing there before he leaves, he looks out to all 1,200 Jewish workers who smile, offer thanks, and wave to him. His emotions overwhelming him, he realizes at this exact moment the magnitude of his efforts to save these Jewish friends from death and is taken by emotion. His manager, now also a free man, and having grown fond of Schindler also, is honored to give him a gold ring with a Hebrew inscription the workers had prepared for Schindler before he left them. The words inscribed on the ring as shared by the manager say, 'A man who saves one life saves a world.' Now swept over by his emotion, Schindler begins to weep uncontrollably, realizing he could have saved more Jews if he had given up more of his worldly possessions like his car, his remaining jewelry, and his clothes. He even states that the gold in the ring he had just received as a gift could have saved one more life. The price of his comfort and his unwillingness to sell everything now becomes evident as he sees the 1,200 waving Jews thankful for the chance at life he gave them. Schindler is a transformed man, now with an openly compassionate heart, willing to wave and reflect back on not only himself but on the needs of others. His realization and his total transformation are a testament to the ability of people to make life-altering change at any stage of their lives.[13]

As we consider Schindler's realization and the personal sacrifice he made, paying the majority of his earthly wealth in trade for the lives of 1,200 Jews, and the eventual lives that followed because of their salvation from extermination, compassion and justice come to mind. Often the least talked about and most admonished virtues in policy, design, and the creation of structure to care for the needs of the under-resourced are compassion and justice. We struggle to understand why our greatness and our wealth, along with our remarkable technological advances cannot reach all those who have desperate lives. Why are so many still dying and suffering? Though our physiological makeup has an enormous capacity to feel and even experience the pain another feels through the mirror neurons of our brain, we seem to falter in our resolution to change the social tribulations of the world.

Yet, we believe Schindler's story and his Polish Jewish workers offers us a glimpse of what might be possible in the world. The seeds for a transformative world lie in the heart of man, in the capacity to love and breed compassion for another's suffering. As we move closer to this ideal and also come closer to God's wisdom and Jesus's love for the poor, our hearts are changed. Our lives and the lives of the afflicted stay connected and we are both able to wave at one another with joyful connection and regard. Indeed it is possible for our world to be full of *wavers*!

Summary Questions for Discussion

1. Mirror neurons in our brain are an important biological system to keep us connected to one another and feel with one another. How have you felt the power of connection motor neurons create in your life when seeing someone suffering?
2. In his book *The Life You Can Save*, Peter Singer revealed the tendency we share to be able to focus on the needs of one individual story over a large group and become more generous. How do you feel about this observation, and have you responded in a similar way?

---

3. Sign language has created a language for the deaf worldwide, and the universal sign for saying hello is a wave. What other universal gestures can you think of that connect all of us? Are there other ways you can think of that we use to communicate with one another universally?

4. Like the example provided in the backdrop of the NBC studios in New York with enthusiastic people waving, is there a time when you were waving to be seen? What prompted your desire to wave and be seen? Did anyone see you and comment later? How did this make you feel?

5. Oscar Schindler's heart changed gradually as he witnessed the atrocities Hitler's army perpetrated on the Jewish people. Why do you think he was able to change his heart and eventually provide such a powerful act of compassion toward the end of the war while there were thousands who continued to persecute the Jewish people?

CHAPTER 10

ANYTHING IS POSSIBLE!

When we try to pick out anything by itself, we find
it hitched to everything else in the universe.
— John Muir

Poverty's Transformation: **"In 1990, almost half of the population in developing regions lived on less than $1.25 a day. This rate dropped to 22% by 2010, reducing the number of people living in extreme poverty by 700 million."** (The Millennium Development Goals Report 2014. United Nations)

Albert Einstein, the great physicist, said we cannot solve a problem with the same thinking that caused the problem in the first place. With Einstein's words serving as our inspiration, if we carefully consider the methodologies being employed today to alleviate poverty, our approach could be improved with fresh insight. Today, poverty around the world is unlike any in the history of man, and our diligence to help people raise the standards of living are incrementally small to bring about widespread change. If we were to take a step back, examine the problems in every nation asking different questions, and involve people who have never had a place at policy discussions, we believe our outcomes could begin to resolve many, if not all, of the tragedies of poverty.

Although daunting and seemingly impossible, creating an environment of conscious effort and work towards solving the world's poverty is certain. In the past century alone, epic milestones have occurred that many thought could never happen. Social walls have literally crumbled, and barriers that kept men separated and unequal have now gone. The desegregation marches of Martin Luther King and his vision to dissolve racial barriers existing for three centuries in America count as one of the most dramatic achievements in world history. Nelson Mandela, imprisoned in South Africa as a political prisoner, eventually gained his freedom from the oppression of Apartheid and went on to become the president of South Africa. The Berlin Wall, rising in East Germany after the tyrannical warring of Adolf Hitler and the Nazi Party, came down! Brick by brick, the Wall was dismantled by young men and women who were determined to express freedom as their choice over separation from their German brothers and sisters born on freedom's wrong side.

Germany had been divided into a communist and non-communist nation as a compromise after World War II. For fifteen years, Berlin's citizens could openly move about from East to West Berlin. But in 1961, East Germany sought to end the freedom of its citizens because millions had left, never to return. The tyranny, fear, and suppression of communism had led millions to leave, and now the Berlin Wall ended the freedom to openly leave East Germany. For nearly three decades the Wall represented all that was considered sterile, undemocratic, and stifling to the communist-governed people of Eastern Europe and the Soviet Union. The Berlin Wall represented and blocked people of East Germany from opportunity and relationships with the outside world. To those who were fortunate to live in democratic nations and had the freedom to exercise free speech and practice liberal ideals, the Wall was dark and foreboding. It represented the inability to pursue one's passions in life in favor of a government that stifled personal expression.

Nevertheless, in November 1989, the Wall and the symbolic meaning it signified came to an end. With the collapsing economies of the east so embattled and riddled with fault, East German officials announced that citizens would be allowed formal passage. Within hours, thousands of East Germans passed to freedom into West Berlin. Officials at the Wall, unable to process the onslaught of travelers were overwhelmed. Eventually, the mob, acting in desperation and with so many years of pent-up frustration, destroyed the Wall. Vivid images of the Wall being torn down by joyously liberated East Germans are still in my memory. An act I thought would never happen in my lifetime had occurred as a triumphant ending to oppressive leadership. A generation of people would never be the same. East and West Germany were divided no more and began to work toward unifying their nation, which had been ripped apart following their crushing defeat in World War II.[1]

Similarly, the long, arduous road toward unifying ethnically divided black and white citizens in the United States was accomplished in the 1960s by the civil rights movement. Though distance still separates our nation's resolve to end prejudice, Martin Luther King, in his famous speech on the steps of the Lincoln Memorial, lauded the possibility where children would not be judged by the color of their skin but by the content of their character. Going further, he lifted his dream and challenged the world to embrace a place "where little black boys and black girls will be able to join hands with little white boys and girls and walk together as sisters and brothers." [2] As a leader in the civil rights movement, King was able to drive policy and change through courageous and carefully planned action. Peaceful protests and use of the first amendment right to free speech, King systematically established a large following of African-American and Caucasian supporters.

The civil rights movement received its launch in 1948 when President Harry S. Truman signed Executive Order 9981, stating, "It is hereby declared to be the policy of the President that there shall be equality of treatment and opportunity for all persons in the armed services without regard to race, color, religion, or national origin." [3] In 1954, the Supreme Court ruled on the famous Brown v. Board of Education of Topeka, Kansas. Their ruling stated it was unconstitutional to have 'separate but equal' facilities and schools. A 'separate but equal' system was itself inherently unequal.[4]

Martin Luther King became involved in the civil rights movement as a young Baptist minister in Alabama when he led a peaceful boycott of the bus system in Montgomery, Alabama. A young black woman, Ms. Rosa Parks, had refused to give her seat near the front of the bus to a demanding white woman. Ms. Parks was removed from the bus and arrested. King, along with the other Montgomery African-Americans, led a lengthy boycott of the bus company lasting over a year. Eventually, the bus company succumbed to the boycott and the negative influence cast upon this nationally reported spectacle. [5]

However, it is important to remember Parks' act was not a lone act occurring randomly as an afterthought of a tired woman unwilling to move to the back of the bus. No, in fact Parks had been a member of her local NAACP for twelve years leading up to this one act of defiance that day on the Montgomery bus.[6] Moreover, her involvement had been spurred by the actions of others who had collectively examined the progress made through challenges to the status quo. The United States Supreme Court's decision banning 'separate but equal in schools' and a successful bus boycott enacted in Baton Rouge two years earlier were seeds for a collective agreement toward using Parks as a vehicle to drive further change in the law. The importance of her act and the process leading up to the boycott emphasize the crucial conviction persistence plays in making any meaningful change. To rehabilitate the *beggars* and strengthen the *wavers* of the world will require persistently critical thinking, wisdom, spiritual guidance, trial and error, and the hand of God. Some regard ending poverty and a vision of a world where no one is forced to beg is utopian. Sure, it may seem impossible and foolhardy to believe we can come together as a planet and work toward egalitarian ideals that don't favor a few over the rights of the many. But remember, ***the Berlin Wall's demise and the successful introduction of a sweeping revolutionary civil rights law in the United States were also not thought to be possible***. History is replete with examples of dramatic shifts in consciousness. As well, we have the capacity, the resources, and the compassion to once again create a world that is compassionate and fair.

As we look over our shoulder, we recognize America's segregated past is no longer as hopeless but still requires enormous commitment to bring us closer as a nation. There was a time when a black child wouldn't have thought he would have an opportunity to be the president of the most powerful nation in the world. But we can now gaze upon this shrinking divide and see the connected link in a broken chain with new hope. As President Barack Obama became the first African-American to become President of the United States, the civil rights injustices challenged by King and others could be fully appreciated. Taking the presidential oath in 2008, I remember fondly the images and the hope many felt. Though our country had still been fairly divided on many of the economic issues, health-care policies, and the socially responsible questions, the emergence of our nation's ability to now represent itself with black leadership is an impressive leap in progress. President Obama not only won in 2008 but was reelected in 2012. His opportunity for this distinction had its genesis in part by the sacrifices of King and others in the civil rights movement. The parallels between the racial unification accomplished in the America and South Africa are a testimony to what is possible!

So what is possible? What can we expect to accomplish in bringing lasting impact in the parts of the world that often seem cut off, disconnected, not allowed to know the fruit of opportunity?

Both China and India are examples of countries making dramatic economic progress. Though both nations still have vast divisions within classes and human rights are devalued, progress from an impoverished economy to emerging and powerful dominance has unfolded. Both nations have created private and public programs of investment that are making an incremental change in their economic terrain. In China, the focus of government investments has been on subsidies and infrastructure, while India's success is attributed mainly to private investment in business growth. China utilizes a strong combination of lower-cost skilled and unskilled labor, which represents one of its strengths in the competitive global market. Similarly, India's lower-cost labor is one of its strengths, while also developing a huge offshore telecommunications network. Anyone who has purchased a computer or an appliance may have spoken with an Indian representative answering calls thousands of miles away. It's extremely common today for companies to use the skills and telecommunications networks created by Indian commerce to provide lower-cost alternatives for their customer-service needs. Though not perfect and often fraught with various complaints, many of the simple procedural questions customers need help with are answered by Indian customer-service agents.

Research on poverty alleviation initiatives in China has discovered that investment in both rural agricultural initiatives and education show great promise. However, efforts that focus on programs that directly affect local agencies and communities demonstrate at times the best source of lasting change. It simply isn't enough to invest in resources nationally without making sure the local agencies and people are ready to utilize the newfound opportunity. The strength China has in the world economy is its people. Holding the largest populace of any nation, China has made dramatic commitments to infrastructure and programs to emerge as an economic world power. But the leadership, in an earnest attempt to grow the nation's GDP, has often taken shortcuts that in the end may lead to their demise. Pollution, waste, and disregard for the environment are profound throughout the industrial regions of China. Their growth and advancing economy are hopeful, but in order to sustain it, there will need to be an adjustment to consider all the extenuating factors that threaten their environment and ultimately their strongest commodity— their people. Moreover, like all the nations of the world, China, India, and the other economic powers will need to heed the warning signs of the ultimate demise of humanity threatening us from the oceans and the very air we breathe. As we detailed in chapter four, the massive accumulation of plastic waste growing in the oceans is a symptom of our consumer-driven society. As well, the huge outpouring of carbon-based emissions is causing profound warming of the earth's surface, causing dramatic weather change. As these factors continue over the next half-century, in all likelihood many, if not all, of the advances we have made as a global society will come to a crossroads.

The Human Soul in Action

In *Soul of a Citizen*, Paul Rogat Loeb takes a thought-provoking look at the calling of each citizen to examine his role in society and where he is called to serve. While it may seem there are times we cannot make a difference, the truth is simple. Every day, citizens make bold choices and change the world as a result. Loeb shares insight into these thoughts as he calls upon the need for citizens to examine when is enough really enough in our lives? As he speaks of his own life's journey, he shares with pride how he has created a self-sustaining energy process in his own home that has led to an electrical meter that actually spins backward! Moreover, as he proposes each citizen examine his/her role, he shares from his favorite Jewish Passover ceremony, 'Dayenu,' which means 'It Would Have Been Enough." [7]

> Had the Lord only brought us out of Egypt…
> it would have been enough.
> Had the Lord only sustained us in the desert…
> it would have been enough.
> Had the Lord only given us the Torah…
> it would have been enough.

As Loeb questions, are we not to examine our hearts and realize God has provided all we require for our happiness if only to know him and trust he has provided completely for our needs? However, such a large hole resides within the spirit of so many and literally tears at the very fabric of our being that a constant need to accumulate ensues. The notion that having the most toys makes us the winner is a trap too many of us fall into. As well, the inner need to draw attention and say, "Look at me!" becomes our preoccupation. These two self-aggrandizing needs override any attempt to consider the inner wealth gained through service and bringing about a balance in nature. Loeb's view ultimately is not hopeful as he believes the imbalance has become corrupted to the point of extinction.[8] While the word 'extinction' may seem strong and unlikely, how are we to know the excess we thrive upon may not be the seeds of extinction of tomorrow's children. As the historian William Appleman Williams writes, "Once people begin to acquire and enjoy and take for granted and waste surplus resources and space as a routine part of their lives, and to view them as a sign of God's favor, then it requires a genius to make a career—let alone create a culture—on the basis of agreeing to limits." Williams' assertion speaks to the insatiable appetite for greed and excess that has left so few with so much and so many with so little.[9]

Williams may very well be speaking to the observations of Paul Hawken, Amory Lovins, and L. Hunter Lovins in their book *Natural Capitalism*. They write that the world has lost a fourth of its topsoil and a third of its forest cover in only the last fifty years. Moreover, our excessive depletion of our resources will lead to a 70% loss of our coral reefs, where 25% of all marine life resides, within our lifetimes. As well, in the last three decades, one-third of the planet's resources —*its natural wealth* —has been consumed.[10]

While this may be sustainable for several more decades, or perhaps even a century, the way we care and use the resources of our planet cannot continue. Each citizen, as Loeb shares, has a moral duty to do something for their planet. It does not take an individual with superhuman capability to change the world, but it does take a will and body of people willing to work together and exerting their courageous expression to effect the transformation. Beginning to steward resources in a new way can be accomplished by simply asking, *"Because I can buy it, does that mean I should?" "Because I can afford it, does that mean I should buy it?" "Because I can use as much as I want does that mean I should use this much?"* Asking questions and deliberating the future consequences of our actions on the current planet and the future residents is crucial to changing the unspoken policy of excess.

Social Entrepreneurship

One of the most powerful developments holding promise to change the world is the emergence of a new type of entrepreneur, the social entrepreneur. "Across the world, the social entrepreneur is demonstrating new approaches to many social ills and new models to create wealth, promote social wellbeing, and restore the environment," says David Bornstein in his book *How to Change the World Social Entrepreneurs and the Power of New Ideas.*[11]

Among the ideas, which have provided promise to thousands around the world, is a program of innovative finance called 'microfinance.' While traditional finance of business often involves a business seeking loans to capitalize projects for infrastructure, growth, purchase of inventory and the like, microfinance does the same, only with smaller loans. Among the early innovators of this method of finance was Bill Drayton. Bornstein tells Drayton's story: In 1978, Drayton was the assistant administrator of the US Environmental Protection Agency and decided to establish an organization to support leading social entrepreneurs around the world. Drayton was interested in looking for the people with compelling visions who possessed creativity and determination to see their vision through to conclusion. Drayton wanted to find people who were seeking to leave their 'scratch on history,' as he coined his want. In his estimation, finding these people and then aiding their work through finance and resources would be the single most powerful thing he could do to speed up development and democratization around the globe.[12]

To bring about his vision, Drayton created the organization Ashoka: Innovators for the Public. Ashoka was a famous Indian emperor of the 3rd century BC and was responsible for unifying much of South Asia. Moreover, he pioneered innovations in both economic development and social welfare. Drayton considered Ashoka one of history's most tolerant, global-minded, and creative leaders. As Drayton and his colleagues began to establish Ashoka, they traveled widely, seeking to learn and interview the brightest and most innovative people they could find in developing nations. Among their innovators they found was forty-five-year-old Gloria de Souza, a teacher in Bombay, India.[13] De Souza had been teaching while harboring a dream to transform education across India. Her experience with students had led her to recognize that a more hands-on approach outside the classroom gave the best results. While the standard during the early 1970s had been a listen-and-repeat-after-me method, she took students on field trips to learn about birds, architecture, and flora and fauna. She pursued an active interest in helping students to place their hands on their learning and to experience it firsthand. Her methods were unappreciated by most of her fellow Indian teachers as she pushed to have schools adopt her method of education. She called it Environmental

Studies (EVS). Resistance was strong for many years but aided by Drayton and Ashoka, De Souza found the time and financial commitment to pursue her dream of nationalizing her educational methods. Eventually, by the end of the 1980s, India had adopted her methods of education as the official standard of instruction for grades one through three. Her work has been a driving force, influencing a generation of teachers and curriculum development in India, and she continues to seek methods to adapt the methods to different environments, such as rural and tribal areas.

In his book *The Life You Can Save: Acting Now to End World Poverty?*, Peter Singer cites several promising examples of microfinance institutions demonstrating positive progress. In 1976, Muhammad Yunus, then head of the Department of Economics at Chittagong University in Bangladesh, established the primary microfinance model. While visiting a village to research poverty, he observed a group of women who were borrowing money from local moneylenders at high interest rates in order to fund their furniture-building business. At the rates established, the possibility of sustained profitability was nearly impossible, so Yunus took the equivalent of twenty-seven dollars US from his own pocket and lent it to the group of forty-two women. With only sixty-four cents loaned per person to forty-two women, Yunus launched these women into independence from moneylenders and toward a meaningful way to work themselves out of poverty. Observing their success, he established a system with the local government to provide small loans to villagers. Over the ensuing six-year period, thousands of loans were made and repaid with an extremely high rate of repayment. As the program expanded, loans were offered across Bangladesh and grew to more than seven million microfinance recipients. Moreover, over six billion dollars of capital was repaid at a 97% repayment rate.[14]

While this program provided a model for microcredit all over the world, 'did it reduce poverty?' To that end, two former hedge-fund employees, Holden Karnofsky and Elie Hassenfeld, had already begun to tackle this important question over a broad spectrum of charitable endeavors. As successful hedge fund analysts, they had begun a system of evaluating charities to determine how effective the organizations were at creating impactful changes. As they embarked on the quest, they created a method to determine results over a broad spectrum of measures. In their study, they evaluated relative costs associated with actual life-saving results and compared this to the stated results that charities claimed. Their findings were enlightening because they substantiated actual true costs associated with saving lives. But saving lives was not the only measure of a relative change in poverty transformation; they looked for further evidence that charities were gaining ground on the poverty of the world. In their research, they discovered evidence that microfinance was impacting the likelihood of gainful employment, hunger reduction in households, and overall impoverished status change. While the numbers were small, an 11% improvement in likelihood of employment, 6% less likely to experience severe hunger, and 7% less likely to be classified as impoverished, these findings were a positive step and demonstrated impact.[15]

Successful strategies using microfinance, educational programming, and active policy change to move away from our need to accumulate over egalitarian fairness will continue to have a major impact. Though the effect may seem small relative to the needs that exist around the world, the only reason the impact is small is because we have not created enough desire on the part of the greater majority of the world to make poverty alleviation a priority. Even in the poorest nations, the desire to help their own poor is surprisingly low. In many instances, because of the outside influences of NGOs, the local people feel it is incumbent upon the NGOs to do the heavy lifting and make the changes for them. This scenario is not unlike the challenges in America we face with entitlement programs. The balance between helping, programming, and letting people do it themselves is like a tightrope walk. The long steadying pole we carry across the divide from poverty to sufficiency has to be carefully balanced, and the walk will take time. But, as we develop and change ourselves as individuals, we will also discover our world will change, too. History is a good measure to examine how we use the knowledge of others to advance our ways of doing things. The Etruscans and other ancient civilizations have provided examples of ingenuity that they used to provide for the needs of the people living during their time.

What Can We Learn from Ancient Civilizations to Help our Problems Today?

The Etruscans were a civilization of significant prominence, which had its most powerful presence during the 8th century BC until the 2nd century BC. Their origins are uncertain, but the Etruscans inhabited the central and northern regions of Italy. Remarkably, they were able to create vast wealth and develop intricate methods for sustaining a rich and powerful life. One of their most remarkable feats of their time was the creation of a vast water and sanitation process capable of handling the dense populace. Their sanitation and aqueduct system became the forerunner for much of the system employed in Rome during its reign and following. Through a vast system of underground water tunnels, the Etruscans created a system to dispose of sewage and waste that would drain into the nearby Tiber River. Though often praised for its inventive methods and the eventual influence on Roman water systems, the sewage system fell short in its intended result. As the populace of city centers continued to grow in ancient Etruria and then Rome, the sewage problem grew steadily with disease a byproduct of the close proximity people to the sewage system. Recycling waste was not one of the original ideas of the Etruscans but came into fashion during the era of Roman Emperor Vespasian in 69-79 AD. Vespasian, seeking solutions to the rising budgetary problems his empire was experiencing, created a system of payment for latrines as a type of tax. He further moved the latrines and their operational process to cleaners who had discovered the ammonia in urine was useful for cleaning clothing, thereby creating a secondary recycling rationale for the human waste previously only thought to be unusable waste. Vespasian recognized that when society connected a value to something previously only thought of as waste, there is a remarkable opportunity to be transformational and solve societal problems.[16]

Similarly, recycling programs are taking root around the world to battle the burgeoning waste problems. In Honduras, plastic bottles, called ecobricks, are used to build walls, homes, and social gathering places. Once considered useless, communities collect the discarded plastic bottles and bags. Then, bricks are created by stuffing the plastic bottles with dirt, sand, and the bags that formerly littered the landscape. The new bricks are stronger than traditional bricks when packed tightly and now provide affordable shelter for families. Andreas Froese Germen, founder of Eco-Tec, began using this technology in 2001 with a vision to eliminate the waste problem in his country and provide economical housing. Since inception, Germen has worked with governments and NGOs to build more than fifty eco-friendly projects in Honduras, Columbia, and Bolivia. He has won numerous environmental awards for innovation, and further developed technology to build water tanks using plastic bottles.[17]

The advantage of using plastic bottles include:

1. Low cost
2. Non-brittle (unlike regular bricks)
3. Absorbs abrupt shock loads: Since they are not brittle, they can take heavy loads without failure
4. Bio-climatic
5. Re-usable
6. Less construction material
7. Easy to build
8. Green construction

India produces over 300,000 tons of e-waste annually. E-waste is discarded computers, cell phones, printers, ink cartridges, monitors, and old television sets. A growing problem in industrialized countries like India, some local residents have discovered ways to capitalize on this waste and turn it into profitable business. In Dharavi, Mumbai, one of the densest slums in the world exists and was the slum immortalized in director Danny Boyle's Oscar-winning film Slumdog Millionaire. Within Dharavi, it is estimated nearly eighty thousand workers have created an informal sector of employment, dismantling and reprocessing roughly half a million tons of e-waste each year. Much of the work is done by hand and without protective gear to guard against the known toxins in old electronics. However, older women, who do much of the segregating and cleaning of waste, are still thankful for the opportunity waste provides them for economic support. Children, working on the periphery, also help by transporting materials by bicycle or foot and sorting through mounds of tiny components pulled from circuit boards. The resourcefulness of this enterprise and the positive environmental impact are remarkable.[18] Still, the piles of garbage, the smelly stench, and disease-laden material that these children and women handle isn't ideal. The tragedy is the absolute lack of waste management and population density that has created this dump. This is the symptom of their poverty and these courageous and resourceful workers are making the best of a bad situation.

Mother's Day and the Heroic Efforts of Two Women to Raise Awareness

Many of our national observances in the United States are steeped in rich historical events leading up their nationalization. Memorial Day and Independence Day are two examples that have a powerful significance and hold great honor for Americans. Another day in which we honor our mothers, which occurs in May, is probably not as well understood for its significance. As well, Mother's Day provides a lesson that every day people who are unwilling to accept the status quo can leave their legacy stamped on history and in the process change millions of lives.

The origin of Mother's Day has its earliest start in the spring celebrations of ancient Greece in honor of Rhea, the Mother of the Gods. During the 1600s, the early Christians of England celebrated Mary, the mother of Christ, as recognition for her gallant effort and gift she provided humanity. Later, as the recognition and observance of this day began to evolve, it was eventually expanded to include all mothers and became known as Mothering Sunday. The day was celebrated on the fourth Sunday of Lent, which was the forty-day period leading up to Easter. Mothering Sunday became a national holiday in England, recognized to pay tribute to the mothers of England.

Traditions began to develop during Mothering Sunday in England, including the restful permission given to servants of the wealthy to return to their homes and honor their mothers. Making a cake, called a mothering cake, was also implemented by many as a way to bring a festive touch to the holiday in honor of all mothers. With time and the spread of Christianity throughout Europe, the holiday began to coexist with and transform to a holiday known as 'Mother Church.' Mother Church provided a day when the spiritual power that gave all people life and protected them from harm was acknowledged.

As exploration abroad and colonial expansion of the Americas continued, the holiday of Mothering Sunday eventually discontinued because little interest existed and time constraints became stronger. It was not until the mid-19th century when American activist Julia Ward Howe suggested a day to promote peace among mothers. She issued a manifesto for peace at the international peace conferences in London and Paris. Howe was horrified with the carnage of the Civil War and the Franco-Prussian War and wanted to bring mothers together to rally for peace and put an end to the senseless killing that had taken millions of young men and women too early.

Her one-woman crusade for peace was an appeal to womanhood to rise against war. Impassioned and resolute, she composed a powerful plea in 1872 called the Mother's Day Proclamation and had it translated into several languages for wide distribution internationally. Her crusade brought her before the Woman's Peace Party Congress that same year as she worked tirelessly to promote a 'Mother's Day for Peace' to be celebrated on June 2.

Her efforts were met with some success in these early days as she was eventually able to organize a Mothers' Day for Peace observance in Boston on the second Sunday in June. The observance took place for ten consecutive years and inspired woman in eighteen cities in America to hold Mother's Day for Peace gatherings. Throughout her lifetime, she championed efforts to sustain the observance and bring attention to the need for peace. However, her effort eventually lost traction to have this day become a national observance when she turned her attentions toward other causes as they related to the observance of peace and end of war. Nonetheless, her sustained role in singularly having a vision and determined action to make her thoughts on war and peace known can be credited as the forerunner of the observance of the Mothers' Day we now have every year in America on the second Sunday of May.

Howe's courage and sustained efforts were not without inspiration and effort from a series of bold acts by a predecessor. Preceding her efforts, in the 1870s Marie Reeves Jarvis, a young Appalachian homemaker, had begun a quest to raise awareness in her community to improve sanitation by having a 'Mothers' Friendship Day.' Jarvis had decided to act in a way unlike the typical women of the day and organize and bring conscious awareness to a problem that required change. Many of her contemporaries were satisfied to primarily take care of their homes and families but Jarvis had her passions on the healing of a nation after the Civil War. In 1868, she worked for better sanitary conditions for both sides of the conflict that had torn America in two during this bloody era. Her efforts toward both Confederate and Union soldiers was equally placed in humanitarian education and aid. Ann was instrumental in saving thousands of lives by teaching women in her Mothers' Friendship Clubs the basics of nursing.[19]

Howe's resolve to bring about peace and end the killing drove her relentless pursuit to see Mother's Day become a national holiday. Her example sheds light on the strong effort and it requires bringing about change in the world. Moreover, she is also another example that one woman, one man can make a difference. If we find our cause, our issue that keeps us up at night thinking, 'This is wrong, people don't deserve to live like this or be treated this way,' we are knocking on the door of the issue we can have the most profound impact to change. Sometimes beginning with small steps first and then larger steps gives more clarity to move your agenda of change forward. Often others come alongside your ideas and vision, and eventually a movement is created. Every great change in the world began with an idea first and then someone who was willing to say, "We can change the world."

Shared Cooperation in our Daily Lives

For a sixteen-year-old in America, the potential for a life of freedom and exploration grows wings through the small business-sized card with a picture and pertinent personal information called a 'driver's license.' However, this card is not easy to obtain without gaining knowledge and understanding of guidelines and laws, the rules of the road. Prior to offering the privilege to a teen, there are classroom requirements to sit in on possible scenarios a driver might experience while navigating the roads behind the wheel of two-ton metal object called a motor vehicle. Following the course of study, a series of lessons are provided by a trained instructor and parent to further help a new driver gain necessary experience to make trusted decisions on the road. All of this effort is provided in the hope the new driver will be safe to himself and to others who are working in a cooperative effort that takes place in virtually all walks and drives of life around the globe. The cooperative effort is called the commute, and billions participate daily from Singapore to Scotland and down to Chile. People are now accustomed to the 'need' for an automobile and the ability to reach places quickly.

But this 'need' and the enormous effort to keep the experience safe for everyone requires a price. The price in some instances can mean the taking of a life or a lifetime of handicap because of carelessness. Although not all accidents are serious, they do have a common element, trauma, associated with them and the possible risk of death. For this reason, drivers are trained over and over again to pay attention, stay alert, avoid accidents, and drive safely. Drive safely! Driving safely is a mantra of cooperation heard around the world. This message is universally accepted to be a good idea and is a shared experience the majority of the world believes in.

With the thought that we need to drive safely, let's take a closer look at the daily commute and how this cooperative effort can shed light on what is possible on our planet and with our collective efforts to work in harmony. Suppose you're driving on the highway in a large metropolitan city in America and you merge onto the highway for your morning commute. It's 8:00 a.m. and you've left in plenty of time to drive and arrive promptly ready to work at 9:00. As you drive along, you are aware of the safe driving distances while applying brake and accelerator accordingly. You are aware of slight variations in road grade and make small adjustments to the steering wheeling as needed. The number of cars on the road and the type of vehicles, along with the conditions of the day, all work in concert in your mind to establish yourself as one among the many cooperating together to move from one place to another, working to arrive at a destination safely. While some will be traveling to a destination near your ultimate stop, many are likely traveling through your city. It's unlikely you will ever know any of the commuters you are choosing to share this cooperative effort with this day. However, your intimate knowledge of their personality, preferences, color of their skin, nationality, or ability does not affect your willingness to share a cooperative effort with them on this morning. ***You have joined them in a cooperative TRUST!***

As you drive on and near your exit ramp, there's a disturbance in the distance. A truck seems to be applying its brake and swerving in a pattern out of character to the other cars speeding along the road. As you see this obvious deviation from normal driving, you imagine a series of possible responses to respond and keep yourself and others around you safe. Your response to this unsafe driving may be slowing down—taking your foot off the accelerator, and applying the brake. You may choose to move over to another lane to distance yourself from the truck ahead. Or you may move all the way over to the shoulder and simply stop your vehicle and allow the swerving truck to continue on as you make a choice to not add more variables to the possible traffic accident event that could unfold.

Your thoughts as you take action may wildly gravitate toward a variance of judgments surrounding the meaning of the swerving truck. You may be angry with the driver for being reckless saying, "What's a matter with that guy up there?!" You may also notice your fear for yourself and others. Your awareness has been heightened and your sensory system is now alarmed regardless of the response you take. Your choices and the emotions you express are a result of a desire to maintain a safe cooperation with others around and to preserve the precious life you live. At this moment, you don't want to die and leave your family! This scenario plays out daily everywhere. Shared cooperation on the road with imperfect humans operating heavy pieces of metal on round rubber wheels is a one of the most common practices today. We expect a cooperative effort and safety.

Yet, we also know it is not entirely safe and being killed in a car accident is a risk associated with driving.

Our awareness of the possible risks of driving a car as a commuter does not stop us from joining in the cooperative effort. Because it's *important* to us, we choose to *take the risk*. We make the choice, ascribing value to the experience and believing the risk–reward ratio is tilted in our favor. Therefore, we get behind the wheel and take to the road. We also recognize there are elements of this daily cooperative effort that we will need to trust our own judgment relative to an unsafe event that could unfold as the reckless truck swerving to and fro on the highway. *Trust* is required. Cooperation between others and ourselves requires trust, and we believe in our system of education and cooperation enough to trust our safety when we venture onto the road with thousands of other commuters.

If cooperative trust is possible on the road in a daily commute, is it not possible in our lives in other places? Pause and ask yourself to think about the things you come to accept and the cooperative efforts you make every day. Reflect for a moment on the areas of your life where trust is slim or nonexistent and why the trust has not grown in these places. If we move back to the hypothetical commuter scenario, let's examine the role of the truck in our mind and where we might find ourselves stuck, or still sitting on the side of the road as the commuters of life whiz by on their way to their destinations. If we'd seen this truck swerving and we made up a belief system in our mind that *all trucks* are unsafe and should be avoided, we would have some fairly hard choices to make before turning the ignition key and getting back on the highway.

If our paradigm from this moment forward went something like this, 'When I see a truck, I don't trust its unfamiliar behavior; it could hurt me or others for whom I care,' then we are paralyzed. There may be thousands of trucks speeding along the highway, and although immense by comparison to our smaller vehicle, they are driving the correct speed and maintaining orderly lane management. However, our one unfortunate observation, which didn't even end in an accident, has paralyzed our trust from entering the highway again. A parallel thought regarding cooperation is also relevant as it relates to working together internationally and locally with people of different ethnic backgrounds. Although we've seen harmful acts on television, listened to radio accounts of bloodshed, or been told by others that certain populations might do harm to us, we must recognize and *trust* our judgment to discern when we should get off the highway or avoid a possible accident rather than completely avoid the 'unsafe truck.' We must recognize when it is safe to trust people who are different than our color, race, nationality, abled ability, or other attributes. ***Diversity in the human species is not supposed to be feared, but instead can be celebrated and, in fact, is necessary to engage the continual improvement in the human species.***

When we accept that all trucks are unsafe or all rich people can't be trusted, we limit our possibilities. ***If we don't allow our families to experience diverse populations around the globe and even in our own community, we handicap our mind, our heart, and our ability to improve the planet and ourselves.*** Our worldview narrows with each passing generation and eventually the puzzle we see as the world becomes virtually so small, is nearly impossible to fit any irregular experiences or opportunity into our matrix of possibilities. We then relegate our lives to a lifetime of struggle and unfulfilled destiny where our life experience will mostly be lived from the side of the road, the bench, or the small closet cell of a shrunken four-roomed box we have created in our mind.

However, if we become willing participants to encounter diversity, trust change, recognize danger and avoid it when required, we come to know a new kind of life filled with cooperative effort. With this newfound cooperation, we recognize we are connected and responsible for caring for one another. We recognize people's needs sooner and act more quickly to help. Our behaviors are learned responses, and just as we have the ability to cooperate on the road with one another, we also have the same ability wired within our consciousness. We are capable of amazing lives! We are capable of creating beautiful lives! We are capable of caring and loving one another and practicing God's second commandment: to love your neighbor as yourself.

Geoffrey Canada: Harlem Children's Zone

Previously in chapter four, we introduced Mr. Geoffrey Canada and his dynamic education program called the Harlem Children's Zone. The hallmark of the Harlem's Children's Zone is a comprehensive approach to solving the truancy, drug addiction, and failed systems plaguing the youth of Harlem. Canada recognized that children growing up in Harlem are less likely to succeed not because they are unable but because the methods and opportunity afforded them are limited. Schools and, more importantly, the home life these youths experience were important factors in ultimate success or failure.

Helping Canada to construct a more successful education program was a discovery he made in children's language development. Hart and Risley, from the University of Kansas, set out to determine the origins of developmental variations that existed from the poorest and wealthiest children. What Hart and Risley discovered was groundbreaking. They found that vocabulary growth differed dramatically by class, and the gap between the poorest and the wealthy opened earlier than originally thought. By studying families closely and spending extensive time within the family structure for an extensive two-year period, they were able to determine that children of professional parents had larger vocabularies. They found the professional, wealthier families would speak more often to their children and with greater use of expanded language. It was discovered by age three that the gap in vocabulary was nearly two to one when comparing professional families to families on welfare. Three-year-olds in professional parent homes had a vocabulary of 1,100 words while welfare parent homes struggled with only a 525-word vocabulary. Moreover, the average IQ of professional children was 117 compared to welfare children's IQ of 79.[22]

Recognizing the distinct differences between the professional and welfare children, Hart and Risley sought to understand what the exact variations were that led to the dramatic differences in these children. What they found was remarkable. In professional homes, children would hear their parents speak 487 separate utterances from one-word commands to full soliloquies every hour, whereas in a welfare home children heard only 178 *words* hourly. Expanding on this discovery, this meant in welfare homes a child was likely to hear around ten million words addressed to him by age three but in a professional home there would be *thirty* million words spoken to a child.[23]

The differences did not stop in the quantity of language spoken, either. Hart and Risley also found children in welfare homes were more apt to hear more words of discouragement than encouragement than their counterparts in professional homes. By age three, the average professional child would hear about five hundred thousand encouraging words while only eighty thousand discouraging. In the welfare homes, *the ratios were reversed.* Welfare homes spoke eighty thousand encouragements and two hundred thousand discouragements. They further found that as a child heard more words, his language complexity also increased. Professional children were afforded additional language cues beyond the normal child-raising basic language commands. Complex sets of extra words and phrases along with additional discussions and abstractions led to more opportunities for professional children to build important and vital language development.[24]

Hart and Risley were further able to demonstrate that IQ was most closely related to the amount and kind of language spoken in a home and not the socioeconomic status, race, or anything else measured. Hearing frequent discouragements along with prohibitions was most closely related to a stifled IQ, whereas affirmations, questions, and complex sentences had a constructive effect on IQ. Because wealthier parents were speaking frequently and with greater affirmation, they were providing an advantage for their children, which continued to grow.[25]

As a result of these findings and other data suggesting early and often intervention was paramount to educational success, Canada embarked on a new paradigm. If parents had to speak to their children differently in poor homes to secure a brighter future, then educating new parents how to speak and act with their babies and young children would certainly be vital. The answer would become 'baby college.' With the help of the

Robin Hood Foundation and T. Berry Brazelton, a basic parenting skills curriculum was created. Covering nine weeks and emphasizing new sets of skills many young parents found foreign, the Baby College program has steadily grown and has been the catalyst to drive the educational process Geoffrey Canada now refers to as the conveyor belt.[26]

The conveyor belt is the ladder to success that Canada has discovered is necessary to thwart the destructive influences of poverty and inner-city chaos taking so many young people today. As he discovered, many of the job training programs, social services, and aid based programs were targeting young people too late. Many of the cognitive skills and social etiquettes were absent or lacking in any significant way to achieve success because they simply were not instituted sooner. As he discovered through James Heckman's work in economics, there was little difference in the cognitive abilities of children born to college graduates and high school dropouts at age one. But by age two, a sizable gap emerged and by age three a small canyon began to unearth.[27]

In consequence, Canada launched a systematic and complete educational program from birth until age eighteen and high school graduation to stop the abysmal failures moving through the school system and into the cultural populace. If the data was correct and the necessary interventions had to occur early and regularly throughout the entirety of the educational process to cease the unending failures, then the only solution would be full educational coverage throughout a child's maturing lifecycle.

As a result, Canada discovered when programs were initiated early to help young parents change their behavior and speak to their babies, their results changed dramatically. Now boasting a 92% acceptance rate into college, children who move through the Harlem Children's Zone process are given similar opportunities to succeed as wealthier children receive. As well, there have been over five thousand graduates of the Baby College program, seeding a transformation and rippling effect of change throughout the community.[28]

Right to Play

Every child has a right to play; of course they do! Every child has a right to play and take part in games of laughter and fun. Children play, that's just what they do! However, for half of the children alive today, this is not the case. Of the 2.8 billion children living on the planet today, over half are in families that live in indescribable poverty. Barely able to survive and without the means to provide the enrichment necessary to foster the emotional and physical rewards of play, over 1.4 billion children live without ever realizing the joy of sport, play, the arts, music, or a vast cultural experience many children receive from parts of the world living in economic prosperity. These remote and sometimes urban settings are devoid of play. As Goossens details in *Right to Play: Every Child Has the Right to Play*, children living in poverty have never known what play means in their lives. They have never had the tools, coaching, or simple mentoring necessary to even teach the most basic childhood games many youngsters play around the world.[29]

For Johann Olav Koss, a triple world skating champion and winner of four Olympic gold medals this was unacceptable. Growing up in Norway with parents who were committed to exposing Johann to a life outside Norway, his parents took him on travels to Egypt, Africa, and India. Johann further had the education and experience garnered from parents who were both doctors and dedicated to the suffering and sick. As he says, he knew early in his life at the age of eleven he wanted to do certain things. "I wanted to be a world champion skater, to study medicine, and to be of help to children."

Lessons he learned in skating transcended and added virtue to his life in meaningful ways. Growing up, he skated with his brother at a local skating club in Norway. He recalls his father's supportive words: "It's more important to get a little better each time than actually winning." He also recalls: "While I was skating, I learned something very important. Athletes—even the most successful athletes, myself included—lose more than they win. Yet there is no harm in that, as we all know that failure is part of the whole. What is more, to become very good we have to accept many mistakes. They teach us a lot, whilst simply to get on with the most important! One can change one's tactics or try out something different, but one should never give up."[30]

Johann goes on to credit his dynamic, caring pursuit to the love of his parents. "Both my father and mother are doctors. Their door was always open to all in need of help. For my part, caring about others and looking after others has always been a natural thing to do."

Guiding principles and moral virtues guided Johann to develop Right to Play. "I founded Right to Play so the world should be a healthier, safer place for children. I think that can happen through sport and play. Why? Take a few hundred boys, put them somewhere where there is nowhere else to go and nothing for them to do. What happens next? They start looking for trouble. In refugee camps and internally displaced camps all over the world there are eleven million men and boys. They have nothing to strive for, no hope of a better life, and there is nothing for them to do. Then the problems start; violence and sexual abuse rear their ugly heads. There is no schooling for the children, and adults start neglecting themselves. Yet if you can give them something to do, such as taking part in sport and in play, some sense of meaning enters their lives. That is what we are doing in Right to Play, we return that power of courage and strength to young and old through sport and play."

One example of the powerful role the message of Right to Play can have on young people is cited in Goossens' book, *Right to Play*. In Sierra Leone, while working with authorities from various organizations including FIFA (Federation International de Football Association), a young girl in despair is discovered by Johann Olav Koss while visiting a local project. Inquiring why her sorrow hangs ominously over her with such power, he learns that while she has been able to secure a job sewing to support her daughter, she had now become an outcast in her own village. Johann learns she had been a child soldier for rebels in her country, providing cooking and cleaning for soldiers while they fought. During this time, she had become pregnant by one of the soldiers and had a baby girl. When peace had returned and she was able to return once more to her village, her parents and the community would have nothing to do with her. Feeling helpless now, she had arrived at her only possible solution, that to have a better life she would have to return to the rebel forces and their way of life.

Knowing this would be a grave mistake, Johann pleads with her not to return and to wait so he can work something out for her. Moving now to action, he develops a plan with members of the Right to Play organization in Sierra Leone to train her as a coach in their program. Every day for an hour or two, they will work with her and give her an opportunity to find new meaning and purpose in her life, alleviating the despair and shame she was experiencing stemming from the judgments of her community.

After some months, Johann receives a letter from this young girl with an upbeat note of possibility. Her life has absolutely changed in remarkable ways as she finds new meaning in taking part in the activities and coaching programs offered by Right to Play. She has found new friends and acceptance in the group. Moreover, in the time that has passed her parents have now softened and come to accept her new situation. Together with her daughter, she has been welcomed home by her family. [31]

Hope is the thread and the tapestry that exists within the Right to Play system and is apparent in all their processes and efforts with children. Every situation, regardless of the country or the dire circumstances, is significant to the people affected by hardships. Whether children, adults, or seniors, all people living desire acceptance, love, hope, and want to feel a sense of being needed for something. The deterioration of the human spirit and the demoralizing downfall into poverty's deepest recesses that can eventually lead to losing hope is sometimes swift and at other times a gradual, slow fall. When a child is the victim, this should incite outrage in anyone who has a conscience and a heart.

Gear for Goals (G4G)

Similar to Johann Olav Koss, one of the most troubling observations I have made in areas of extreme poverty is the lack of equipment children have available to play sports and thus garner the emotional and physical rewards sports can provide. The same blighted lack also exists for musical instruments and resources in the arts genre. The enormous holes poverty leaves in most of the world and the lack of adequate attention afforded this vital need by charities, NGOs, and local governmental leadership is unfortunate. As Johann recognized, and I have also witnessed when children are provided with access to play, sports, and the equipment necessary to have fun and competition, they thrive. Hope is palpable in the eyes of a child who has the opportunity to kick a soccer ball, catch a baseball, toss a Frisbee, or paint a picture. Learning how to play a chord on a guitar or blow a series of notes on a clarinet are all ways to open and unlock vast areas of resources untapped by poverty alleviation methods currently.

As I discovered in the establishment of our sports and arts program, called Gear for Goals (G4G), there are billions of dollars in sports items and musical instruments going unused in America. They sit in garages, basements, and in closets, waiting for a child to use them like the unwanted toys in the movie Toy Story. At one time, old bats, baseball mitts, and soccer balls were used and cared for by a child, but as children grow up and move on to other interests, often these once-cherished items become an afterthought. However, we recognized an opportunity and created methods to access this sports/music/arts equipment and get it into the hands of needy children domestically and internationally.

Using drives with clubs, schools, and churches, our Gear for Goals project has been able to provide new and gently used sports equipment to over 450,000 children in twenty-nine countries since 2012. Every month this number grows, and our eventual mission is to see that every child living in poverty has a chance to discover the arts and sport. Now children in the Dominican Republic who long to one day be the next Miguel Cabrera or Albert Pujols have their own mitt and ball to practice. No small achievement, many of the children who love baseball in the Dominican Republic play baseball although the entire sports league might have only eight or nine mitts, one helmet, and two bats for over two hundred children. In Kenya, an average mid-grade number five soccer ball, which costs fifteen to twenty dollars in the US costs thirty to fifty, the extra costs related to taxes, tariffs, and shipping. While fifty dollars would be expensive in the Unites States, it is nearly impossible for anyone living in the poorest regions of Kenya and the rest of East Africa to afford a soccer ball. Why? Well, the average man or woman in Kenya earns only about thirty to fifty dollars a month! If you think about this, it would be like a soccer ball costing two to three thousand dollars in the United States on the average wage of an entry-level worker in the US. The same is true for baseball bats in the Dominican Republic, as the average baseball bat costs $150 to $250, and most people earn this in a month. So once again, it becomes almost impossible to ever buy a baseball bat for a son or daughter who may want to pursue a passion for baseball. Yet, in America we have millions of baseball bats that are now unused. This same scenario plays out across the board with other sports, arts, and music resources.

Where few commodities exist and there are limited opportunities for young people to achieve an education or move ahead economically, using athletic ability or artistic prowess are ways to overcome adversity and poverty. Certainly in the Dominican Republic, the game of baseball has had a powerful impact on the economy of the nation. While only ten million people live in the Dominican Republic on this tiny island shared with Haiti, there is a disproportionate number of Major League Baseball Players coming from the Dominican Republic relative to other nations, including the United States. The desire and the access to warm weather have fueled this explosion of talent, with huge economic impact. Now Major League Baseball funds programs, sports academies, and helps develop talented players. But there are still too many children who are excluded because the funding and availability of coaching and sports gear are restricted. Still, the salaries paid to professional players in Minor League Baseball and Major League Baseball, along with the positive impact of money spent in the Dominican economy, is a valuable example of the way sports can improve economic opportunity.

Summary Questions for Discussion

1. Rosa Parks' courageous decision to remain seated in the front of the Alabama bus she rode set the stage for a dramatic shift in America. But the process leading up to her act took many years of sacrifice. How do you imagine Rosa Parks might have felt that day? How do you believe it made others feel who challenged the status quo of America and said valiantly we deserve equality and the freedom the US Constitution guarantees?

2. History is replete with examples of systems created long ago that are still in use today. The Etruscans' sewage and waterway system is one such example. Can you think of other systems created in the past century, or even longer ago, that led to the modern-day examples we use today? How would your life be different if you did not have these modern day devices? Can you see the enormous capacity people have to change the world by the numerous examples of ingenuity we use today?

3. As Geoffrey Canada discovered while developing the Harlem Children Zone, children growing up in poverty fall behind early in life academically and intellectually because their parents' communication is often negative and insufficient. What steps or ideas can you come up with that could be a solution to this problem in addition to the Baby College program Canada created?

4. Gear for Goals (G4G) is a sports and arts charity that provides hope to children around the world living in poverty. What items that you are not using could help a child or a community? Create a plan for sharing your resources with others. Time, talent, and materials are all resources needed by people living in under-resourced regions of the world.

In Closing

As you can see from the examples discussed in this book, there is a commonality we all share with one another, and our ability to accept the similarities and look past the differences can be the beginning of something altogether remarkable. *We are all born with inherent needs from the moment we take our first breath, and the fact we were given a right to live is proof enough there is a God who loves us and wants us here.* However, when our internal desires to exercise greed, power, and domination over the weak and gentle within society incites our darker sides, the seeds of evil emotional darkness take hold of our hearts, and conscious acts of love and kindness become unattainable. It is only through an awakening, and sometimes enlightenment in the form of tragedy, are we reminded of our humanity and connection to the most desperate. As the great leader of India, Mahatma Gandhi said and was quoted previously in this book: "Earth provides enough to satisfy every man's need, but not every man's greed."

As Thom Hartmann writes in *The Last Hours of Ancient Sunlight*, cooperation was paramount to the survival of ancient civilizations that lived for thousands of years in peace. War, domination, and the desire to have more than were required for basic necessities of life were nearly absent in their cultures. Instead, cooperative efforts created a thoughtful democracy in which every member of a tribe would exercise a vote and the conscious decisions that would affect everyone within the community were valued. But many of these civilizations eventually perished when explorers came to their lands and cultivated their resources to enrich the mother nations in search of new wealth. The disease, hardships, and expectations, along with the brutal killing and enslavement of many, ultimately led to the annihilation of millions in various global regions of the world.[32]

Some argue that the destruction and eventual end to entire cultures that had survived for perhaps ten thousand years or more would only indicate they were not that strong, and that evolutionist ideals where the most powerful and dominant survive is correct. Therefore, the cultures of European and other societies who came and changed their ways of life and destroyed them were part of the natural order of the planet. However, we cannot make such assumptions in the short timeframe of only a few hundred years relative to the lifetime of planet earth, the solar system, and the many galaxies. The unfolding paradoxes and understanding we have of our planet, humanity, and all of creation give us small peeks of wonder with each new discovery. Like a curtain opening on a stage play where we are the audience and God is the playwright, our lives have significance. Every last one of God's creations has a purpose and relevance. They are interconnected from the smallest single-cell organism to the largest mammal, the whale.

Our interconnected lives are part of the master plan of God. We are created to need one another and cannot survive as newborn infants without care. If a new baby is left uncared for, abandoned, he will die without the nurturing of a caregiver. He needs food, shelter, clothing, the human touch, and language to bond and develop all of his faculties of life. There is an intelligent design that can be seen in the need for human care in a baby's survival. Even further, if we consider our connections as strands of love that piece us all together in a beautiful and colorful carpet, we will recognize our world can no longer be thought of as *us* and *them*. The time has come for our love and desire to act to simply come from a place of *us*. We are the makers of history and the determinants in the future of the planet. I have heard it said that God does not always demonstrate His loving desire through the supernatural, but instead uses our hands and hearts to be His extension. God used Moses in this way when Moses was called to lead the Hebrew people from their bondage in Egypt. He used Paul to preach the gospel of Jesus Christ and guided him almost single handedly to start the movement of Christianity. Moses did not come from royal lineage or have any special gifts that would have led people to see his emergent leadership as the entity that would free the Hebrew slaves from bondage. Though he was raised as a prince, his bloodline pointed to humble origins.

In the same way, we each must examine our calling and the prompting we may be hearing as a whisper from God that we are to do something. What is that something that is calling you? What is unacceptable to you that you know needs to change and maybe you have been talking about but not doing anything about? We all have things we complain about. We know there are significant problems that need our attention but we sit back and wait for someone else to lead. Why? Hopefully, you have gained some encouragement from the ideas and inspirations Todd and I have shared throughout this book. We've made a thorough examination of the causes of poverty and given a new way to look at the subject that has never been talked about before. As we stated in the introduction, it is our hope this book and the metaphors of the *waver* and *beggar* will become a launching point for a new conversation about poverty.

Hopefully, when you are given an opportunity to volunteer, to visit a country and help under-resourced people, or give financial assistance to a cause you are passionate about, you act with resolve to be a more active participant in the needed changes required to heal the dis-ease of the planet we've discussed. The issues of society facing us today are real and need our immediate attention. Poverty, illiteracy, gender inequality, hunger, lack of clean water, inadequate healthcare, ecological damage, human trafficking, genocide, civil war, terrorism, and so many issues need our attention.

As you consider your life's legacy you wish to leave, there are two questions to ask and contemplate. Perhaps taking time to pray, meditate, and journal your thoughts can crystalize your answers and give you some direction. As you finish this book, **let this be the start and not the end to your call to action**. Ask yourself these questions:

1. *Why am I here?*

In other words, why are you alive and what is your purpose? Every one of us has purpose or we would not have been born. But too often the purpose is lost or unclear. Even *beggars* have a purpose, as we detailed earlier in the book.

2. *What will I leave behind when I am no longer here?*

What is that *one* thing you want to be remembered for? We all are going to die; so when we have gone home with the Lord and our loved ones are mourning, what will they remember about you? Walt Whitman wrote in the poem, *O Me! O Life!* That "the powerful play goes on, and you may contribute a verse."

What will your verse be?

What will others who never knew you read about your life or share about the people you impacted? Impacting lives doesn't have to be magnanimous. Sometimes, believing our work has to be grand paralyzes the start to act. My mother taught me in the most gentle of ways with love and compassion that the message Jesus taught in the Good Samaritan parable is all that really needs to take place to be significant in the world. Many years ago, when she began working as a missionary in Kenya, she was boarding a bus with my younger brother in the busy bus stop area of Nakuru. Hundreds of buses were being loaded and they were parked in a seemingly chaotic, yet organized, stream. Thousands of people speaking many tribal languages loaded their belongings with some of their personal items being secured on the roofs of the buses. Seeing the organized chaos and calamity would make most of us uncomfortable and likely be insulated and highly protective for fear of harm or thievery. But in the midst of this chaos, my younger brother shared with me recently how my mother acted, how she did the one single thing we have written about throughout this book: she helped a woman who was beaten down by life and lying in a ditch. My mother, who passed away suddenly in February of 2016, aware of the needs of the most vulnerable all the way up to her death, spotted a woman lying half-naked in a ditch by the bus being jeered and laughed at. Onlookers gawked and made fun of her dirty, partially naked body as she ranted and lay in the ditch unable to stand on her feet. The woman was probably mentally sick. She was crazy, so people made fun of her instead of helping!

How often does this scenario play out around the world in exactly this way with mentally sick people, and on a larger scale with whole segments of populace that are the weak and the oppressed? People beaten by life, weak, fragile, broken, and needing someone to care about them and act for them are left to die alone in a ditch while being made fun of and criticized?

This was the *unacceptable* to my mother, and probably the reason it has become the same for me. Instead, though it embarrassed my younger brother and there was chaos all around, she went to her. She stopped what she was doing, boarding the bus, and went to this weakened and dirty, smelly woman, being laughed at and knelt down to her. She picked her up in her arms and told her God loves her and that she loved her, too. She touched her forehead and caressed her face gently with her hand, telling her how beautiful she was. She assured her that God loved her and she mattered to Him.

As my brother shared this story he admitted, in this moment he was embarrassed by the onlookers' critical judgment and jeers. But this didn't stop my mother from going to this woman and helping her. Leaving an indelible memory for my brother, I wonder again:

How many times do the criticisms and judgments we think may follow stop our call to act? How many times have we chosen to play small, to be safe, and to not act?

As we sat around the house on the day following my mother's passing, my stepfather recanted a story, again about my mother, that illustrated this question in action. Providing ministry in remote Nyahururu, Kenya, a woman wielding a large two-foot knife called a *panga* came storming into the church. Many in attendance, knowing this woman was crazy, were frightened and moved away to protect themselves from her. Onlookers who knew her said she had been crazy for many years and was dangerous! But my mother's courage and ultimate faith in Jesus instead led her to do something no one had the courage to do before: she held her arms open and went toward the ranting, insane woman. As she moved toward her and spoke, the woman allowed my mother to hug her and tell her simply,

"Jesus loves you." At that moment, the woman began to weep and dropped the *panga*, holding tightly to my mother's waist, and laid her head on my mother's shoulder. Instantaneously, she was healed and when my mother, stepfather, and younger brother left Nyahururu, residents said she never returned to her former self. From that moment, she was freed of the evil that had taken her soul.

But what would have happened to this woman if my mother had not had the courage to act? What if she had not trusted her instinct to embrace instead of run? I can honestly say I probably would have run or moved for protection if I was in that church on that day, too. But, my hope is that I will one day understand and have the trust in God to act selflessly and do what is right all the time because spirit leads me and not personal interests or fear. As I continue to grow in my love of Jesus and serving the poor, I grow with every experience of service, and I am still humbled and recognize I have a long way to go. You may also see in yourself the distance you need to travel to become the loving servant you are called by God to become.

I'll urge you again: ***don't let circumstances or the fact you don't have it all figured out stop your desire to act.***

Just start! Start digging a foundation of change and look around you. You'll find there are others who want to dig alongside you. Everyone has something they care about, and when you begin your journey, those who are drawn to the passionate cause you stand for will become your ally. Eventually, your small group will become an army and then a social revolution. ***Every great change started with an idea*** and a small group of dedicated servants. Servants I call Agents of Social Change have been the motor that has moved society to become better.

What will I leave behind when I am no longer here? On behalf of my mother, I'll answer this question mentioned earlier.

Amongst many other things, my mother leaves behind a woman who was changed not by force but by love. The community of Nyahururu said from that moment on, the crazy woman in the church never returned to her former self but was healed of her sickness and is no longer a danger to anyone. One life touched by a simple, selfless act of love.

Though my mother's passing has only occurred within hours of the time of this writing, I am certain the ripples of impact her life has had on thousands in Africa and around the world will reveal themselves in time. In the same way, we can each be determinants of the impact we will have by our decisions to act, serve, and care with compassion for others. My mother's life, and those of so many other people I admire, gives me inspiration and desire to become an Agent of Social Change, too.

What will be *your legacy* and what change do you want to see? As you take time to review the appendix of this book and begin to feel the call to action, remember the *waver* and *beggar* is inside everyone of us. We all have a *waver* and a *beggar* connecting us together, especially as we recognize that the two archetypes in ourselves make us similar, not different, from our brothers and sisters of the world. Whether you are serving in your own community near your home or halfway around the world, there are no true barriers between us. Our community is planet earth and we are all brothers and sisters.

It is no longer *us* and *them*, it is time to become just *US*.

BIBLIOGRAPHY

Chapter One

1   Strack, Fritz, Martin, Leonard L. and Stepper, Sabine. "Inhibiting and Facilitating Conditions of the Human Smile: A Nonobtrusive Test of the Facial Feedback Hypothesis." *Journal of Personality and Social Psychology* 54.5 (1988): 768-77. Web

2   Kahneman, Daniel. *Thinking, Fast and Slow*. New York: Farrar, Straus and Giroux, 2011. Print

3   *NIV Bible*. London: Hodder & Stoughton, 2007. Print

4   *Delta boys*. Dir. Andrew Berends. Perf. Nigerian Citizens. Storyteller Productions, 2012. Film.

5   *NIV Bible*. London: Hodder & Stoughton, 2007. Print

6   *NIV Bible*. London: Hodder & Stoughton, 2007. Print

Chapter Three

1   *The End of Poverty?* Dir. Philippe Diaz. Perf. Various. Ironweed Film Club, 2011. Film.

2   Jamison, Dennis. "Christopher Columbus and the Taino People." *Examiner. com*, n.p., n.d. Web. 22 Oct. 2014. http://www.examiner.com/article/christopher-columbus-and-the-taino-people

3   "Christopher Columbus: Explorer – EnchantedLearning.com." *Christopher Columbus: Explorer – EnchantedLearning.com*, n.p., n.d. Web. 20 Oct. 2014. http://www.enchantedlearning.com/explore

4   Encyclopedia Britannica. "Araucanian (people)." *Encyclopedia Britannica Online*, n.d. 22 Oct. 2014. Web.

5   Morris, Charles. *The great republic by the master historians*. New York: R.S. Belcher Co., 1902. Print.

6   Ferraro, Vincent and Rosser, Melissa. "Global Debt and Third World Development," in *World Security: Challenges for a New Century*, edited by Michael Klare and Daniel Thomas. St. Martin's Press, New York, 1994. 332-355.

7   *Park Avenue: Money, Power, and the American Dream—Why Poverty?* Dir. Alex Gibney. Danish Broadcasting Corporation, 2012.

8   "Milestones | Heartland Health Centers." *Heartland Health Centers*. Heartland Health Alliance, n.d. 08 Nov. 2014. Web.

9   Twist, Lynne and Barker, Teresa. *The Soul of Money: Transforming Your Relationship with Money and Life*. New York: Norton, 2003. Print.

10 "Climate Stabilization Targets." Climate Change at the National Academies. National Academy of Engineering, Institute of Medicine, National Research Council, 2012. Web.

Chapter Four

1   Roth, Mark. "Growing up Poor Can Affect Brain Development." Pittsburgh Post-Gazette. 1 Aug. 2010.

2   Roth, Mark. "Growing up Poor Can Affect Brain Development." Pittsburgh Post-Gazette. 1 Aug. 2010.

3   ""Epigenetics" Means What We Eat, How We Live and Love, Alters How Our Genes Behave." – Duke Medicine. Duke Medicine and News, 25 Oct. 2005.

4   "Your DNA May Carry a 'Memory' of Your Living Conditions in Childhood." Home Page. 20 Oct. 2011.

5   Jimmy Carter for the Nobel Foundation, "Text from the Nobel lecture given by the Nobel Peace Prize Laureate for 2002," Jimmy Carter Library and Museum, http://www.jimmycarterlibrary.gov/documents/jec/nobel/phtml.

6   Humes, Edward. *Garbology: Our Dirty Love Affair with Trash*. New York: Avery, 2012. Print.

7   Humes, Edward. *Garbology: Our Dirty Love Affair with Trash*. New York: Avery, 2012. Print.

8   Humes, Edward. *Garbology: Our Dirty Love Affair with Trash*. New York: Avery, 2012. Print.

9   Tough, Paul. *Whatever It Takes: Geoffrey Canada's Quest to Change Harlem and America*. Boston: Houghton Mifflin, 2008. Print.

Chapter Five

1   Stearns, Richard. *The Hole in Our Gospel*. Nashville, TN: Thomas Nelson, 2009. Print.

2   Hopper, Kim. *Reckoning with Homelessness*. Ithaca: Cornell UP, 2003. Print.

3   "World Giving Index 2013, A Global View of Giving Trends." Charities Aid Foundation, 1 Dec. 2013. Web.

4   Stearns, Richard. *The Hole in Our Gospel.* Nashville, TN: Thomas Nelson, 2009. Print.

5   "WORKING FOR THE FEW Political Capture and Economic Inequality." *Oxfam.org.* Oxfam, 20 Jan. 2014. Web. 4 Dec. 2014.

6   "Mahatma Gandhi Quotes." ThinkExist.com, n.d. Web. 4 Dec. 2014.

7   Aleem, Zeeshan. "The 85 Richest People in the World Now Own as Much Wealth as the Poorest 3.5 Billion." *Mic.* Policy. Mic, 24 Nov. 2014. Web. 4 Dec. 2014.

8   Ryall, Jenny. "The Giving Pledge: How to Join the New Billionaires' Club." NewsComAu. News Limited, 22 Nov. 2013. Web. 02 Mar. 2015.

9   "WORKING FOR THE FEW Political Capture and Economic Inequality." Oxfam.org. Oxfam, 20 Jan. 2014. Web. 4 Dec. 2014.

10 "WORKING FOR THE FEW Political Capture and Economic Inequality." Oxfam.org. Oxfam, 20 Jan. 2014. Web. 4 Dec. 2014.

11 "WORKING FOR THE FEW Political Capture and Economic Inequality." Oxfam.org. Oxfam, 20 Jan. 2014. Web. 4 Dec. 2014.

12 "World Poverty Statistics." Statistics Brain Research Institute, 8 July 2014. Web. 4 Dec. 2014.

13 "World Poverty Statistics." Statistics Brain Research Institute, 8 July 2014. Web. 4 Dec. 2014.

14 . "World Poverty Statistics." Statistics Brain Research Institute, 8 July 2014. Web. 4 Dec. 2014.

15 "World Poverty Statistics." Statistics Brain Research Institute, 8 July 2014. Web. 4 Dec. 2014.

16 "World Poverty Statistics." Statistics Brain Research Institute, 8 July 2014. Web. 4 Dec. 2014.

17 Scott, Matt. "40 Shocking Facts about Water." Matador Network, 30 June 2009. Web. 09 Dec. 2014.

18 Scott, Matt. "40 Shocking Facts about Water." Matador Network, 30 June 2009. Web. 09 Dec. 2014.

19 "World Poverty Statistics." Statistics Brain Research Institute, 8 July 2014. Web. 4 Dec. 2014

20 Scott, Matt. "40 Shocking Facts about Water." Matador Network, 30 June 2009. Web. 09 Dec. 2014.

21 Scott, Matt. "40 Shocking Facts about Water." Matador Network, 30 June 2009.

22 Scott, Matt. "40 Shocking Facts about Water." Matador Network, 30 June 2009. Web. 09 Dec. 2014.

23 "Matters of Scale – Spending Priorities." Worldwatch Institute, 1 Feb. 1999. Web. 4 Dec. 2014.

24 Scott, Matt. "40 Shocking Facts about Water." Matador Network, 30 June 2009. Web. 09 Dec. 2014.

25 "World Poverty Statistics." Statistics Brain Research Institute, 8 July 2014. Web. 4 Dec. 2014.

26 "Daily Amount of Food Waste in America Enough to Fill a Football Stadium." Natural News, n.d. Web. 13 Apr. 2015.

27 "7 Shocking Food Waste Statistics." *Chow The CHOW Blog*, n.p., n.d. Web. 13 Apr. 2015.

28 Britt, Robert Roy. "Global Food Shortage Becomes Urgent as Planet Warms." LiveScience. TechMedia Network, 05 June 2011. Web. 13 Apr. 2015.

29 "Global Illiteracy & Global Literacy Statistics." Global Illiteracy & Global Literacy *Statistics*, n.p., n.d. Web. 13 Apr. 2015.

30 "Matters of Scale – Spending Priorities." Worldwatch Institute, 1 Feb. 1999. Web. 4 Dec. 2014.

31 "2013 World Hunger and Poverty Facts and Statistics by World Hunger Education Service." World Hunger Education Service. Web. 4 Dec. 2014.

32 Castillo, Michelle. "U.S. Has Highest First-day Infant Mortality out of Industrialized World, Group Reports." CBSNews. CBS Interactive, 7 May 2013. Web. 09 Dec. 2014.

33 "Matters of Scale – Spending Priorities." *Worldwatch Institute*. Worldwatch Institute, 1 Feb. 1999. Web. 4 Dec. 2014

34 "National Debt of the United States." *Wikipedia*. Wikimedia Foundation, 12 May 2014. Web. 10 Dec. 2014.

35 "National Debt of the United States." *Wikipedia*. Wikimedia Foundation, 12 May 2014. Web. 10 Dec. 2014.

36 "National Debt of the United States." *Wikipedia*. Wikimedia Foundation, 12 May 2014. Web. 10 Dec. 2014.

37 Watts, Duncan J. *Six Degrees: The Science of a Connected Age*. New York: Norton, 2003. Print.

38 Huitt, W. and Hummel, J. *Educational Psychology Interactive: Cognitive Development*. n.p., 2003. Web. 08 Dec. 2014.

39 Bellis, Mary. "The History of Rubik's Cube – Erno Rubik." *About.com Inventors*. About.com, n.d. Web. 11 Dec. 2014.

40 Marinoff, Lou. The Middle Way: Finding Happiness in a World of Extremes. New York: Sterling Pub., 2007. 47-61. Print.

41 Marinoff, Lou. The Middle Way: Finding Happiness in a World of Extremes. New York: Sterling Pub., 2007. 47-61. Print.

42 Marinoff, Lou. The Middle Way: Finding Happiness in a World of Extremes. New York: Sterling Pub., 2007. 47-61. Print.

43 Marinoff, Lou. The Middle Way: Finding Happiness in a World of Extremes. New York: Sterling Pub., 2007. 47-61. Print.

44 Levi, Primo, S. J. Woolf, S. J. and Roth, Philip. *Survival in Auschwitz: The Nazi Assault on Humanity.* New York: Simon & Schuster, 1996. Print.

45 "The Freezing Homeless Child! (Social Experiment)." YouTube, n.d. Web. 13 Apr. 2015.

Chapter Six

1 Gans, Herbert J. *The War against the Poor: The Underclass and Antipoverty Policy.* New York, NY: Basic, 1995. Print.

2 "Born Good? Babies Help Unlock the Origins of Morality." *CBS News.* CBS Interactive, 18 Nov. 2012. Web. 12 Nov. 2014.

3 Gans, Herbert J. *The War against the Poor: The Underclass and Antipoverty Policy.* New York, NY: Basic, 1995. Print.

4 "Matthew 6:25-26." The Holy Bible: New International Version, Containing the Old Testament and the New Testament. Grand Rapids: Zondervan Bible, 1978. Print.

5 "2013 Poverty Guidelines." *ASPE.* U.S. Department of Health and Human Services, 24 Jan. 2013. Web. 11 Nov. 2014.

6 "Facts About the Minimum Wage." *The Heritage Foundation.* 30 Jan. 2014. Web. 13 Nov. 2014.

Chapter Seven

1 "Bible Gateway Passage: Isaiah 58:10 – New International Version." Bible Gateway, n.d. Web. 13 Nov. 2014.

2 "Bible Gateway Passage: Luke 10:25-37 – New International Version." Bible Gateway, n.d. Web. 13 Nov. 2014.

3 "Deuteronomy 10 NIV." Bible Hub, n.d. Web. 13 Nov. 2014.

4 "Psalm 82:4 NLT." Bible Hub, n.d. Web. 13 Nov. 2014.

5 "Isaiah 1:17 NLT." Bible Hub, n.d. Web. 13 Nov. 2014.

6 "Matthew 19:30 NIV." Bible Hub, n.d. Web. 13 Nov. 2014.

7 "How Many times Is the Word Poor in the Bible?" Answers Corporation, n.d. Web. 13 Nov. 2014.

8 "What the Bible Says About Poverty." Compassion International, n.d. Web. 13 Nov. 2014.

9 "Deuteronomy 8:3 NIV." Bible Gateway, n.p., n.d. Web. 13 Nov. 2014.

10 "Matthew 4:4 NIV." Bible Gateway, n.p., n.d. Web. 13 Nov. 2014

11 "Isaiah 41:17 NIV." Bible Gateway, n.p., n.d. Web. 14 Nov. 2014

12 "Luke 6:20-21 NIV." Bible Gateway, n.p., n.d. Web. 14 Nov. 2014.

13 "Matthew 5:3." Bible Hub: Search, Read, Study the Bible in Many Languages, n.p., n.d. Web. 14 Nov. 2014.

14 Donin, Hayim. *To Be a Jew: A Guide to Jewish Observance in Contemporary Life.* New York: Basic Books, 1972. Print.

15 "Helplessness (Forerunner Commentary)." Bible Tools, n.p., n.d. Web. 14 Nov. 2014.

16 "Helplessness (Forerunner Commentary)." Bible Tools, n.p., n.d. Web. 14 Nov. 2014.

17 "Isaiah 61:1 NIV." Bible Gateway, n.p., n.d. Web. 14 Nov. 2014.

18 "Matthew 10:30." Bible Hub: Search, Read, Study the Bible in Many Languages, n.p., n.d. Web. 14 Nov. 2014.

19 "Deuteronomy 15:7 NIV." Bible Gateway, n.p., n.d. Web. 14 Nov. 2014.

20 "Matthew 7:7-8 NIV." Bible Gateway, n.p., n.d. Web. 14 Nov. 2014.

21 Merriam-Webster's Collegiate Dictionary. Springfield: Merriam-Webster, Inc., 2003. Print.

Chapter Eight

1 "Maimonides Principles of Tzedakah." *Maimonides Principles of Tzedakah.* Ed. Rabbi Efraim Davidson. Do Jewish. Web. 19 Nov. 2014

2 Marinoff, Lou. *The Middle Way Finding Happiness in a World of Extremes.* New York: Sterling Ethos, 2007. Print

3 Hartmann, Thom. *The Last Hours of Ancient Sunlight: The Fate of the World and What We Can Do before It's Too Late.* Rev. and Updated ed. New York: Three Rivers, 2004. Print.

4 Poole, Robert M. "What Became of the Taíno?" Smithsonian Institute, 1 Oct. 2011. Web. 19 Nov. 2014.

5 Hartmann, Thom. *The Last Hours of Ancient Sunlight: The Fate of the World and What We Can Do before It's Too Late.* Rev. and Updated ed. New York: Three Rivers, 2004. Print.

6 Corbett, Steve and Fikkert, Brian. *When Helping Hurts: How to Alleviate Poverty without Hurting the Poor—and Yourself.* Chicago, IL: Moody, 2009. Print.

7 Corbett, Steve and Fikkert, Brian. *When Helping Hurts: How to Alleviate Poverty without Hurting the Poor—and Yourself.* Chicago, IL: Moody, 2009. Print.

8 Stern, Ken. *With Charity for All: Why Charities Are failing and a Better Way to Give.* New York: Doubleday, 2013. Print.

9 Stern, Ken. *With Charity for All: Why Charities Are failing and a Better Way to Give.* New York: Doubleday, 2013. Print.

10 Stern, Ken. *With Charity for All: Why Charities Are failing and a Better Way to Give.* New York: Doubleday, 2013. Print.

11 Hogan, Tori. *Beyond Good Intentions: A Journey into the Realities of International Aid.* Berkeley, CA: Seal, 2012. Print.

12 "Nova." *Newton's Dark Secrets.* Public Broadcasting Service, n.d. Television.

13 "Newton's Three Laws of Motion." Web. 21 May 2015. http://csep10.phys.utk. edu/astr161/lect/history/newton3laws.html

14 "Newton's Three Laws of Motion." Newton's Three Laws of Motion. Web. 21 May 2015. http://csep10.phys.utk.edu/astr161/lect/history/newton3laws.html

15 Watts, Duncan J. *Six Degrees: The Science of a Connected Age.* New York: Norton, 2003. 67-68. Print.

16 Mullainathan, Sendhil and Shafir, Eldar. *Scarcity: Why Having Too Little Means so Much.* New York: Macmillan, 2013. Print.

17 Mullainathan, Sendhil and Shafir, Eldar. *Scarcity: Why Having Too Little Means so Much.* New York: Macmillan, 2013. Print.

18 Mullainathan, Sendhil and Shafir, Eldar. *Scarcity: Why Having Too Little Means so Much.* New York: Macmillan, 2013. Print.

19 Mullainathan, Sendhil and Shafir, Eldar. *Scarcity: Why Having Too Little Means so Much.* New York: Macmillan, 2013. Print.

20 Mullainathan, Sendhil and Shafir, Eldar. *Scarcity: Why Having Too Little Means so Much.* New York: Macmillan, 2013. Print.

21 Mullainathan, Sendhil and Shafir, Eldar. *Scarcity: Why Having Too Little Means so Much.* New York: Macmillan, 2013. Print.

22 Murali, Vijaya and Oyebode, Femi. "The World Health Report 1995 – Bridging the Gaps." World Health Organization, n.d. Web. 21 June 2014.

23 Murali, Vijaya and Oyebode, Femi. "The World Health Report 1995 – Bridging the Gaps." World Health Organization, n.d. Web. 21 June 2014.

24 Funk, Dr. Michelle, Drew, Natalie, and Robertson, Patricia. "Mental Health, Poverty and Development." *Mental Health, Poverty, and Development.* World Health Organization, n.d. Web. 21 Nov. 2014.

25 "Horace Mann Biography." Bio.com. A&E Networks Television, n.d. Web. 19 Nov. 2014.

26 "A Solvable Problem." Teach for America, 2012. Web. 22 Nov. 2014.

27 "Education." *For All.* World Bank, 4 Aug. 2014. Web. 22 Nov. 2014.

28 Hillman, Arye and Jenkner, Eva. Economic Issues No. 33 – *Educating Children in Poor Countries.* International Monetary Fund, 2004. Web. 22 Nov. 2014.

29 Hillman, Arye and Jenkner, Eva. Economic Issues No. 33 – *Educating Children in Poor Countries.* International Monetary Fund, 2004. Web. 22 Nov. 2014.

30 Cardoza, Kavitha. "Graduation Rates Increase Around The Globe As U.S. Plateaus." *WAMU 88.5.* American University Radio, 21 Feb. 2102. Web. 22 Nov. 2014.

31 Cardoza, Kavitha. "Graduation Rates Increase Around The Globe As U.S. Plateaus." *WAMU 88.5.* American University Radio, 21 Feb. 2102. Web. 22 Nov. 2014.

32 Kahlenberg, Richard D. "To Raise Graduation Rates, Focus on Poor and Working Class Kids." The Chronicle of Higher Education, 28 May 2011. Web. 22 Nov. 2014.

Chapter Nine

1   Rifkin, Jeremy. "The Brain's Circuitry May Hold the Key." *The Empathic Civilization: The Race to Global Consciousness in a World in Crisis*. New York: J.P. Tarcher/Penguin, 2009. 84-87. Print.

2   Rifkin, Jeremy. "The Brain's Circuitry May Hold the Key." *The Empathic Civilization: The Race to Global Consciousness in a World in Crisis*. New York: J.P. Tarcher/Penguin, 2009. 84-87. Print.

3   Rifkin, Jeremy. "The Brain's Circuitry May Hold the Key." *The Empathic Civilization: The Race to Global Consciousness in a World in Crisis*. New York: J.P. Tarcher/Penguin, 2009. 84-87. Print.

4   Rifkin, Jeremy. "The Brain's Circuitry May Hold the Key." *The Empathic Civilization: The Race to Global Consciousness in a World in Crisis*. New York: J.P. Tarcher/Penguin, 2009. 84-87. Print.

5   "History of American Sign Language." Start ASL, n.d. Web. 21 Nov. 2014.

6   "United Nations Millennium Development Goals." UN News Center. United Nations, n.d. Web. 21 Nov. 2014.

7   "United Nations Millennium Development Goals." UN News Center. United Nations, n.d. Web. 21 Nov. 2014.

8   "United Nations Millennium Development Goals." UN News Center. United Nations, n.d. Web. 21 Nov. 2014.

9   "United Nations Millennium Development Goals." UN News Center. United Nations, n.d. Web. 21 Nov. 2014.

10   Singer, Peter. *The Life You Can Save: Acting Now to End World Poverty*. New York: Random House, 2009. Print.

11   Gleeson, Renny. "TED: Ideas worth Spreading." TED Talks, Feb. 2009. Web. 20 Nov. 2014.

12   Hamblin, Dora Jane. "Has the Garden of Eden Been Located at Last?" Lambert Dolphin's Library, Sept. 1983. Web. 22 Nov. 2014.

13   *Schindler's List*. Dir. Steven Spielberg. Prod. Steven Spielberg. By Steven Zaillian. Perf. Liam Neeson, Ben Kingsley, and Ralph Fiennes. Universal Pictures, 1993. DVD.

Chapter Ten

1   "Berlin Wall." History.com. A&E Television Networks, 2009. Web. 22 Nov. 2014.

2   White, Deborah. "What Martin Luther King Said in His Iconic 'I Have a Dream' Speech." About News, 2014. Web. 23 Nov. 2014.

3   "EXECUTIVE ORDER 9981." The Truman Library, 26 July 1948. Web. 23 Nov. 2014.

4   Fruchtman, Jr., Jack. "Separate But Equal?" The Baltimore Sun, 05 Apr. 1992. Web. 23 Nov. 2014.

5   "Rosa Parks Biography." Bio.com. A&E Networks Television, 2014. Web. 20 Nov. 2014.

6   "Rosa Parks Biography." Bio.com. A&E Networks Television, 2014. Web. 20 Nov. 2014.

7   Loeb, Paul Rogat. "Davenu – It Would Have Been Enough" *Soul of a Citizen: Living with Conviction in a Cynical Time*. New York: St. Martin's Griffin, 1999. Print.

8   Loeb, Paul Rogat. *Soul of a Citizen: Living with Conviction in a Cynical Time*. New York: St. Martin's Griffin, 1999. Print.

9   Loeb, Paul Rogat. "William Appelman Commentary." *Soul of a Citizen: Living with Conviction in a Cynical Time*. New York: St. Martin's Griffin, 1999. Print.

10 Hawken, Paul, Lovins, Amory B., and Lovins, L. Hunter. *Natural Capitalism: Creating the next Industrial Revolution*. Boston: Little, Brown, 1999. Print.

11 Bornstein, David. *How to Change the World: Social Entrepreneurs and the Power of New Ideas*. Oxford: Oxford UP, 2004. Print.

12 Bornstein, David. *How to Change the World: Social Entrepreneurs and the Power of New Ideas*. Oxford: Oxford UP, 2004. Print.

13 Bornstein, David. *How to Change the World: Social Entrepreneurs and the Power of New Ideas*. Oxford: Oxford UP, 2004. Print.

14 Singer, Peter. "The Grameen Bank." *The Life You Can Save: Acting Now to End World Poverty*. New York: Random House, 2009. Print.

15 Singer, Peter. *The Life You Can Save: Acting Now to End World Poverty*. New York: Random House, 2009. Print.

16 Hansen, Roger D. "Water and Wastewater Systems in Imperial Rome." WaterHistory.org. Metropolitan Fire, n.d. Web. 20 Nov. 2014.

17 Sparx, N. "How to Construct Houses with Plastic Bottles!!" Instructables.com. n.d. Web. 23 Nov. 2014

18 Sohrabji, Sunita. "India's Poor Recycle World's E-Waste into Wealth." New America Media, 20 Mar. 2010. Web. 23 Nov. 2014.

19 History.com. "Mother's Day." History.com. A&E Television Networks, 2011. Web. 23 Nov. 2014.

20 Tough, Paul. *Whatever It Takes: Geoffrey Canada's Quest to Change Harlem and America*. Boston: Houghton Mifflin, 2008. 41-43. Print.

21 "Geoffrey Canada." Bio. A&E Television Networks, 2014. Web.

22 Tough, Paul. "Hart and Risley Research." *Whatever It Takes: Geoffrey Canada's Quest to Change Harlem and America*. Boston: Houghton Mifflin, 2008. Print.

23 Tough, Paul. "Hart and Risley Research." *Whatever It Takes: Geoffrey Canada's Quest to Change Harlem and America*. Boston: Houghton Mifflin, 2008. Print.

24 Tough, Paul. "Hart and Risley Research." *Whatever It Takes: Geoffrey Canada's Quest to Change Harlem and America*. Boston: Houghton Mifflin, 2008. Print.

25 Tough, Paul. "Hart and Risley Research." *Whatever It Takes: Geoffrey Canada's Quest to Change Harlem and America*. Boston: Houghton Mifflin, 2008. Print.

26 Tough, Paul. "Baby College, T. Berry Brazelton, MD." *Whatever It Takes: Geoffrey Canada's Quest to Change Harlem and America*. Boston: Houghton Mifflin, 2008. Print.

27 Tough, Paul. *Whatever It Takes: Geoffrey Canada's Quest to Change Harlem and America*. Boston: Houghton Mifflin, 2008. 41-43. Print.

28 "HCZ's Goals and Achievements | Harlem Children's Zone." Harlem Children's Zone, n.d. Web. 09 Apr. 2015.

29 Goossens, Jesse and Tilleard, John. *Right to Play: Every Child Has the Right to Play*. New York: Lemniscaat, 2011. Print.

30 Goossens, Jesse and Tilleard, John. *Right to Play: Every Child Has the Right to Play*. New York: Lemniscaat, 2011. Print.

31 Goossens, Jesse and Tilleard, John. *Right to Play: Every Child Has the Right to Play*. New York: Lemniscaat, 2011. Print.

32 Hartmann, Thom. *The Last Hours of Ancient Sunlight: Waking up to Personal and Global Transformation*. New York: Harmony, 1999. Print.

Appendix

The information contained herein is provided as a summary of possible ways readers who are interested in beginning to work toward poverty alleviation can become involved.

Creating a Mission Statement of Action for Your Cause

The foundation for effective action and understanding the primary motivating issues that drive your desire to act arise from your personal mission. If you understand the issues that are significantly upsetting to you and you want changed, then the places to provide time, money, and talent become clear. Answer these five questions to help formulate a mission statement for your passions to serve.

1. Do you have a personal relationship with God and how does your relationship shape your thoughts of personal duty and calling to help others?
2. Describe the importance of family, community, and country to you.
3. What is your educational background and what skills, knowledge, and talents are you ready to share with the world?
4. Have you experienced any significant hardships in your life; what were they and how did they change you?
5. If you could change three problems in the world that you feel are extremely troubling and are morally wrong, what would you change?

These questions are a launching point to consider the causes and the challenges that will inspire you to ACT! As we have detailed throughout *Wavers & Beggars*, acting and not talking about 'what is wrong with the world' is the beginning to change. Having a sense of your calling and mission drives you and makes taking the action to change circumstances less like work and more like purpose.

A mission statement should be as succinct as possible using the fewest words that clearly define what you want to do and act upon in your life. As an example, a mission statement would read like this:

My personal mission is to create a world that allows all children equal access to an education so they fulfill their potential and destiny to create a world that embraces diversity and change.

Volunteer

- Schools
- Churches
- Homeless shelters and food kitchens
- Senior centers
- Prison ministries
- Helping neighbors
- Acting as a surrogate parent
- Coaching children's sports
- Teaching musical instruments – art instruction
- Non-profit charities
- Recycling and community clean-up
- Short-term and long-term mission trips
- International aid and education

Volunteering 10% of your time is a strategy for success in this area and will bring more fulfillment to your life

---

Giving Gifts/Donations

- Non-profit organization
- Churches
- Shelters and food kitchens
- Help a neighbor in need
- School programs in need of money
- Educational programming
- Arts programming
- Sports programming

Goal Setting

- Use your mission statement as a starting point to set goals
- Create short term goals of change (less than 3 months)
- Create medium-term goals of change (3–12 months)
- Create longer-range goals (1–3 years)
- Create vision goals (3–10 years)
- Goals need to be measurable

To write goals, prepare a statement as if the goal has already been accomplished:

I am excited and happy with the results of the local charity fundraiser we provided raising over $2500 to help in the alleviation of domestic hunger challenges.

Partnerships

- Create relationships with multiple charities to create the greatest impact
- Focus on the results and the impact and not on who is receiving the credit

- Partner with business (e.g., Whole Foods Dime a Bag Program)
- Partner with schools, churches, civic organizations, government organizations
- Family and other community members

Examples of Charities Working Toward Poverty Alleviation

United Way – www.unitedway.org

Summary: United Way Worldwide is a leadership and support organization for the network of nearly 1,800 community-based United Ways in 41 countries worldwide. The focus is to ignite a worldwide social movement, and thereby mobilize millions to action to give, advocate and volunteer to improve the conditions in which they live. In addition, United Way seeks to galvanize and connect all sectors of society—individuals, businesses, non-profit organizations, and governments—to create long-term social change that produces healthy, well-educated, and financially stable individuals and families.

Salvation Army – www.salvationarmyusa.org

The Salvation Army is an integral part of the Christian Church, although distinctive in government and practice. The Army's doctrine follows the mainstream of Christian belief and its articles of faith emphasize God's saving purposes. Its objects are 'the advancement of the Christian religion… of education, the relief of poverty, and other charitable objects beneficial to society or the community of mankind as a whole. The movement, founded in 1865 by William Booth, has spread from London, England, to many parts of the world.

The movement's partnership with both private and public philanthropy continues to bring comfort to the needy, while the proclamation of God's redemptive love offers individuals and communities the opportunity to enjoy a better life on earth and a place in Christ's everlasting Kingdom.

Dreamweaver International – www.dreamweaver911.org

At no time in the history of mankind has the chasm between the rich and the poor been greater than in the 21st century. Over 1 billion children live in poverty with little or no hope for a better future. Countless generations of people around the world have suffered and endured hardships for too long with limited opportunity and no provision to change much of anything in their lives. Dreamweaver believes everyone deserve a chance at a future of promise and hope.

To alleviate poverty around the globe, Dreamweaver's sole purpose is 'to help the needy become the needed.' When people are needed, valued, and contribute to the economy of life, their lives and the lives of those around them improve. They are able to lift themselves from the depths of poverty and move to sustainability. Dreamweaver provides models of care in three primary areas: education, health care, and compassion care.

Dreamweaver has the world's largest sports and arts charity project in the world, collecting and distributing sports-, music-, and arts-related material. The Gear for Goals (G4G) project is an eco-friendly campaign that collects new and used sports, music, and arts items and distributes them to under-resourced children domestically and internationally. The Gear for Goals project has also created a unique sports gifting program called One Gives One, which enables supporters to purchase sports items for personal use, and for every item purchased, sports items are donated to schools, orphanages, and individual children.

Task Force for Global Health – www.taskforce.org

The Task Force for Global Health was founded as the Task Force for Child Survival in 1984. The Task Force was initially tapped to serve as a secretariat for a consortium of global health organizations: UNICEF, WHO, The Rockefeller Foundation, The United Nations Development Program, and the World Bank. These organizations sought Task Force support for a collaborative effort to improve child wellness and survival strategies. With the Task Force as secretariat for the network, they resolved to work together to develop and implement a plan for global immunization efforts and measures to promote and maintain healthy children and families.

Over its 28-year history, its role as neutral convener and collaborator has expanded. Its programs include work in three sectors: health system strengthening, immunization and vaccines, and neglected tropical diseases. In each of these areas, Task Force works with partners and communities around the world to provide and improve the resources necessary for better global health for those in need. The Task Force for Global Health is a nonprofit, public health organization, recognized as a 501(c)(3) corporation. The organization is based in Atlanta, Georgia.

Feeding America – www.feedamerica.org

For 35 years, Feeding America has responded to the hunger crisis in America by providing food to people in need through a nationwide network of food banks.

The concept of food banking was developed by John van Hengel in Phoenix, AZ in the late 1960s. Van Hengel, a retired businessman, had been volunteering at a soup kitchen trying to find food to serve the hungry. One day, he met a desperate mother who regularly rummaged through grocery store garbage bins to find food for her children. She suggested that there should be a place where, instead of being thrown out, discarded food could be stored for people to pick up—similar to the way banks store money for future use. With that, an industry was born.

Van Hengel established St. Mary's Food Bank in Phoenix, AZ as the nation's first food bank. In its initial year, van Hengel and his team of volunteers distributed 275,000 pounds of food to people in need. Word of the food bank's success quickly spread, and states began to take note. By 1977, food banks had been established in 18 cities across the country.

As the number of food banks began to increase, van Hengel created a national organization for food banks, and in 1979 he established Second Harvest, which was later called America's Second Harvest the Nation's Food Bank Network. In 2008, the network changed its name to Feeding America to better reflect the mission of the organization.

Today, Feeding America is the nation's largest domestic hunger-relief organization—a powerful and efficient network of 200 food banks across the country. As food insecurity rates hold steady at the highest levels ever, the Feeding America network of food banks has risen to meet the need. It feeds 46.5 million people at risk of hunger, including 12 million children and 7 million seniors.

Young Life – www.younglife.org

Young Life doesn't start with a program. It starts with adults who are concerned enough about kids to go to them, on their turf and in their culture, building bridges of authentic friendship. These relationships don't happen overnight—they take time, patience, trust, and consistency.

So Young Life leaders log many hours with kids—where they are, as they are. Young Life listens to their stories and learns what's important to them because they genuinely care about kids' joys, triumphs, heartaches, and setbacks.

Young Life believes in the power of presence. Kids' lives are dramatically influenced when caring adults come alongside them, sharing God's love with them. Because their Young Life leader believes in them, they begin to see that their lives have great worth, meaning, and purpose.

This is the first step of a lifelong journey; the choices they make today, based upon God's love for them, will have an impact on future decisions—careers chosen, marriages formed, and families raised—all ripples from the time when a Young Life leader took time to reach out and enter their world.

Business Advocacy

Microfinance Organizations

Accion – accion.org

Founded in 1961, Accion has helped build 62 microfinance institutions in 31 countries around the globe. Their reach extends to 4.9 million clients in the US, Mexico, Latin America, Africa, and Asia. They provide instruction and assistance to microfinance institutions worldwide, offering guidance in management, investment, and governance. Accion uses its impressive breadth to orchestrate growth in the microfinance industry.

Grameen Foundation – grameenfoundation.org

Grameen Foundation helps the world's poorest people reach their full potential, connecting their determination and skills with the resources they need. They provide access to essential financial services and information on agriculture and health, assistance that can have wide-scale impact by addressing the specific needs of poor households and communities. They also develop tools to improve the effectiveness of poverty-focused organizations.

Opportunity Fund – opportunityfund.org

From Opportunity Fund website:

"Twenty years ago, when we launched Opportunity Fund, I had no idea what we would become. Just getting to a million dollars in microloans, I thought, that would be amazing. It was hard to think far beyond that as we took our first wobbly steps in 1994. Four years later, we threw our "Million Dollar Party," celebrating the milestone of our first million in microloans. My vision for what we could become started to expand.

Today, we lend more than $2 million every month and help people save over $1 million each year. Last year for the first time, we cracked 1,000 loans in a single year. Over the past five years, we invested $36 million in entrepreneurship, education, and everyday savings, benefiting clients who usually get left out of the financial picture. In the next five years we will invest $100 million.

These are loans to women selling tamales and hot dogs from carts on the street, to family-run restaurants and dry cleaners. These are savings accounts for single moms who seek to build stability and strength for their children, and for students who will be the first in their families to graduate from college.

For Californians yearning for opportunity, your donations provide the fuel. Through our loans and savings programs, we are entwined in the life stories of thousands – some 2,800 Californians every year. We are helping Californians rewrite their futures, one microloan and one micro savings account at a time."

Kiva – kiva.org

From Kiva website:

"*Why we do what we do*

We envision a world where all people – even in the most remote areas of the globe – hold the power to create opportunity for themselves and others. We believe providing safe, affordable access to capital to those in need helps people create better lives for themselves and their families.

How we do it

Making a loan on Kiva is so simple that you may not realize how much work goes on behind the scenes. Kiva works with microfinance institutions on five continents to provide loans to people without access to traditional banking systems. One hundred percent of your loan is sent to these microfinance institutions, which we call Field Partners, who administer the loans in the field. Kiva relies on a worldwide network of over 450 volunteers who work with our Field Partners, edit and translate borrower stories, and ensure the smooth operation of countless other Kiva programs."

Compassion and Justice

Exodus Cry – exoduscry.org

From Exodus Cry website:

"Sex trafficking thrives when it is hidden in the shadows. It becomes a well-kept secret—an out-of-sight, out-of-mind tragedy with victims who are unable to speak for themselves. By bringing light into the darkness and forcing the issue to the forefront of collective awareness, we become a voice for the victims. We become advocates for awareness. As long as we are silent, the injustice will continue. Together we must create social awareness and call for an end to sex trafficking around the world. Our awareness and training efforts seek to inform and educate the public about the issue and also give ways to work toward the prevention and eradication of sex trafficking. Raising public awareness is a critical part of prevention work. Ignorance fosters the growth of this insidious industry in our cities and nations. We are working tirelessly to bring sex trafficking to an end, but we can't do it alone. We need your help! In the late 1700s, William Wilberforce initiated an aggressive grassroots campaign to bring the horrors of the slave trade to public awareness. In order to bring about the societal change of heart necessary for the ending of modern-day slavery, we must follow Wilberforce's example and expose how far reaching the injustice is."

Free the Slaves – freetheslaves.net

Free the Slaves recognizes that slavery flourishes when people cannot meet their basic needs, and lack economic opportunity. Moreover inadequate education, deplorable health care, and dishonest government are all faulty systematic problems which further drive human slavery. Free the Slaves takes a holistic approach to eradicating slavery by working with grassroots organizations where slavery flourishes. They record the stories so people in power can see slavery and be inspired to work for freedom. Moreover, there is a movement to enlist businesses to clean slavery out of their product chains and empower consumers to stop buying into slavery. Governments are motivated by advocates to produce effective antislavery laws then held to their commitment to end slavery.

Polaris Project – polarisproject.org

Polaris is connecting with hundreds of anti-trafficking and related-issue hotlines and organizations from around the world. They have worked closely with the Freedom Fund, the Walk Free Foundation, and partner organizations to establish the Global Modern Slavery Directory—a first-of-its-kind publicly searchable database of over 770 organizations and hotlines working on human trafficking and forced labor. By enabling actors in the anti-human trafficking field to better locate, identify, and connect with each other, the tool will help connect victims of human trafficking and at-risk populations to the help they need.

Compassion International – compassion.com

Compassion International exists as a Christian child-advocacy ministry that releases children from spiritual, economic, social, and physical poverty and enables them to become responsible, fulfilled Christian adults. Founded by the Rev. Everett Swanson in 1952, Compassion began providing Korean War orphans with food, shelter, education, and health care, as well as Christian training. Today, Compassion helps more than 1.5 million children in 26 countries.

International Justice Mission – ijm.org

International Justice Mission seeks Justice system transformation. They don't stop at rescuing people after they have been abused; the ultimate goal is to prevent the violence from happening in the first place.

The unique model drives maximum impact and long-term change. They partner with local governments and communities to meet both urgent and long-term needs. The result? Powerful changes that protect the poor from violence.

Charity Rating Agencies

Donors considering thoughtful giving can use charity rating agencies as a guide. Many charities create significant impact and positive change with their resources, but may find their ratings either not rated or not among the top charities rated. The ratings should not necessarily determine your decision to support, volunteer, or work with the charity. Using financial metrics only in the absence of understanding the day-to-day activities and the people who work within a charity give only part of the picture. Use charity rating agencies as a guide along with your own investigations into the leadership, the programs, and the mission of any charity you are considering supporting.

Charity Navigator – charitynavigator.org

Charity Navigator works to guide intelligent giving. By guiding intelligent giving, we aim to advance a more efficient and responsive philanthropic marketplace, in which givers and the charities they support work in tandem to overcome our nation's and the world's most persistent challenges.

Charity Navigator is a 501 (c) (3) non-profit organization under the Internal Revenue Code and does not accept any contributions from any charities we evaluate.

Charity Watch – charitywatch.org

CharityWatch is America's most independent and assertive charity watchdog. Rather than merely repeat charities' self-reported finances using simplistic or automated formulas, we delve deep to find the real story of how efficiently charities use your donations to fund the programs you want to support. Founded in 1992 as the American Institute of Philanthropy (AIP), CharityWatch continues to expose nonprofit abuses and advocate for your interests as a donor.

Give Well – givewell.org

GiveWell is a nonprofit dedicated to finding outstanding giving opportunities and publishing the full details of our analysis to help donors decide where to give. Unlike charity evaluators that focus solely on financials, assessing administrative or fundraising costs, we conduct in-depth research aiming to determine how much good a given program accomplishes (in terms of lives saved, lives improved, etc.) per dollar spent. Rather than try to rate as many charities as possible, we focus on the few charities that stand out most in order to find and confidently recommend the best-giving opportunities possible.

THE AUTHORS

Dr. Warren Bruhl

Dr. Warren Bruhl is Executive Director of Dreamweaver International, a non-profit charity devoted to poverty alleviation by investment in education, healthcare, and compassion work. Dr. Bruhl is the author of *The Chiropractor's Exercise Manual* and has written extensively for professional publications and news media. He's been featured on television and radio for his progressive healing and charity work. He is the creator of the dynamic sports charity project, Gear for Goals (G4G), which provides sports and musical equipment to children living in extreme poverty. When asked to describe what he does for an occupation, his answer is, "I am social change engineer!" He has traveled extensively in East Africa, Central America, and the Caribbean to visit and serve the poor and bring hope. Dr. Bruhl is married with three grown children and resides in the Chicago area.

Todd Love Ball, Jr.

The author of two fictional books, *Love Against Society* and *Members Only Northshore Confessions*, Todd works professionally as a fitness educator and philanthropist. Involved in international relationship building with African-American communities and Polish communities, Todd is a bilingual speaker of English and Polish, and has traveled to Africa and Poland in efforts of community building. Todd lives with his wife and two children in the city of Palatine, IL.

IN MEMORIAM

Sandra Taylor was born on February 9, 1944 in Benton Harbor, Michigan. Sandra was a graduate of Shiloh Christian Institute in Hamilton, Montana, earning her ministerial degree and becoming an international missionary. During her career in ministry she was recognized as one of the most dedicated and selfless servants of the poor. Working in Spain and Kenya, East Africa, Sandra and her husband, Kenneth Taylor, were responsible for ministering to thousands of people and took part in beginning new churches throughout Kenya.

Believing all people, regardless of their financial circumstances, deserve an education and a chance at a better life, the Taylors founded the Kimana School of Leadership and Professional Studies in Kimana, Kenya. The courageous and difficult work the Taylors engaged in to bring hope to people in the bush of Kenya has become a remarkable education center and continues to develop programs in education, healthcare, and compassion. In 2012, Sandra became a founding director of Dreamweaver International, a 501c3 non-profit with offices in Kenya and the United States. It was her desire to help seed the dreams of the under-resourced and give them the necessary education so they could climb from the deep hole of poverty. She personally oversaw all functions of the Kimana School of Leadership and Professional Studies, and together with the school director, Mr. Joseph Nkaapa, organized and built the Kimana Christian Academy on the ten-acre campus property the Taylors own in Kenya. The Kimana Christian Academy, a school for the young, ages three to fourteen, opened its doors in January 2016.

Wanting to be sure that no one had to endure the horrific trials of poor healthcare found where their primary mission is located, Mr. and Mrs. Taylor teamed up with Dr. Scott Smith, an osteopathic physician in Florida, to build Kilimanjaro Mission Hospital. Now under construction, the hospital will serve a strategic and vital life-saving role in the Kimana and Latoikitok communities of Kajado County in Kenya.

Anyone who knew Sandra never forgot her! She had a special way of engaging people, communicating her mission, and she took a uniquely special interest in the lives of everyone she met. Her greatest gift she brought the world was her compassion and love for people, who many passed over or treated unfairly. Often Sandra dug into her pocket to give a poor mama, who had hungry babies, shillings for milk or food. As well, she arranged school fees and scholarships for children who had lost parents through tragic circumstances and made sure everyone who worked for her was cared for and their families were taken care of.

Her dedication to serving the poor and giving selflessly, have inspired me to become a steward of the poor and angered me to act on behalf of the people oppressed by injustice. As I completed this book in the days that followed my mother's passing, I realized her teaching, love, and discipline live inside me and spurred me to write Wavers & Beggars. We would frequently have conversations about her work in Kenya and how important education and proper healthcare were to changing the circumstances of people in our Kenyan community. I was awed and moved by her life and though it was not always easy being her son, she always called me to be better and gave me the foundation I will need to carry her work forward. I will miss my mother and I know thousands of others are mourning her loss to the world. But, the Lord needed her more than we did here, and I can only hope my life becomes an inspiration like hers has been.

Dr. Warren Bruhl